Beyond Sacred Violence

Beyond Sacred Violence

A Comparative Study of Sacrifice

Kathryn McClymond

The Johns Hopkins University Press
Baltimore

Printed in the United States of America on acid-free paper
9 8 7 6 5 4 3 2 1

The Johns Hopkins University Press
2715 North Charles Street
Baltimore, Maryland 21218-4363
www.press.jhu.edu

Library of Congress Cataloging-in-Publication Data

McClymond, Kathryn, 1960–
Beyond sacred violence : a comparative study of sacrifice / Kathryn McClymond.
p. cm.
Includes bibliographical references and index.
ISBN-13: 978-0-8018-8776-5 (hardcover : alk. paper)
ISBN-10: 0-8018-8776-3 (hardcover : alk. paper)
1. Sacrifice. 2. Violence—Religious aspects. I. Title.
BL570.M33 2008
203′.4—dc22
2007036104

A catalog record for this book is available from the British Library.

The Johns Hopkins University Press uses environmentally friendly book materials, including recycled text paper that is composed of at least 30 percent post-consumer waste, whenever possible. All of our book papers are acid-free, and our jackets and covers are printed on paper with recycled content.

Contents

Acknowledgments

No author produces a body of scholarship without the support and assistance of countless others: colleagues, university staff, students, friends, and family. I thank all those who have contributed to this work in large and small ways. In particular, I thank Georgia State University for the financial support of two Research Initiation Grants, which made trips to India possible. I am also grateful to the staff of the Bhandarkar Oriental Research Institute in Pune, who facilitated my research on several trips, and to the staff at the Johns Hopkins University Press, particularly executive editor Henry Tom and copy editor Grace Carino.

I also appreciate the personal and professional support of the faculty and staff of the Religious Studies department at Georgia State University: Tim Renick, John Herman, John Iskander, Claire Murata Kooy, Ellen Logan, Caroline Nikitas, Felicia Thomas, Lou Ruprecht, Kenny Smith, and Christopher White. Numerous students read drafts of various chapters, especially Russell Cambron, Tony Petro, and John Rivenbark. Special thanks to Andrew Durdin and Sherry Morton, who worked through the copyediting of the manuscript with me.

Colleagues in other departments have also given helpful feedback, either at conference presentations of this material or informally. In addition to several anonymous readers along the way, I especially want to thank Steve Berkwitz, Francis X. Clooney, Sara Karesh Coxe, William Gilders, Robert Goldenberg, Richard Hecht, Barbara Holdrege, Tim Lubin, Laurie Patton, Ellen Posman, Brian K. Smith, Gregory Spinner, Ivan Strenski, Michael Swartz, Thomas Wilson, and the members of the Comparative Studies in Hinduisms and Judaisms Group for their comments on this work at various stages and for their general encouragement.[1]

Most important, I express my deep appreciation to my family. My

daughter, Sarah, will never know how much joy she brings to my life on a daily basis. My parents, Gretchen and Ferdinand Schoch, have demonstrated completely unconditional faith and support, even during dark times. More than anyone else, these two people have sacrificed to make good things possible for me, and so I dedicate this book to them.

Abbreviations

Indological Sources

AitBr	Aitareya Brāhmaṇa
ĀpŚS	Āpastamba Śrauta Sūtra
ĀśvŚS	Āśvalāyana Śrauta Sūtra
AV	Atharva Veda Saṃhitā
BhŚS	Bhāradvāja Śrauta Sūtra
BrhUp	Bṛhadaraṇyaka Upaniṣad
BŚS	Baudhāyana Śrauta Sūtra
ChāndUp	Chāndogya Upaniṣad
HŚS	Hiraṇyakeśin Śrauta Sūtra
JaiŚS	Jaiminīya Śrauta Sūtra
JB	Jaiminīya Brāhmaṇa
KB	Kausīṭaki Brāhmaṇa
KŚS	Kātyāyana Śrauta Sūtra
MS	Manu Smṛti
PB	Pañcaviṃsa Brāhmaṇa
RV	Ṛg Veda Saṃhitā
ŚB	Śatapatha Brāhmaṇa
ŚŚS	Śāṅkhāyana Śrauta Sūtra
TS	Taittirīya Saṃhitā
VārŚS	Vārāha Śrauta Sūtra
YV	Yajur Veda Saṃhitā

Judaic Sources

References to the Hebrew Bible follow standard abbreviations.

Tractates of the Mishnah:

M. Kin.	Kinnim
M. Men.	Menāḥôt
M. Sab.	Šabbāt
M. Suk.	Sûkkāh
M. Zeb.	Zebāḥîm

References to the Tosefta are prefixed by T.

Midrashic Collections:

Lev. R.	Leviticus Rabbāh
Pesiq. Rab Kah.	Pesîqtā' de-R. Kahana
Sif. Num.	Siprê on Numbers

Secondary Sources

AGNI	Staal, *Agni: The Vedic Ritual of the Fire Altar*
HD	Kane, *History of Dharmaśāstra*

Beyond Sacred Violence

Introduction

> In this trial, we have been reminded, and the world has seen, that our fellow Americans are generous and kind, resourceful and brave. We see our national character in rescuers working past exhaustion; in long lines of blood donors; in thousands of citizens who have asked to work and serve in any way possible. And we have seen our national character in eloquent acts of sacrifice.
>
> —GEORGE W. BUSH

> A sacrifice is the best deed. — ŚATAPATHA BRĀHMAṆA

Sacrifice, like religion, appears to be nearly universal in human culture. We find sacrificial systems in virtually every time and place where human communities have developed. Consequently, it seems important to be able to understand the role that sacrifice plays in human society. Yet sacrifice, like religion, appears nearly impossible to define. For those of us who study sacrifice in the context of world religions, sacrificial phenomena prompt a host of questions: What characterizes a sacrifice? Can we discern a single defining characteristic of sacrifice? What distinguishes sacrifice from other kinds of ritual activity? What, if anything, links sacrifice as a religious phenomenon across religious traditions? From an academic point of view, these questions get at the very heart of the nature of sacrifice.

In addition, sacrifice is important in the popular imagination. The term is used to legitimize and valorize the loss of life, liberty, and honor in various contexts, often as a way of investing loss with meaning. In the post–September 11 world, sacrifice has been used to characterize death, material loss, military service, and volunteerism. The term is used broadly, extending beyond "traditional" expressions of sacrifice to incorporate thousands of individual and community acts. Consequently, *sacrifice* has become an active word in our national vocabulary, making it a topic that interests scholars and popular audiences alike. So we return to the question, what *is* sacrifice?

In this book I outline a multipronged approach to the study of sacrifice, setting aside any expectation of finding a single essential or defining quality. I approach sacrifice as a complex matrix of varied and interrelated procedures and, instead of defining it, focus on identifying basic activities that characterize sacrificial events. The book also examines several of the issues raised by the execution of these activities. In addition, I explore the implications of such an approach, tracing how the elements and authority of traditional sacrifice have been appropriated by other activities. Finally, by drawing data from non-Christian—specifically Vedic and Jewish—traditions, I argue that sacrifice as a category of religious experience has largely been shaped by Protestant Christian thought.

In the process of examining the full spectrum of sacrificial offerings (animal, vegetal, and liquid) and exploring the multiple ways in which offering substances are manipulated, a more general question is addressed: How does an investigation of sacrifice with an emphasis on the manipulation of the offering substance contribute to our understanding of religion in general? We can begin this study with the assumption that humans construct "sacred substance," just as they construct "sacred space" and "sacred time." Societies set aside material offerings for specific purposes and invest those offerings with religious value at the same time that they shape, divide, destroy, reconfigure, and consume them. This study is mainly concerned with the broader question of how the manipulation of various offering substances shapes and reflects the religious world in which it takes place.

Why Study Sacrifice?

As I have explained this polythetic approach to sacrifice in various venues, I have frequently been asked, why study sacrifice? For many of us, sacrifice is what "they" do, not what "we" do. Even if it was an important feature of ancient India or biblical Judaism, *sacrifice* seems to be little more than a metaphor in contemporary American life. Traditional sacrifice is associated with the primitive, the exotic, even the savage. Despite (and perhaps because of) these assumptions, there are several very good reasons to continue to consider sacrifice a critical topic in religious studies. First, sacrifice continues to be a central feature of many of the world's religions. Despite temptations in the modern West to associate sacrifice with the past (and a primitive past at that), traditional sacrifice is very much alive and well. It flourishes on all the major continents, including

North America, and thus deserves thoughtful study as an element of contemporary religious life.

Second, sacrifice is often the arena in which certain people distinguish themselves from others, community versus community, social rank versus social rank, modern religion versus ancient religion. Communities sacrifice specific offerings in specific ways that are different from the offerings and ways of their neighbors. For example, the biblical texts instruct Israelites to orient a bull's head in a specific direction to distinguish their sacrifice from that of their neighbors, in which a bull's head would be oriented in another direction. How we execute, slaughter, and offer *our* bull is different from how *they* do it—and, of course, our way is better.

Third, we have long been aware that "sacrifice" as an authoritative concept is often appropriated within streams of religious communities to authorize practices other than traditional sacrifice. Sacrifice becomes a metaphor for other activity. For example, within Judaism, prayer and Torah study are often characterized as sacrifice. Within Hinduism, ascetic traditions liken their spiritual disciplines to sacrifice. How is it that these practices are widely accepted as variations on sacrifice? How is it that President George W. Bush, quoted at the opening of this chapter, can characterize post–September 11 volunteerism as a form of sacrifice?

The power and presence of sacrifice lie precisely in the fact that it cannot be reduced to a single phenomenon. Sacrificial rituals are, in fact, often lengthy, elaborate, complicated, and unbearably detail-oriented. Sacrifice can involve ritual killing . . . and so much more. Sacrifice can involve a communal meal . . . and so much more. If sacrifice were simply one activity or another, it would not have the authority or "staying power" that it has as a multidimensional phenomenon. If we are to continue to learn from these rituals, we must engage sacrificial events in their full complexity, much as a fine wine. Before I outline the approach to the study of sacrifice used in this book, however, it may be useful to orient the reader by reviewing the dominant approaches to sacrifice within the history of religions.

Approaches to Sacrifice

History of religions as a distinct field of study in the West came into being in the late nineteenth century.[1] Since its inception, it has been an interdisciplinary field, and this interdisciplinary character is reflected in the

varied theoretical approaches scholars have taken to sacrifice. It would be impossible to summarize within these pages all the approaches to sacrifice that have been offered. It may be helpful, however, to situate the present study in the context of the most influential approaches, particularly those that currently dominate the study of sacrifice. Numerous theories and models can be classified into six basic streams of thought: those that view sacrifice as dramatized myth, those that view sacrifice as exchange, those that view sacrifice as cuisine, structuralist approaches, feminist approaches, and approaches that view sacrifice as death or violence.

Sacrifice as Dramatized Myth

One of the most common ways to interpret ritual in general and sacrifice in particular is as dramatized myth. Specifically, sacrifice has often been understood as the (re)enactment of various creation myths, linking each individual sacrificial act to a primal act that brought humanity in general or specific communities into being. Adolf E. Jensen first propounded this theory in the mid-1900s, arguing that religious myths contain stories about a primordial time (prehuman) when divine beings existed.[2] This primordial period ended when one of these divine beings was killed. According to this school of thought, the sacrificial killing of animal victims (which may include humans) among primitive peoples dramatizes the cosmogonic event.

In addition, sacrificial ritual may contribute to the ongoing maintenance of the material and metaphysical infrastructure of the universe. (Classic examples of this might include the self-sacrifice of Puruṣa/Prajāpati in the Vedic creation stories.) Over time, however, the underlying cosmogonic myth is often forgotten. As Joseph Henninger explains, "Once the myth had been largely forgotten or was no longer seen to be connected with ritual, rites involving slaying were reinterpreted as a giving of a gift to divinities (who originally played no role in these rites, because the primordial divine being had been slain); blood sacrifices thus became 'meaningless survivals' of the 'meaningful rituals of killing' of the earlier food-growing cultures. Magical actions are likewise degenerate fragments of the originally meaningful whole formed by the mythically based rituals of killing."[3] In other words, although sacrifice may no longer be characterized as the reenactment of a creation myth, it must be understood as arising from such a myth. This myth (which may be long forgotten) is the key to understanding sacrifice.

There are several problems with understanding sacrifice primarily as dramatized myth. Most important, this approach assumes the logical and chronological priority of belief over ritual. In other words, it assumes that the myths and doctrines of a specific people must develop earlier than the ritual practices. Yet historical and textual evidence does not support such a view. As Henninger's words suggest, this position often requires scholars to posit the earlier existence of "lost" myths or to forge connections between myths and rituals that are not readily apparent. Consequently, although this assumption was popular for a time, it is now commonly recognized as inaccurate and simplistic. As a result, contemporary scholars are more open to examining ritual on its own merits, rather than as the ugly stepsister to myth.

Sacrifice as Exchange

Sacrifice has also been characterized as an exchange of material goods that bonds human to human, community to community, or ritual participant to deity. The concept of exchange comes to the study of religion largely through anthropologists of religion such as E. B. Tylor, who argued that sacrifice must always involve some quality of "abnegation," the giving up of something valuable.[4] Émile Durkheim, the famous French sociologist of religion, inaugurated a school of thought that countered Tylor and others.[5] Durkheim redirected scholars' attention to the collective effects of religious practice. He argued that society has its roots in religion and that religion has its roots in sacrifice. Marcel Mauss, Durkheim's nephew and student, continued the Durkheimian approach in his classic work *The Gift* (1950), in which he argued that sacrifice is a means of exchange in primitive societies. More important, Mauss asserted that there is no such thing as a "free gift." Rather, systems of giving require, and in fact are dependent upon, reciprocity. Sacrifice in this sense is gift giving that situates participants in alternating roles of givers and receivers, constructing a never-ending cycle of reception and obligation. Mauss explained:

> One of the first groups of beings with which men had to enter into contract, and who, by definition, were there to make a contract with them, were above all the spirits of both the dead and of the gods. Indeed, it is they who are the true owners of the things and possessions of this world. With them it was most necessary to exchange, and with them it was most dangerous not to exchange. Yet, conversely, it was with them that it was

> easiest and safest to exchange. The purpose of destruction by sacrifice is precisely that it is an act of giving that is necessarily reciprocated.[6]

Building on this general view, Mauss developed a theory of "contract sacrifice," in which an individual or community gives small gifts to the god(s) in exchange for larger gifts. The obligations and exchanges between parties may be expressed in mythic or symbolic forms, but these obligations are very real. In accepting a gift—whether from a human or from a deity—one has implicitly agreed to reciprocate, therefore continuing the cycle.

The concept of "exchange" continues to be a popular way of making sense of certain religious practices. The recently edited *Guide to the Study of Religion* (2000) includes a chapter on "exchange."[7] Gregory Alles, the author of this chapter, characterizes sacrifice as one expression of exchange: "Exchange did provide one of the oldest theoretical models for understanding the widespread ritual of sacrifice: the notion that sacrifices are gifts given to the gods or ancestors in the hope of receiving a gift in return. This perspective is often summed up in three Latin words: *do et des*, 'I give [to you], so that you will give [to me].' "[8] Exchange in religious contexts involves the transfer of not only material goods but also intangible goods, such as offspring, honor, deferred rewards in the afterlife, and so forth.[9] Exchange also reflects and constructs social relationships. Religious exchange, therefore, includes but is not limited to an economic transfer of material goods.

The concept of exchange raises the issue of motivation. What am I thinking about when I sacrifice? Theorists disagree over whether religious exchange is always self-interested or whether there can be altruistic exchange. Melford Spiro notes, for example, that Burmese monks and nuns receive far more in material goods than they give in return—at least materially.[10] He concludes that this uneven exchange reflects the monks' and nuns' dominant social standing. People lower in the socioreligious hierarchy (the lay people) acknowledge the status of those higher in the socioreligious hierarchy (monks and nuns) by offering them gifts. Another interpretation, however, is that the lay people simply expect a deferred gift that has equal (or greater) value according to their own reckoning, despite its immateriality. At issue is whether a broad understanding of exchange effectively means that all sacrificial activity is self-interested.

Examining "exchange" as a dimension of sacrificial activity directs our attention to the social context in which religious activity occurs and the

social relations that are negotiated via sacrificial activity. For example, the act of communion can be viewed not only as an exchange between the communicant and the divine but also as an occasion for the negotiation of power relations between the lay communicant and the priest who consecrates and sanctifies the bread, relations that persist beyond the communion event into other social, so-called nonritual or nonreligious, settings. Exchange highlights religion's interconnection with the mundane, the political, and the social, collapsing absolute distinctions between the sacred and the profane.

Sacrifice as Cuisine

Another common way to understand sacrifice has been to imagine it as a ritual meal. W. Robertson Smith is generally credited with introducing this understanding to the field of religious studies. In his classic *Lectures on the Religion of the Semites* (1889), Smith presented a model of sacrifice that he regarded as universal. Smith writes largely in response to E. B. Tylor, who characterizes sacrifice as an evolutionary phenomenon that developed in three stages.[11] In the second of these evolutionary phases, sacrifice involves "homage" to the god(s) in the form of a communal banquet. During this meal the ritual participants ate an animal victim, and the god received the spirit of the victim.

Smith, in response, argues that this communion meal is primarily important because it strengthens community ties. Within certain communities, specific animals come to be viewed as material representations of the community deity. When crises develop, these "totems" are consumed in sacrificial banquets. According to Smith, consuming animal totems repairs a broken relationship between a community and its deity, and it also strengthens community ties and values. Smith's theory has been found faulty on several fronts (particularly his evolutionary views of sacrifice), but his work is foundational because he is the first scholar who asserted the primacy of ritual over belief. For this reason, Smith's work has been tremendously influential in ritual studies in general as well as sacrificial studies in particular.

More recently, Marcel Détienne and Jean-Pierre Vernant have characterized sacrifice as "cuisine," but in a very different way than did Smith. Their edited volume *The Cuisine of Sacrifice among the Greeks* (1989) should be required reading for anyone interested in theoretical treatments of sacrifice. Drawing primarily from Greek practices as represented in

classical writings and pottery images, Détienne and Vernant argue that sacrifice is a political and social "cuisine" that serves a variety of social functions, including the establishment of political power: "Political power cannot be exercised without sacrificial practice." Their approach assumes "the political and alimentary vocation inherent in sacrificial practices. . . . Expressed in actions and carried out since time immemorial in eating habits, the sacrificial system eludes clear and explicit analysis."[12] Thus sacrifice is, fundamentally, political cuisine.

Détienne and Vernant make a number of important points in their volume. They state up front that their focus is specifically Greek blood sacrifice. Therefore, their work focuses on the manipulation of animal victims (the only sacrificial substances that involve blood). They draw attention to the manipulation of oblations that occurs after the death of the victim. Like the noted historian of religions Jonathan Z. Smith, they argue that sacrifice is work, labor, intentionally directed activity. Nevertheless, Détienne and Vernant continue to imply that sacrifice can be understood as having a single distinguishing feature, the consumption of a cooked oblation. They go to great pains to distinguish sacrificial cuisine from mundane cooking, and they are among the few scholars who note the nuances of the manipulation of the oblation after its slaughter (a point that we will return to later). Fundamentally, however, they still suggest that sacrifice can be understood through one defining element, the metaphor of cuisine.

Détienne and Vernant are not the only recent theorists to focus on the alimentary nature of sacrifice. Charles Malamoud, in his classic study of Vedic sacrifice *Cooking the World* (1996), characterizes Vedic sacrifice in a similar vein. He sums up Vedic sacrificial practice by saying, "[I]f we attempt to describe, rather than define, the sacrifice, we come to acknowledge that it is essentially a matter of cooking: it is the preparation, sometimes through the combination, but always through the cooking, of edible substances."[13] One of the many strengths of this volume is Malamoud's awareness of vegetal (grain cake) and liquid (soma, milk, ghee) oblations within the Vedic system, as well as animal offerings. He is one of a handful of scholars who pay serious attention to nonanimal offerings, which are often at the forefront of sacrificial activity. In addition, Malamoud notes the significance of the apportionment of oblations. The thrust of Malamoud's book, however, is to view Vedic sacrifice through a culinary lens. The culinary metaphor is helpful, and particularly well suited to Vedic

sacrifice, but it would be a mistake, I believe, to reduce sacrifice in general to alimentary activity. Other activities are performed with oblations that cannot easily be adapted to a culinary metaphor, activities that we will explore later in this volume.

Structuralist Approaches to Sacrifice

Other scholars have developed various structuralist approaches to sacrifice, focusing on the oppositional relations between elements of activity rather than attempting to find meaning in the myriad activities performed. Claude Lévi-Strauss, a student of Marcel Mauss, was strongly influenced by Swiss linguist Ferdinand de Saussure. Saussure posited a dichotomy between language and speech in which language is spiritual and speech is embodied. Consequently, the spirit is viewed as perfect and sacred, whereas the body is considered imperfect and profane. Lévi-Strauss builds on this dichotomizing approach, polarizing totemism and sacrifice. According to Lévi-Strauss, totemism is true, but sacrifice "adopts a conception of the natural series which is false."[14] Sacrifice is false because it falls within the realm of "continuity," which for Lévi-Strauss means disorder.

Frits Staal is perhaps the best-known contemporary scholar of sacrifice within the structuralist line. His book *Rules without Meaning: Ritual, Mantras and the Human Sciences* (1993) continues to generate controversy within ritual studies circles. In this volume Staal examines Vedic sacrifice, specifically the complex *agnicayana* ritual, to outline his theory. He argues that ritual, like any other human activity, can be studied scientifically. Drawing on linguistic distinctions between language and speech, he posits a similar opposition between meaning and rules. He argues that "the home of meaning is language," whereas ritual, which is governed by rules, is meaningless. "Ritual is pure activity, without meaning or goal. . . . To say that ritual is for its own sake is to say that it is meaningless, without function, aim or goal, or also that it constitutes its own aim or goal."[15] In a passage well known to ritual theorists, Staal explains,

> A widespread assumption about ritual is that it consists in symbolic activities which refer to something else. It is characteristic of a ritual performance, however, that it is self-contained and self-absorbed. The performers are totally immersed in the proper execution of their complex tasks. Isolated in their sacred enclosure, they concentrate on correctness of act, recitation and chant. Their primary concern, if not obsession, is

> with rules. There are no symbolic meanings going through their minds when they are engaged in performing ritual. . . . [W]hen we ask a Brahmin explicitly why the rituals are performed, we never receive an answer which refers to symbolic activity.[16]

Staal has made several important contributions to the study of ritual in general and sacrifice in particular. First, like a number of other scholars, he rejects the primacy of belief over ritual practice, thus eliminating the need for sacrifice to be understood as a dramatic presentation of myth or dogma. Second, Staal is quick to point out that sacrificial events are not necessarily dramatic in nature; nor do they build toward a decisive, climactic moment. Rather, it is more accurate to think of sacrifice as a complex sequence of events that unfold rather evenly. Third, Staal illuminates an orderliness to Vedic sacrifice in the relationship between different rites, an orderliness that has eluded many other scholars. He has become well known for arguing that complex Vedic rituals are understood more accurately as combinations of simpler rites organized in discernible patterns. This point is significant because many scholars have been willing to throw up their hands in despair of ever finding rhyme or reason in Vedic ritual. Staal himself quotes a well-known deprecatory remark by Julius Eggeling, the translator of the Śatapatha Brāhmaṇa: "For wearisome prolixity of exposition, characterized by dogmatic assertion and a flimsy symbolism rather than by serious reasoning, these works are perhaps not equalled [*sic*] anywhere."[17] Eggeling's words reflect the views of many scholars who, failing to discern rationality in complex sacrificial systems, simply assumed rationality was not there to be found. By bringing to light patterns in the unfolding of sacrificial rites, Staal demonstrates that there may be syntactic orderliness underlying seemingly disorganized practices. In doing so he demonstrates that the *relationship* between different activities performed in a ritual deserves as much attention as the individual activities themselves, if not more. We will see that this point is a crucial issue in understanding sacrificial ritual in general.

There are, however, a number of concerns with Staal's work. First, he arbitrarily chooses to restrict the term *sacrifice* in the Vedic system to "a ritual in which an animal is ritually killed," even though he is aware of the full complement of Vedic *śrauta* ("public") ritual offering substances.[18] Second, he focuses on what participants are thinking about during the course of a ritual and concludes from his informal questioning of priests

that since the priests are not thinking about what the ritual means *while they are performing sacrifices*, but rather about what to do next, the ritual ultimately has no meaning. In my own conversations with Vedic priests, however, it is clear that the priests take the meaning of sacrificial ritual very seriously. Otherwise, they would not perform it. Finally, much of Staal's work begins with assumptions about language and the relationship between the written and spoken word which many contemporary scholars reject. Despite these problems, however, Staal's attention to the interaction of sacrificial elements is a valuable contribution.

Feminist Scholarship and Sacrifice

One of the greatest challenges that the study of sacrifice presents is the blatant chauvinism that seems to run throughout sacrificial activity across time and space. Sacrifice, for the most part, has been largely an arena for men. In most cultures men have created the rules, dominated the ritual activity, and transmitted the oral and written sacrificial traditions. Sacrifice seems to have been one of the original boys' clubs.

Despite—or because of—this, several recent scholars have argued that sacrifice is also a critical arena in which gender roles are formed and played out. Consequently, the study of sacrifice can yield fresh insights into the construction of male and female identity. In addition, feminist theory can contribute much to our understanding of sacrifice. Two authors in particular have drawn attention to gender issues associated with sacrificial practice. Stephanie Jamison, examining Vedic sacrifice, builds on the notion of sacrifice as "cooking" or "hospitality," situating these activities in broader concepts of hospitality. In *Sacrificed Wife/Sacrificer's Wife* (1996), Jamison examines women's activity in Vedic sacrificial practice, particularly the sacrificer's wife (*patnī*). She argues:

> The elaborate codes of hospitality exist in order to exert some measure of control over potentially dangerous contact between strangers. Contact between men and gods is even more perilous, since the gods hold most of the cards. The fantastic intricacy of śrauta ritual can be interpreted again as a control mechanism, to regulate the damage that can result from such meetings. . . . Though we tend to think of these relationships as forged between males (and indeed they are, in some sense), the pivotal, mediating figure between the males is frequently a woman. She often dispenses hospitality and, perhaps more important, she is often the means of mak-

> ing alliances—through marriage. She performs this mediating role not only between *human* males but also between men and gods.[19]

Women, therefore, play a key role in sacrifice by mediating social relations as they are being negotiated in the sacrificial context. This perspective has been largely ignored by sacrificial studies and deserves further attention.

Nancy Jay takes a slightly different approach. She begins her book *Throughout Your Generations Forever: Sacrifice, Religion, and Paternity* with the bold claim, "In no other major religious institution is gender dichotomy more consistently important, across unrelated traditions, than it is in sacrifice." She goes on to argue that the practice of sacrifice is "remedy for having been born of woman."[20] Throughout her book she argues that sacrifice is placed in opposition to childbirth, the shedding of sacrificial blood in contradistinction to the blood shed by women in childbirth, a shedding of blood, by the way, that produces a far better result than woman's childbirth. Sacrifice is, in effect, childbirth envy run wild.

Feminist approaches address the importance of women's engagement with sacrifice at a number of levels. First, they examine previously ignored ritual activity performed by women within indigenous traditions. Second, they illuminate "patriarchal presuppositions" that have driven sacrificial theorizing, presuppositions that universalize male experience and ignore women's distinctive and marginalized experiences.[21] Finally, the work of scholars such as Stephanie Jamison and Nancy Jay brings women's voices into academic conversations about sacrificial theory, conversations still dominated by men to this day.

Both Jamison and Jay raise important issues, not just regarding women and sacrifice but also related to the study of women and ancient cultures more broadly. First, they draw attention to the "situatedness" of sacrificial activity. The nature of sacrifice is not the same in every culture, and the experience of sacrifice is not the same for all participants. In addition, Jamison and Jay raise issues about the study of minority communities through texts controlled by a dominant elite. Sources that contribute to the study of the religious elite may or may not be helpful for the study of women's activity. Jamison, for example, notes that many of her colleagues "believe that *no* trustworthy work can be done on gender issues for cultures we know only or primarily through texts, especially 'institutional,' not private texts." She confesses that her work "must all take place in what may seem like the most unpromising of verbal territory: texts preserved by men

for men as the foundation and support for an elaborate, well-organized, institutionalized religious system." Jamison argues, however, that research on women's experience *can* be done by making "the texts tell us things that their composers did not think they were saying; we must read between the lines."[22] Scholars interested in the feminine dimension of sacrificial activity are often forced to become ritual "detectives," generating a coherent picture by compiling scattered, seemingly unrelated pieces of data. Jamison, Jay, and other feminist scholars model a method for critical textual study with their work, opening avenues that promise fresh insights, not just about women but about any marginalized community that is represented textually by a small group of religious elite.

Sacrifice as Violence

In modern Western thought, sacrifice is most frequently associated with death, violence, and bloodshed. Consequently, it is no surprise that the most influential theories of sacrifice—certainly at the popular level, and even within academic circles—begin with the assumption that sacrifice involves the death of animal victims, including humans. A handful of scholars have dominated the field, characterizing sacrifice as various forms of destruction or violence. Henri Hubert and Marcel Mauss, Durkheim's foremost students, are generally credited with the first theoretical treatment of sacrifice that influenced religious studies as a discipline. Their collaborative work *Sacrifice: Its Nature and Functions* (1898) established the definitive perspective on sacrifice for the twentieth century. Hubert and Mauss's model claimed to provide a general schema for all sacrificial rituals. Drawing largely upon examples from Vedic and Jewish sacrificial traditions, they argued that all sacrifices occur in three stages: entry into the sacrificial arena, destruction of the victim, and exit from the arena. Hubert and Mauss note that the first phase (entry into the sacrificial arena) imparts a religious quality to the participants: "Sacrifice is a religious act that can only be carried out in a religious atmosphere and by means of essentially religious agents. But, in general, before the ceremony neither sacrifier [ritual patron] nor sacrificer [ritual priest], nor place, instruments, or victim, possess this characteristic to a suitable degree. The first phase of the sacrifice is intended to impart it to them. They are profane; their condition must be changed."[23] Thus Hubert and Mauss make a clear distinction between the realms of the sacred and the profane.

Destruction of the sacrificial offering is the defining characteristic of

sacrifice in their model: "[W]e must designate as sacrifice any oblation, even of vegetable matter, whenever the offering or part of it is destroyed."[24] The killing of the victim is absolutely essential; it is the climactic moment of the drama. In its destruction the victim's nature is fundamentally changed as it moves from the profane world to the sacred world.

According to Hubert and Mauss, sacrificial performances always involve a ritual patron, usually the person who is meant to benefit from the sacrifice; a ritual expert or priest, who usually performs or directs the sacrifice; and a victim. These three participants are the focus of Hubert and Mauss's study, with particular emphasis on the ritual patron. The purpose of their study is to modify the religious state of the ritual patron through manipulation of the victim: "Sacrifice is a religious act which, through the consecration of a victim, modifies the condition of the moral person who accomplishes it or that of certain objects with which he is concerned."[25] The death of the victim benefits the ritual patron.

Even though the destruction of the victim receives considerable attention in Hubert and Mauss's analysis of the sacrifice, the victim is significant only in relation to the ritual patron. Hubert and Mauss are primarily interested in how the manipulation of the victim benefits the ritual patron, and they argue that those benefits are acquired through the victim's death. Consequently, their approach to sacrifice focuses almost exclusively on the killing of the animal victim, and they virtually ignore all the other procedures to which the victim is subjected. As an object of scholarly interest, the victim is really secondary to the ritual patron in Hubert and Mauss's research, and they are therefore not concerned with the myriad other ways in which the victim is manipulated during the sacrifice.

Hubert and Mauss established the prevailing approach to sacrificial interpretation for many years to come. Sacrifice in their model is a drama, the unfolding of a story with a predetermined conclusion. The victim in this drama is a gift offered to the appropriate god(s). The offering of the victim, according to the rules of the sacrificial game, requires that the deity give something in return: "*do et des.*" The offering itself is acceptable as a gift only because it represents the ritual patron of the sacrifice. Until recently, most scholarship on ritual has accepted Hubert and Mauss's interpretation of the sacrifice in general and the victim in particular. As a result, although the sacrificial offering has been acknowledged as a pivotal element in the sacrifice, it has not received adequate attention in and of

itself as a helpful starting point for ritual scholarship because it has been viewed as "only" a substitute for the ritual patron himself.

Several modern scholars have recently begun to challenge Hubert and Mauss's model, approaching sacrifice from different perspectives. In particular, René Girard and Walter Burkert, building on the general theoretical work of Sigmund Freud, have developed approaches to the study of sacrifice which differ from that of Hubert and Mauss but still focus on the death of an animal victim. These approaches have gained increasing acceptance and now have as much influence in some circles as Hubert and Mauss's work. Girard, in his groundbreaking work *Violence and the Sacred* (1972), begins with the "violence" he sees inherent in sacrifice. "If sacrifice resembles criminal violence, we may say that there is, inversely, hardly any form of violence that cannot be described in terms of sacrifice." The sacrificial victim in Girard's scheme is the locus for violence that has been redirected from within human society onto a substitute animal victim that serves as a scapegoat. Consequently, religion can and should be studied in terms of this violence. In fact, Girard focuses on violence as the defining characteristic of sacrifice because of his broader interest in the principle of scapegoating. "[M]y research always leads me to emphasize scapegoating as the generative principle of mythology, ritual, primitive religion, even culture as a whole." Drawing largely upon Greek tragedy as his primary material, Girard argues that in sacrifice "society is seeking to deflect upon a relatively indifferent victim, a 'sacrificeable' victim, the violence that would otherwise be vented on its own members, the people it most desires to protect."[26] In Girard's view sacrifice has nothing to do with the guilt or innocence of the victim, or even the guilt or innocence of the individual whom the sacrificial victim represents. In addition, sacrifice has virtually nothing to do with deities or a divine realm. Rather, it has primarily to do with constructing a legitimate channel for the expression of society's aggression against its own members: "[Sacrifice] is a substitute for all the members of the community, offered up by the members themselves. The sacrifice serves to protect the entire community from *its own* violence; it prompts the entire community to choose victims outside itself. The elements of dissension scattered throughout the community are drawn to the person of the sacrificial victim and eliminated, at least temporarily, by its sacrifice."[27] In Girard's scheme, the participants are not aware of the scapegoating involved: "The celebrants do not and must not comprehend the

true role of the sacrificial act. The theological basis of the sacrifice has a crucial role in fostering this misunderstanding."[28] Maintaining the illusion that the sacrifice is required by an outside deity is essential.

Since sacrifice is the means of diverting violence in an acceptable fashion, the victim is important primarily as the object of that violence. The victim's identity is virtually inconsequential. Beyond the slaying of the victim, none of the other activities performed in relation to the victim draw Girard's attention because his views of the victim and sacrifice are secondary to his concerns about redirected human aggression.

Walter Burkert, like Hubert, Mauss, and Girard, focuses primarily on the death of animal victims, but for different reasons. Burkert assumes that sacrifice is rooted ultimately in hunting practices. In particular, he bases his approach to sacrifice on the hunting practices of Paleolithic culture. "I have attempted to derive sacrificial ritual from Paleolithic hunting. . . . The central, practical, and necessary act would be to kill animals for food. Sacrifice is ritual slaughter."[29] Like Girard, Burkert draws his data most heavily from Greek sacrifice, although he focuses on historical records rather than the Greek tragedies. In *Homo Necans* (1983), Burkert argues that the decisive moment of the hunt was the kill. Aggression engendered by intracultural conflict was redirected in the hunt for animal prey. According to Burton Mack's introduction to Burkert's work, "Aggression found its outlet by being projected on the prey, and this projection both heightened the significance of the hunt and the kill and provided the focal point for its ritualization." Rituals evolved that were centered on the kill, and myths developed as ways of reflecting upon the kill. Sacrifice in this context "functions as a dramatization of an activity around which society can be structured for the satisfaction of basic survival needs."[30] As in Girard's model, Burkert's work views the victim primarily as the site for redirected social aggression. Consequently, Burkert also focuses on the violence done to the victim, not on any other handling the victim receives.

Hubert, Mauss, Girard, and Burkert have each contributed in important ways to contemporary understandings of sacrifice. Although each scholar has his own unique approach to the study of sacrifice, they all share some features in common, features that tend to dominate—and limit—the current study of sacrifice. First, all three approaches emphasize the destruction of the animal victim and find in that activity the defining point of sacrifice. Hubert and Mauss put it most succinctly: "Through this act of destruction the essential action of the sacrifice was accomplished."[31]

Each of these scholars ignores or minimizes the other activities that are applied to the sacrificial offering, and in so doing they exaggerate the importance of killing, characterizing it as the essential feature of sacrificial activity. Second, all these scholars focus almost exclusively on animal offerings, rather than discussing the full complement of animal, vegetal, and liquid oblations that are used in various sacrificial rituals. Although some lip service is paid to the notion that sacrifice can involve nonanimal offerings, all three approaches largely ignore nonanimal offerings in their broader conclusions.

This brief review is by no means comprehensive, but it does delineate the basic approaches to sacrifice that dominate the field today. Certain common assumptions continue to persist. First, there is a fixation on animal sacrifice to such an extent that vegetal and liquid oblations are virtually ignored in theorizing, even though these substances are used far more frequently than animal offerings. Related to this focus on animal oblations is the assumption that sacrificial activity is violent, usually involving blood and gore. As we explore examples of sacrifice from brahmanical Hinduism and biblical and rabbinic Judaism and develop an approach to sacrifice grounded in these two complex traditions, we will gain a different perspective on sacrificial activity.

The Comparative Enterprise

This book is unapologetically comparative. We will be examining data from a number of religious traditions across space and time, with a particular focus on brahmanical Hindu and biblical and mishnaic Jewish textual representations of sacrifice. Yet the comparative study of religion has frequently been surrounded by controversy and criticism, often for good reason, so it deserves some comment before we begin. Many of the early comparativists oversimplified individual religious traditions in their search for universal religious elements. Such comparativists, perhaps most notably represented in the scholarly world by Mircea Eliade and in the popular world by Joseph Campbell, generated ahistorical, acontextual, consensual models of religious traditions. In other words, they largely glossed over differences and ignored sociohistorical contexts in their quest for universal religious elements. As a means of countering and correcting this universalizing tendency, one response within religious studies has been to give more emphasis to area studies. This approach is tradition-

specific in nature and in some circles has been presented as the only responsible way to do scholarship. An area studies approach has been celebrated as the disciplinary orientation that respects the individuality and complexity of each religious tradition.

More recently, however, a new brand of comparativism has been developing. A principal exponent of the need for responsible comparative work is Jonathan Z. Smith, one of the most influential religious studies scholars of his generation. Smith has asserted the importance of comparison as an integral part of the scholarly enterprise: "Comparison, as seen from such a view, is an active, at times even a playful, enterprise of deconstruction and reconstitution which, kaleidoscope-like, gives the scholar a shifting set of characteristics with which to negotiate the relations between his or her theoretical interests and data stipulated as exemplary. The comparative enterprise provides a set of perspectives which 'serve different analytic purposes by emphasizing varied aspects' of the object of study."[32] Smith has argued repeatedly for the importance of responsible comparison in several of his works. In doing so he situates himself in a lineage of scholars such as Morris Jastrow Jr., who advocated the comparative method at the beginning of the twentieth century: "A matured comparative method is as much concerned with determining where comparisons should not be made as with drawing conclusions from comparisons instituted."[33] Such comparison recognizes the value of discovering differences because it forces scholars to recognize subtleties in religious traditions that might otherwise seem unremarkable. Comparison also reveals the subjective nature of our scholarly categories and assumptions, which have often been treated as objective, because it often reveals that "universal truths" are, in fact, not universal at all.

A new generation of comparative scholars is becoming increasingly vocal. These scholars argue for a comparative methodology that recognizes the value of difference as well as that of similarity. For example, a recent volume of essays, *A Magic Still Dwells: Comparative Religion in the Postmodern Age*, asserts in multiple voices that comparative analysis has a critical role to play in the academic study of religion.[34] The present study situates itself within the broader context of contemporary comparative research.

Vedic and Jewish Sacrifice

In the following pages we will examine sacrifice in various religious traditions, with special emphasis on two sacrificial systems: brahmanical Hinduism and biblical and mishnaic Judaism. There are several reasons for focusing on these specific traditions. First, the Vedic tradition within Hinduism and the biblical and rabbinic traditions within Judaism include extensive, detailed primary texts for study because of the central role sacrifice has played as an authoritative category of religious experience. Staal has commented regarding the Vedic tradition: "Vedic ritual is not only likely to be the oldest surviving ritual of mankind, it also provides the best source material for a theory of ritual. This is not because it is close to any alleged 'original' ritual. Vedic ritual is not primitive and it is not an *Ur*-ritual. It is sophisticated and already the product of a long development. But it is the largest, most elaborate, and (on account of the Sanskrit manuals) best documented among the rituals of man."[35] The biblical and rabbinic texts also present elaborate and extensive descriptions of ancient Jewish sacrifice. Both traditions contain literally thousands of pages of primary material describing sacrificial procedures in exhausting detail. These traditions include extensive commentary literature that sheds light on how sacrifice in general and offering substances in particular are viewed within their own respective traditions.

The central importance of the brahmanical Hinduism and rabbinic Judaism sacrificial traditions is further evidenced by the fact that the founding fathers of sacrificial studies, Hubert and Mauss, chose these two traditions as the focus of their own landmark work. It seems only appropriate to draw upon the same sources they used. In addition, Hananya Goodman, in his edited volume *Between Jerusalem and Banares,* reminds readers that comparison between Hinduism and Judaism is nothing new. He notes that such efforts "have been an important thread woven into the fabric of Western intellectual thinking for centuries. Placing Hinduism and Judaism side by side has played an important part in European discussions of spirituality, primitivism, idolatry, theories of language and race origins, universalism and particularism, comparative mythology, and oriental studies."[36] Yet within religious studies, comparison between historically or geographically unrelated communities has often been frowned upon. No major study since *Sacrifice: Its Nature and Functions* (1898) has

compared the great sacrificial traditions of brahmanical Hinduism and biblical and rabbinic Judaism.

Until recently sacrifice has been examined independently within Vedic studies and Jewish studies. In both cases, research has been dominated by textual and philological work. Following the lead of the nineteenth-century Indologist F. Max Müller, early scholars of Vedic studies tended to give precedence to Vedic mythology, with a corresponding neglect of Vedic ritual. Prominent Indologists such as Müller and Julius Eggeling dismissed Vedic sacrifice as "magical" and nonsensical and characterized the ritual taxonomies described in the Brāhmaṇas, the sacrificial manuals, as arbitrary, inconsistent, and absurd. Consequently, far greater scholarly attention was lavished on Vedic myths than on the sacrificial rituals, which were viewed as hopelessly mired in elaborate and seemingly incoherent detail. Among early Indologists, Sylvain Lévi was one of the few scholars who sought to counter this trend by asserting the primacy of ritual as constitutive of Vedic religions.[37]

In recent decades the central importance of Vedic ritual has been championed by several scholars, who have argued, contrary to earlier critiques, that Vedic ritual is a coherent and well-ordered system. The historian of religions Brian K. Smith is the most eloquent proponent of such a view and has developed a theory of Vedic ritual to explicate the sacrificial system. In *Reflections on Resemblance, Ritual and Religion* he argues,

> Vedic "equations" are neither absurd nor random but are rather systematic expressions made possible (and logical) by fundamental Vedic principles of metaphysics and epistemology—of how the world is and how humans know and represent their knowledge. . . . [R]itual action was presented in Vedic texts not as symbolic or dramatic playacting, magical hocus-pocus, or "pure," transcendent, or meaningless activity. Rather, the sacrifice was displayed as a *constructive* activity, creating the human being (ontology), the afterlife (soteriology), and the cosmos as a whole (cosmology). It was also, of course, a social instrument—constructing individuals as part of a class and defining both the classified individual and the classes themselves from within the universe of the ritual. In sum, I will maintain that Vedism was a coherent and comprehensive system of doctrine and practice.[38]

I quote Smith at length here because the present study situates itself within the recent body of scholarship that views Vedic sacrifice as orderly, coherent, and an authoritative organizing category in brahmanical Hindu

society. Jan C. Heesterman, Charles Malamoud, Brian K. Smith, and Frits Staal have also argued that there is structure and coherence to Vedic ritual, although each of these scholars has developed his own distinctive theory to explain the significance of the ritual.[39]

Like early studies of Vedic sacrifice, scholarship on sacrifice in the Jewish tradition has been dominated by textual and philological approaches, with an emphasis on biblical studies or theological concerns. Jacob Milgrom's work on Leviticus in the Anchor Bible series is a definitive example of biblical studies work regarding sacrifice. Milgrom presents a thoughtful, detailed study of the biblical text, analyzing etymology and grammatical constructions and discussing sacrifice in the broader ancient Near Eastern context. Baruch Levine has also established himself as a preeminent scholar of biblical and rabbinic texts regarding sacrifice.[40] Although works such as Levine's and Milgrom's are invaluable resources for the study of Jewish sacrifice, they do not approach the category of sacrifice from the perspective of a comparative historian of religion.

Howard Eilberg-Schwartz is perhaps the best-known modern scholar of Jewish ritual working from a religious studies perspective, applying anthropological and historical methods to the biblical and rabbinic texts. In his introduction to *The Savage in Judaism*, he acknowledges the novelty of his approach: "[In the field of Jewish studies] certain kinds of questions are asked rather than others, . . . particular types of comparisons are considered fruitful while others are treated as uninteresting or irrelevant, and . . . certain methods are adopted to answer the questions interpreters deem important."[41] In particular Eilberg-Schwartz argues that "savage" elements have been largely excluded from scholarship on Judaism, partly in an attempt to distinguish Judaism from surrounding "primitive" religions and partly as an attempt to suppress the "savage" elements of the tradition such as sacrifice and circumcision.

Comparative work using data from Jewish sacrificial traditions has primarily focused on either highlighting similarities and differences between Jewish and Christian traditions, particularly early Christianity, or examining Jewish traditions in relation to cultures of the ancient Near East that were geographically close to the ancient Israelites. Both of these types of comparison have depended almost entirely on textual-philological or archaeological evidence. As Eilberg-Schwartz has emphasized, very few studies have attempted to compare Jewish traditions with religions, such as the Vedic tradition, that are not historically or geographically related.

> [C]omparisons between Israelite religion and non–Near Eastern religions have been unthinkable for mainstream interpreters of ancient Israel in the twentieth century. . . . [I]n the study of Israelite religion and ancient Judaism there has been a strong tendency to ignore anthropological theory, ethnographic literature, and cross-cultural studies. . . . When comparisons are tolerated, they are almost all of the metonymic variety, that is, between cultures and religions that are in a single geographical area and hence "in context." But there is a lack of interest in, and hostility toward, metaphoric comparisons, comparisons that are drawn between religions and cultures that are similar in some respect but are separated in place and perhaps also in time.[42]

Contrary to the dominant trend, I would argue that, irrespective of whether the Jewish and Vedic traditions are historically or geographically connected, a comparative study of these traditions' sacrificial systems can contribute in significant ways to an understanding of the category of sacrifice. Indeed, as Hubert and Mauss recognized, the ancient Jewish and Vedic traditions constitute the most appropriate candidates for such a study, for they have perhaps the most sophisticated, elaborate, and well-developed sacrificial systems in the world.

Fortunately, comparative work between Hinduism and Judaism more broadly has finally begun to receive sustained attention. Barbara A. Holdrege's *Veda and Torah: Transcending the Textuality of Scripture* (1996) is indicative of a growing interest in comparative research specifically on these two traditions. In 1995 the Comparative Studies in Hinduisms and Judaisms Consultation first convened a panel at the national meeting of the American Academy of Religion (AAR). That consultation has since been granted the official status of an AAR Group, and a number of published papers have been generated by conference presentations. The *Journal of Indo-Judaic Studies*, founded by Nathan Katz, is devoted exclusively to Hindu-Jewish comparisons, and other journals publish Indo-Judaic comparative work as well. Clearly, there is a growing recognition of the value of studying these two major world religions in relationship with one another.

The present study thus coincides with the recent upsurge of scholarly interest in the comparative study of Hindu and Jewish traditions. Through the comparative analysis of these traditions' sacrificial systems, I hope not only to contribute to the specialized corpus of scholarship on Vedic sacri-

fice and Jewish sacrifice respectively but also to challenge scholars to rethink the category of sacrifice as a cross-cultural category in the history of religions.

Comparison is, of course, a methodological approach, not a conclusion. In the following comparative analysis of the Vedic and Jewish sacrificial systems, the differences between the traditions will be just as significant as—if not more important than—the similarities. William Paden defines comparison as "the study of two or more objects in terms of a common factor, a common factor in relation to which either the differences or the similarity of the objects can become explicit and understood."[43] In this study the methods of manipulating the offering substance provide the "common factor." In other words, the focus is on the sacrificial oblation rather than the sacrificial actors. By focusing on the ritual substance (rather than ritual actors), we will focus on the *how* of sacrifice and allow ourselves to linger over the complexity of ritual activity rather than leaping ahead to questions of symbol or meaning. In addition, this study draws from two major sacrificial systems. If we want to be able to speak generally about the phenomenon of sacrifice, we must draw from more than one tradition in order to guard against generalizing cultural characteristics. Given the dominant influence that Protestant categories have had in shaping the discipline of religious studies in general and the characterization of sacrifice in particular, it will be immensely helpful to examine sacrifice from the perspective of two non-Christian traditions with extensive textual resources for such a study.

As mentioned earlier, we work in a time when renewed interest in comparison as a valid research approach is emerging within religious studies after years of severe criticism. Various scholars are articulating a disciplinary need for comparative work in the academy. William Paden goes so far as to assert that "it is the comparative, cross-cultural nature of religious subject matter which constitutes and justifies religious studies as a secular field of knowledge."[44] *Beyond Sacred Violence* is intended to contribute to religious studies generally, as well as to Vedic and Jewish studies specifically, by using the comparative method to challenge dominant conceptions of sacrifice that have largely been driven by Protestant Christian models.

The following chapters identify various elements of sacrifice and then approach these elements as "lenses" through which we can examine specific examples of sacrifice. Each chapter focuses on a particular dimension of

sacrificial activity, using that dimension as the stepping-off point for a certain line of inquiry. Chapter 1 lays out my overall approach, re-imagining sacrifice as a dynamic matrix of activity. After identifying individual sacrificial elements, we will examine how these elements interact to generate complex sacrificial events. Chapter 2 takes on the popular (but incorrect) assumption that sacrifice is simply ritual killing. It reevaluates the role that killing plays in sacrificial rituals, noting limitations on its scope as well as its interdependence with other activities. We will also note often overlooked issues prompted by killing, such as the presence or absence of bloodshed and the killing of plant oblations. Chapter 3 spotlights vegetal oblations, substances that are commonly used and yet just as commonly overlooked by sacrificial theorists. Chapter 4 focuses on liquid oblations, including blood, ghee, milk, and wine, which are commonly employed as sacrificial offerings yet commonly overlooked in sacrificial theorizing. We will see how the sacrifice of liquid substances involves distinct manipulations, manipulations with their own distinctive purposes. Chapter 5 continues to highlight the constructive and transformative dimensions of sacrifice, shifting our attention to the division and distribution of sacrificial offerings. We will see that offering substances in their "natural" forms have to be shaped and divided into ritually appropriate oblations, often involving the "trick" of transforming one substance into many whole oblations. Chapter 6 focuses on consumption, noting its constructive and mediating functions. We will see that consumption involves far more than eating; it raises issues surrounding hospitality, the transformation of sacrificial substances, and exchange. Finally, the Conclusion explores the continuities between traditional sacrifice and other forms of ritual activity that appropriate the term *sacrifice*. Over time many activities appropriate sacrificial terminology to authorize their inclusion within certain religio-cultural systems. In addition we will discuss how our examination of the various sacrificial elements challenges Protestant-based paradigms that dominate religious studies.

The following pages are meant to be suggestive, not comprehensive. I hope that by pursuing a polythetic approach, we can recognize sacrifice as a complex, dynamic, and persistent category of religious experience that continues to wield tremendous authority within religious communities and which promises to yield fresh insights for students of religion.

CHAPTER ONE

Re-imagining Sacrifice

> The notion of sacrifice is surrounded by considerable confusion.
> —JAN C. HEESTERMAN

Despite the importance of sacrifice as a phenomenon of religious experience, scholars have had considerable difficulty explaining it. One has the gut feeling that certain acts (e.g., a Roman Catholic Mass) are more sacrificial, others (e.g., a county fair pie-eating contest) less so. Why is this? What is it about certain events (and not others) that prompts us to think of them as sacrificial? I am going to suggest that a helpful starting point is to shift the question from "What is sacrifice?" to "What makes an event sacrificial?" It is a subtle shift but an important one. Throughout the following chapters I encourage the reader not to think of rituals as either "sacrifice" or "not sacrifice" but rather to view some rituals as more or less sacrificial than others. In so doing, we forgo the need to identify essential or defining characteristics of sacrifice. Instead, we recognize a wide spectrum of ritual activity in which certain ritual events are more or less sacrificial than others, depending upon several criteria.

In taking this approach we find ourselves in a long line of religious studies scholars building on the work of Jonathan Z. Smith. Perhaps more than any scholar of his generation, Smith has reshaped the disciplines of religious studies in general and ritual studies in particular. He draws from

Wittgenstein's understanding of "family resemblances" and applies this concept to religion, rejecting the notion that there are essential beliefs or practices that mark various religious traditions. In chapter 1 of his classic work *Imagining Religion*, for example, Smith argues that no single essential criterion can be found that definitively characterizes Judaism. He maintains instead that "[a] set of characteristics . . . may be used as one cluster toward the eventual polythetic classification of Judaism. What has animated these reflections and explorations is the conviction that students of religion need to abandon the notion of 'essence,' of a unique differentium for early Judaism. . . . We need to map the variety of Judaisms, each of which appears as a shifting cluster of characteristics which vary over time."[1] In other words, religious phenomena should not be defined so much as characterized. Throughout this book I take a similar approach to sacrifice. We will see that sacrificial rituals should be understood and studied as dynamic combinations of activities that vary from sacrificial event to sacrificial event. No individual element is definitive or essential to sacrifice; rather, distinctive combinations of basic activities generate rituals that are more or less sacrificial in nature.

Such an approach can be constructive for a number of reasons. Most important, understanding sacrifice as a matrix of interconnected events encourages us to replace cut-and-dried categorizations of ritual phenomena (sacrifice/not sacrifice) with a more nuanced understanding of ritual activity. Certain activities are *more* sacrificial than some but *less* sacrificial than others. In addition, such an approach encompasses the full range of activities that are performed in the course of a sacrificial event without looking for one defining activity.

This approach flies in the face of many popular notions of sacrifice. Many people—scholars and lay people alike—assume that there must be one essential or definitive element of sacrifice that distinguishes it from other ritual activity. At the very least, they look for an overarching metaphor that characterizes sacrifice. For example, the most common image associated with sacrifice is killing, and many people argue that killing is a definitive, essential element of sacrifice. Even those who oppose killing as a defining element usually respond by suggesting an alternative essential element. For example, in the entry "Sacrifice" in *The Encyclopedia of Religion*, author Joseph Henninger argues that " 'killing' can be applied only to living beings, human or animal, and thus does not cover the whole range of objects used in sacrifice as attested by the history of religions. *A*

truly essential element, on the other hand, is that the recipient of the gift be a supernatural being."[2] It is tempting to try to discover the one true key that will unlock the mysteries of sacrificial activity. Alas, such a key does not exist. In fact, searching for such a key oversimplifies sacrificial phenomena and seals off many productive avenues of investigation.

Re-imagining sacrifice as a dynamic matrix of activity also underscores the fact that no single activity (such as eating, killing, or exchange) is inherently "sacrificial." Rather, certain actions become sacrificial when they collaborate dynamically with other actions. For example, the person who consumes the wafer at the Roman Catholic Mass would never confuse the consumption of that wafer with the consumption of Grandma's pie at the county fair three hours later. "Consumption" in and of itself is not sacrificial. But consumption in collaboration with other activities (association of the wafer with Christ's death on the cross; apportionment of the wafer under the direction of ritual elite) generates a sacrificial event. A polythetic approach to ritual draws attention to the importance of the interactions *between* activities. Understanding the polythetic nature of sacrifice will prevent us from focusing inappropriately on any single activity (e.g., killing, consumption) or overlooking the significance of others (e.g., apportionment, heating).

In addition, the polythetic approach helps us to understand how the term *sacrifice* can be applied to activities that are not traditional sacrifices but which effectively appeal to the authority of sacrifice as a religious phenomenon. For example, it is common in contemporary culture to view certain acts involving setting aside time, material goods, status, or even physical well-being as "sacrifice." One need not conclude from this observation that sacrifice equals "setting aside." Rather, we can acknowledge that the apportionment of material or immaterial resources, as one strand of sacrificial activity, occurs in other contexts and that, through a specific interpretation of apportionment, individuals and communities are able to appropriate sacrificial authority in certain contexts. This acknowledgment does not make apportionment a definitive sacrificial element. Rather, it suggests that a number of traditional sacrificial activities—including but not limited to apportionment—can be found in other activities that can then successfully appropriate the language and authority of traditional sacrifice.

In the following pages I identify basic activities that generate sacrificial events when they are combined with one another. Certain rituals are more or less sacrificial, depending on (1) how many of these activities are pres-

ent and (2) how formally and intimately these activities are related to one another. Throughout the rest of this book we will be examining these activities, exploring how and in what contexts they contribute to sacrificial rituals. In the process, three important conclusions will become apparent. First, despite the emphasis on death and violence in the most popular treatments of sacrifice, sacrifice does not equal "killing." In some sacrifices, there is no killing at all. In the sacrificial rituals that do involve killing, it occurs in unexpected forms, and in many rituals killing is not the primary act.

Second, sacrificial oblations include animal, vegetal, and liquid substances. Most theoretical approaches to sacrifice, however, focus exclusively on animal offerings. This arbitrary and uneven treatment leads to several misconceptions about sacrificial rituals. It focuses attention on a subset of oblations (animals) rather than encompassing the wide variety of oblation material, including vegetal and liquid substances such as grains, wine, milk, and ghee (clarified butter). As a result, it tends to highlight activities frequently conducted with animal oblations, such as violence, bloodshed, and death. However, in many traditions animal sacrifices occur far less frequently than do nonanimal sacrifices. Purely pragmatically, animal offerings are more costly than grain offerings, so they are performed more rarely. Consequently, theoretical approaches that are driven by animal sacrifice do not address the full spectrum (or even the majority) of sacrificial oblations or activity.

Finally, many approaches to sacrifice grounded in the academic study of religions still arise out of a paradigm shaped by Protestant Christian thought and practice. As Barbara Holdrege notes,

> brahmanical "Hinduism" and rabbinic "Judaism" represent two species of the same genus and provide a model of "religious tradition" that is distinctly different from the prevailing Christian-based model that has tended to dominate the academic study of religion. . . . The brahmanical and rabbinic traditions . . . provide an alternative paradigm of "religious tradition," in which priority is given to issues of practice, observance, and law, and notions of tradition-identity are delineated primarily in terms of ethnic and cultural categories that reflect the predominantly nonmissionary character of these traditions.[3]

Current thinking about sacrifice reflects historical biases toward Christianity that pervade our discipline.[4] By focusing on Vedic and Jewish

sacrificial systems and by taking a polythetic approach, the present work is intended to offer an important corrective, not only for the study of sacrifice but more broadly for the comparative study of religion.

The Elements of Sacrifice

Several activities occur regularly during sacrificial events, and these basic "building blocks" of activity combine in various ways to generate sacrificial events. I argue that these activities tend to fall into several general types: selection, association, identification, killing, heating, apportionment, and consumption. I explore each of these in more detail in the following chapters, grounding them in specific examples, but let me offer a brief overview here.

Selection

"Selection" refers to the activities involved in procuring the appropriate sacrificial substance. Selection involves obtaining the correct general type of offering (bull, goat, soma stalk), as well as satisfying specific criteria that determine the suitability of any particular offering (age, gender, unblemished appearance). Often the act of selection in and of itself indicates the purpose of a sacrifice or at least narrows the options somewhat. For example, the selection of a bull oblation within the Jewish system can indicate that one is about to perform an *ʿōlâ* or a *ḥaṭṭāʾt* rite, whereas a grain offering generally indicates a *minḥâ,* both of which serve very different purposes. In past theorizing, the selection of the offering has not been considered part of the ritual itself; rather, it has been treated as a necessary —but uninteresting—prelude. But the choice of oblation material often indicates the intent of the sacrifice and in some cases inaugurates the sacrificial time frame. In addition, the presentation of the prescribed oblation, animal or nonanimal, in suitable physical condition, is necessary for any of the other activities to occur.

Association

"Association" refers to the activities that publicly link an oblation with one or more deities. Sometimes an oblation is automatically associated with a particular deity. For example, in Vedic thought, goats are traditionally associated with Agni. No ritual action is required because there is already a cultural understanding that links the animal with the deity. In

other cases, some sort of activity must be performed to associate an oblation with a particular deity. For example, the Jewish sacrificial system requires that the animal victim be oriented in a particular cardinal direction, publicly associating the sacrifice with YHWH.[5] In either case, at some point during the ritual the offering is often associated with a particular god.

At first glance, it might seem that association would be important in polytheistic traditions (in which there are a number of deities with whom an offering might be associated) but not in monotheistic traditions (in which there seems to be only one possible association). After all, Israelite sacrifices were all directed to YHWH, so why would one need to associate an oblation with him? We find, however, that certain activities were performed to associate an offering with one community's preferred deity in contradistinction to the god(s) of surrounding communities. For example, as mentioned earlier, a bull intended for YHWH was supposed to be slaughtered with its head to the south and its face turned toward the west.[6] Surrounding non-Israelite communities, in contrast, slaughtered their bulls facing downward or upward, so the very method of slaughter associated the offering with YHWH and distinguished the Israelites from other communities at the onset of ritual activity. Association, therefore, sometimes denotes interreligious differences as well as intrareligious preferences.

Identification

"Identification" refers to the practice of correlating an offering with a ritual patron, the one who benefits from the sacrifice. Some action occurs, usually early in the ritual, that publicly identifies the offering substance with an individual or group. For example, in Jewish animal sacrifice, Leviticus specifies that an individual should lay hands on an animal victim's head in the ritual arena prior to its slaughter (Lev. 1:4, 3:2, 3:8, 3:18). This act identifies the individual (or the community that the individual represents) with the animal. From this point on the offering is usually understood to "stand in" or substitute for this individual or group. Acts of identification vary from tradition to tradition, even from offering substance to offering substance, but generally some public action is performed to indicate the beneficiary of any particular sacrifice.

Killing

"Killing" refers to the intentional execution of the offering. I choose to use the term *killing* as we address issues surrounding the death of an

offering for several reasons. Most important, the concept of killing is tremendously influential in the dominant theories of sacrifice, so it is important to keep the term as we explore its nuances and limitations. However, at least within the pages of this book, killing does not mean the same thing as destruction or violence. Each of these terms suggests distinctive activities that are often, but not always, related and which must not be conflated.

In addition, the term *killing* is important for our study because of the language frequently interpreted to refer to killing in the Vedic and Jewish texts. When we begin to examine vocabulary specifically referencing killing, we find somewhat surprising results. Sometimes terms explicitly referring to killing do not occur where one might expect them (as in Vedic animal sacrifice). I argue that we can learn as much about killing's proper significance in sacrifice from noting when killing is *not* mentioned as from noting when it *is* mentioned. In addition, language referring to killing occurs unexpectedly in other contexts (as in Vedic soma sacrifice, which focuses on a plant stalk as its central offering). The surprising presence or absence of killing language in certain sacrificial contexts has important implications for sacrificial theorizing, especially when that theorizing depends upon images of death, substitution, and bloodshed.

Finally, we will note how killing is related to other activities in sacrificial rituals, such as identification of the victim with a sacrificial patron or apportionment of the offering. Killing never stands alone in sacrifice; it is always combined with other actions, some of which may actually have more ritual significance than the act of killing itself. In light of these issues, although I acknowledge the importance of killing in certain sacrificial contexts, I argue that killing has often been overrated and oversimplified in sacrificial theorizing. In the following pages, I suggest that we can learn more about the nature of sacrifice by situating killing in the broader context of and in relationship with several other types of sacrificial activity. Such an approach should prompt new appreciation of what killing does—and does not—accomplish.

Heating

"Heating" refers to placing an offering on top of a sacrificial fire, either directly or in some kind of container. I prefer to use *heating* rather than *cooking* for several reasons. First, heating is a broad concept that can encompass a number of activities, including but not limited to cooking

(which I understand to be preparation for consumption). For example, some oblations are heated in order to purify them or to transform them for subsequent ritual manipulation. It is important to distinguish the different reasons for which an oblation is heated.

When heating does refer to cooking, we also need to note that there are different methods of cooking oblations (e.g., boiling, baking, roasting, frying) and that each cooking method serves a distinct purpose. The general term *heating* can encompass the different ways offerings are cooked. In addition, just as some oblations are heated without necessarily being cooked, similarly some oblations are "cooked" without being heated (at least in the traditional sense). For example, Charles Malamoud has argued that, within the Vedic sacrificial system, soma juice is "cooked" in milk: "Mixed together with a cooked substance—including milk—*soma* is thus considered to be cooked."[7] The broader term *heating* allows us to note various types of and purposes for heating without conflating it with cooking.

Apportionment

"Apportionment" refers to the division of a single offering unit into multiple pieces or portions and the assignation of these portions to specific ritual participants, including the ritual patron, various priests, and the god(s). For example, in the Jewish sacrificial system, the fat (*ḥēleb*) and the blood (*dām*) must be given to YHWH. No human is permitted to receive either of these animal elements, and a sacrifice would be invalidated if these elements were distributed improperly. The process of apportionment makes it possible for one substance to generate multiple discrete offerings, each of which plays a distinct role within the sacrificial ritual.

The apportionment of oblations plays a key role within sacrificial ritual, often indicating the personality of individual sacrifices. In addition, apportionment often displays and reinforces the relationships between the ritual players. Consequently, the distribution of sacrificial portions is a key procedure in sacrificial activity. As such, it deserves further attention than it has received to date, since it brings to light the constructive dimensions of sacrifice. We will see that sacrifice is not primarily about destruction but about the construction of new elements and the redistribution of those elements.

Consumption

"Consumption" refers to the ingestion of the sacrificial offering either by the ritual participants—priest or laity (or both)—or by the god(s)

involved in the sacrifice. For example, in the Jewish *šĕlāmîm,* the altar fire consumes the fat (as YHWH's rightful portion), but "the breast meat shall belong to Aaron and his sons" (Lev. 7:31). Consumption includes but is not limited to "eating." We will see, for example, that inhaling the aroma of an oblation is sometimes referred to as consumption, indicating that a sacrificial oblation can be ingested in various forms. In addition, some sacrificial events prohibit consumption of certain portions of an oblation, but others do not. For instance, in the Jewish sacrificial tradition, a bull offering may be presented in the context of an *ʿōlâ* ritual and a *šĕlāmîm* ritual. None of the *ʿōlâ* offering may be consumed by any human being, but portions of the very same animal offering may be consumed by priests and laity when it is used in the *šĕlāmîm* ritual. Fundamentally, certain offerings are always "off limits" to ritual participants. Within the Jewish system, the blood and fat may never be consumed by YHWH's followers. These portions belong solely to him, marking Judaism as distinct from other ancient Near Eastern sacrificial systems. The actions involved in and rules governing consumption play a crucial role in distinguishing certain sacrificial rites—and, in fact, entire sacrificial systems—from others.

The Polythetic Approach

Combinations of the seven activities described above—selection, association, identification, killing, heating, apportionment, and consumption—characterize sacrificial ritual, primarily in brahmanical Hinduism and biblical and rabbinic Judaism but also in other religious traditions. These activities may occur in different sequences. For example, sometimes an oblation is heated before it is divided into portions; at other times it is divided first. In addition, sometimes all seven activities are performed; sometimes only a few occur. The presence of many or a few of these activities makes a ritual more or less sacrificial in nature.

In addition, each of these elements becomes more sacrificial in nature as it is more formally or intimately connected with other elements. For example, killing alone is not sacrifice. But the killing of a preselected animal victim, which is subsequently divided according to traditional guidelines by ritual experts and apportioned to individual participants according to social and religious ranking, is highly sacrificial. Killing gains sacrificial authority by being performed within the context of other activities, all of which reinforce one another's sacrificial (and authoritative) status.

Why is any of this significant? What is helpful about characterizing sacrificial events as clusters of different types of activities? We will see that there are several important benefits. First, such an approach honors the complexity of sacrificial activity without being overwhelmed by it. Rather than circumscribing sacrifice with one well-intentioned but oversimplistic metaphor (such as death or a meal), the polythetic approach focuses on the broad complex of activity involved in sacrificial events. Second, such an approach reflects the priestly discussions of sacrifice found within traditional sacrificial texts without being beholden to them. That is, the model proposed is grounded in the authoritative textual representations of sacrificial traditions (particularly the Vedic and Jewish traditions), discussions that commonly focus on specific aspects of sacrificial events. At the same time, this approach does not allow any individual tradition to dictate the language or parameters of the discussion. Finally, this approach draws our attention to the multiplicity of sacrificial activity, which in turn brings to light ritual substances that are frequently overlooked, such as vegetal (grain, soma stalks) and liquid (blood, wine, ghee) substances.

Perhaps most helpful, a polythetic approach sheds light on the connections between traditional sacrifice and the appropriation of "sacrifice" as a way of describing other activities. For example, rabbinic Judaism characterized prayer and Torah study as sacrifice in the post-Temple Jewish world. How were the rabbis able to take a term that originally referred to animal, grain-cake, and wine offerings in a Temple setting and apply it successfully to prayer and the study of a text? Obviously, many complex historical and sociocultural factors are at play here, but I argue that, at least in part, prayer and Torah study were able to be characterized as sacrifice because they include some of the sacrificial activities discussed above. Similarly, within Hinduism, certain yogic self-disciplines accomplish the same result as Vedic sacrifice, transforming elements of sacrificial activity while relinquishing others. Closer to home, notions of civil sacrifice that underlie individual actions in the twenty-first century also have roots in the elements of traditional sacrifice that we will examine in the coming pages. Consequently, individual and national acts of "self-sacrifice" are able to appropriate some of the authority of traditional sacrifice. Generally speaking, an increased recognition of the polythetic nature of sacrifice will be helpful not only in studying traditional sacrificial activity but also in guiding research into other practices that tap into the authoritative category of sacrifice.

Vedic and Jewish Sacrifice

For the reasons set forth in the Introduction, this study depends largely on data drawn from the Vedic and Jewish sacrificial systems. The primary material we will be examining, however, does not necessarily represent the historical actualities of Vedic and Jewish sacrifice; rather, these priestly discussions represent sacrifice from the perspective of the religious leadership in each community. These texts present sacrifice in the ideal and cannot be interpreted as records of historical sacrifices that were actually performed. Priestly manuals were prescriptive, not descriptive, in nature. To make things more complicated, the ritual texts often present contradictory accounts and, paradoxically, significant omissions, largely because they include information meant to be transmitted over a long period of training within the context of a priestly school. It would be impossible to reconstruct either Vedic or Jewish sacrifice on the basis of the texts alone.

At the same time, the textual traditions available to us (originally oral transmissions) provide invaluable data for understanding sacrificial procedures. Priestly records can be helpful when understood as representations of the ritual arena as the religious elite wanted it to be conceptualized. Although we cannot assume that these textual representations describe what actually happened, we can conclude that the texts available to us describe sacrificial ritual as the religious leadership thought it ought to be represented. For readers unfamiliar with these traditions, I provide a brief overview of the Vedic and Jewish sacrificial systems below.

Vedic Sacrifice

The complex and elaborate practices of Vedic sacrifice (usually equated with the Sanskrit term *yajña*) were most prevalent in India from approximately 1000 BCE to 200 BCE. Although the practice of Vedic sacrifice has declined, it is still very much alive, particularly in South India. Most of what we know about Vedic *śrauta* ("public") ritual comes from ancient texts, and several sources are particularly relevant for our purposes. The Vedic Saṃhitās (ca. 1500–800 BCE), the oldest ritual texts, are collections of mantras, which are recited by ritual participants during sacrificial rites. The Brāhmaṇas (ca. 900–650 BCE), although composed later than most of the Saṃhitās, explain the meaning and purposes that underlie the ritual performances. The Brāhmaṇas focus on the creator deity Prajāpati, who inaugurates sacrificial practice in his cosmogonic activity. The Śrauta

Sūtras (ca. 800–300 BCE) provide an enumeration of the sacrificial rules and meta-rules, describing in detail what each ritual participant is required to do in various sacrifices. The Śrauta Sūtras developed out of various priestly schools, and some differences between distinct priestly traditions are reflected in the texts. The bulk of the information for the present study is taken from the Śrauta Sūtras, the foundational discussions of Vedic sacrifice.

The Vedic sacrificial system is characterized primarily by substances offered into fire. Vedic sacrifice is divided into two main types of rituals: *śrauta* (public) and *gṛhya* (domestic). The *śrauta* rituals are generally thought to be older and more complex than the *gṛhya* rituals, which focus on life-cycle events such as birth, initiation, marriage, and death.

Vedic *śrauta* rituals can be divided into two types of sacrifices: obligatory (*nitya*) and optional (*kāmya*). Obligatory sacrifices are required of each twice-born (*dvija*) married male who has established the sacrificial fires at his own household.[8] The obligatory *śrauta* rituals should be performed on a daily, monthly, or annual basis (correlated with lunar dates in the calendar) or when certain events occur. For example, every twice-born male is required to perform a simple obligatory ritual daily: simply pouring ghee into fire. Optional sacrifices, in contrast, are performed according to an individual's desire. These are performed if the ritual patron, the *yajamāna*, wants to obtain special worldly ends (such as wealth, cattle, progeny) or when he wants to ensure that he will go to heaven after his death. For our purposes, it is important to note whether a sacrifice is obligatory or optional because the designation affects one's ability to alter or adapt the sacrifice in any way. For example, in obligatory sacrifices only "the principal part must be performed, for it in itself is sufficient to incur the intended object ([Mīmāṃsā-sūtra] 6.3.1–4). An optional rite, on the other hand, must be performed in its entirety because the principal part, having no connection with the 'fruit' of the rite, cannot achieve the desired result (6.3.8–9)."[9] In other words, since an obligatory sacrifice is by definition required, accommodations to the procedures are permitted so that if one can perform only the main part of the rite, it is considered sufficient. Optional sacrifices, however, allow for no such accommodation; they must be performed in their entirety, with no corners cut.

Śrauta rituals are also divided into three categories depending upon the nature of *dravya*, or primary offering substance: *iṣṭi* sacrifices, *paśubandha* sacrifices, and soma sacrifices.[10] *Iṣṭi* sacrifices, which vary in complexity,

use as their primary offerings vegetal substances such as rice or barley grains. The *darśapūrṇamāsa* (new- and full-moon sacrifice) is considered the prototypical *iṣṭi. Paśubandha* sacrifices use animals as their main offering, primarily goats.[11] The term *paśubandha*, meaning "binding of the animal victim," refers to the tying of the animal to the sacrificial post, a central feature of the ritual. *Paśubandha* sacrifices are either performed independently or incorporated into more complex soma sacrifices. The third category of sacrifices, soma sacrifices, is named for the plant soma, the primary offering substance in the ritual. The central activity of the soma sacrifice is the repeated pressing of the soma plant to extract its juice so that participants can drink the juice, which is said to be a hallucinogen. Soma sacrifices range from the simple *agniṣṭoma* to the complex twelve-day *agnicayana*. Both the animal and the soma sacrifices are considered "great sacrifices."

The different types of *śrauta* rituals belong to a hierarchy that becomes increasingly complicated as one moves from *iṣṭi* to *paśubandha* to soma sacrifices. More complicated rituals, positioned higher in the hierarchy, incorporate within them less complicated rituals ranked lower on the hierarchy. It may be helpful to think of the sacrificial system as a series of concentric circles rather than as distinct, separate sacrifices. Every *paśubandha* sacrifice includes a number of *iṣṭi* sacrifices, and every soma includes a number of *iṣṭi* and *paśubanda* sacrifices. The Vedic *śrauta* system, then, begins with building blocks of relatively simple sacrifices and combines them into increasingly complex, elaborate sacrifices. Each of the rituals, from the simplest *agnihotra* to the complex *agnicayana*, is considered a *yajña*, or sacrifice within the tradition itself.

In this study we will focus on the manipulation of the primary offering substance in each sacrifice.[12] KŚS 1.2.4 explains that the primary offerings are subjected to "the critical actions in the ritual procedures for the attainment of the purpose and 'fruit' [= results]." These substances are manipulated by one or more priests. These priests are all *brahmin* men, and thus both genealogy and gender determine whether an individual is qualified to perform ritual practices. Each priest is trained in one of a variety of schools that instruct priests regarding their responsibilities during the performance of certain sacrificial rituals. During the Saṃhitā period four main classes of priests developed (*adhvaryu*, *hotṛ*, *udgatṛ*, and *brahman*), each with different responsibilities. The *adhvaryu* priest, for example, is responsible for performing most of the ritual activity, including the ma-

nipulation of the oblations while pronouncing the *yajuses* of the Yajur-Veda Saṃhitās. The *brahman* priest is responsible for overseeing the entire sacrificial ritual. He is trained to correct mistakes made by other priests through the use of expiatory formulas (*prāyaścittas*). Sacrifice also requires the participation of the *yajamāna* (the ritual patron) and the *patnī*, his wife. The *yajamāna*, like the priests, must be twice-born, that is, from one of the three highest classes (*varṇas*) of Indian society. The differentiation of responsibility is thus highly developed in Vedic ritual.

Vedic sacrifices are generally performed in temporary ritual spaces constructed outdoors for particular sacrificial performances. The ritual area is oriented to the four cardinal directions. An enclosure is constructed for the *iṣṭi* rites. A second enclosure is constructed to the east of this for *paśubandha* and soma sacrifices. A *havirdhāna* area is constructed within the eastern enclosure for use in soma sacrifices only. Three fires are situated within the ritual arena. The *āhavanīya* fire is where the offerings are presented. The *gārhapatya* fire is where the offerings are prepared. The *dakṣināgni* fire is ritually relatively less important. It is used to prepare a meal for the ritual participants and to cook rice balls offered to the ancestors in one rite.

Jewish Sacrifice

The Jewish sacrificial system, outlined originally in the Bible and elaborated upon in the rabbinic texts, is traditionally held to be a central component of the divinely ordained commandments (*mitzvoth*) prescribed for the Jews. According to the Bible, the sacrificial code, along with other socioreligious guidelines, was given by YHWH and presented through Moses to the Israelites just as they were about to enter the Promised Land.[13] The rules for sacrifice were integral to the Israelites as they began to occupy Canaan and to establish the civil, religious, and social community ordained for them.

Jewish sacrifice is discussed in great detail in Leviticus and less extensively in Numbers and Exodus. In particular, "P," the Priestly source, is credited with the strands of literature within the Pentateuch that explicitly discuss priestly functions. P is preoccupied with the priestly responsibilities for sacrifice, presumably sacrifice in the Tabernacle, or Tent of Meeting (*'ōhel mô'ēd*), before the establishment of centralized cultic practice in Jerusalem. The redactor P, therefore, offers a kind of prototype of the sacrificial system, not a historical account. Like the Śrauta Sūtras, the

biblical texts are more prescriptive than descriptive, discussing how sacrifice was *supposed* to be performed, not necessarily what *actually* occurred.

Sacrifices were performed originally in the Tabernacle, which traveled with the Israelites, and, as the northern and southern kingdoms developed, various cultic centers arose.[14] Under King David and his son Solomon (ca. 1020–922 BCE), sacrificial practices began to be gradually concentrated in Jerusalem in the Temple. The ground plans of the Tabernacle and the Temple were, of course, different, but the layout of the area specifically concerned with sacrificial activity varied only slightly. Eventually worship was centralized in the Temple in Jerusalem, where the priestly community continued sacrificial practice until the Temple was destroyed in 70 CE by the Romans.

The Mishnah (ca. 220 CE) includes the earliest rabbinic discussions of the sacrifices to be performed at the Temple in Jerusalem. It records various rabbis' opinions regarding the most minute ritual details. Indirectly it provides insight into priestly activity that must have actually occurred, since certain passages seem to allude to problems that arose during the execution of specific rites. For example, M. Zebāḥîm 2.1 refers to an accidental spill and discusses whether the subsequent offering could be considered valid. Between the Bible and the Mishnah we have detailed information about various models for and actual performances of sacrificial activity. Consequently the present study is drawn primarily from the discussions of sacrifice in the Bible and the Mishnah.

The Jewish sacrificial system consists of five basic sacrificial rites: the *ʿōlâ*, the *ḥaṭṭāʾt*, the *ʿāsām*, the *šĕlāmîm*, and the *minḥâ*. Each of these rites is distinguished by its intended effect, by the procedures involved in performing the sacrifice and, most important, by the offering substance used in the sacrifice. These five sacrificial rites are basic building blocks, either performed independently or combined with one another to create more complex rituals. Individual building blocks are combined to create the specifically named sacrifices, such as the *tāmîd* (twice-daily offerings) or Yom Kippur (Day of Atonement). The Bible classifies the basic sacrificial rites in different ways. For example, the *ʿōlâ*, the *šĕlāmîm*, and the *minḥâ* are voluntary offerings; the *ḥaṭṭāʾt* and the *ʿāšām* are mandatory.[15]

The *ʿōlâ*, or "whole burnt" offering, ranks first in order of importance in the Jewish sacrificial system. The *ʿōlâ* expunges guilt generated by the neglect of the positive commandments.[16] Jacob Milgrom states that its purpose was "to elicit the favor of the deity."[17] Baruch Levine comments

that the *ʿōlâ* "was offered up with the objective of evoking an initial response from the deity prior to bringing the primary concerns of his worshippers to his attention."[18] In the *ʿōlâ* an animal offering is burned in its entirety on the altar as a gift to YHWH, offered principally to ask for expiation. As such, the *ʿōlâ* was performed as the principal daily offering. According to Leviticus 6:9, "The burnt offering shall be on the hearth upon the altar all night until morning, and the fire of the altar shall be kept burning on it."

The *ḥaṭṭāʾt*, or "transgression" offering, is the second most important sacrificial rite. The *ʿōlâ* is probably more ancient than both the *ḥaṭṭāʾt* and the *ʾāšām*, but gradually the *ḥaṭṭāʾt* and the *ʾāšām* developed into the two principal expiatory (*kippēr*) sacrifices.[19] The *ḥaṭṭāʾt*, which involves an animal offering, is required when inadvertent, unintentional (*šegāgâ*) sin occurs. Specifically, it expiates inadvertent violations of prohibitive commandments (what one should not do) rather than the neglect or omission of positive commandments (what one is obliged to do).[20] The *ḥaṭṭāʾt*, thus, cannot expiate intentional violations of the law. T. Shabbāt 1.1 makes the distinction clear: "One cannot bring something out from a private place into a public place. Nor can someone bring something in from a public place into a private place. If someone brought something out or in unintentionally, he is liable for a transgression [*ḥaṭṭāʾt*] offering; if he did so deliberately, he is punishable by being cut off [Hebrew root *krt*] or by stoning." The *ḥaṭṭāʾt*, thus, has limited but targeted efficacy.

The *ḥaṭṭāʾt* can be offered on behalf of the community as a whole or for individuals. When the community sins, the *ḥaṭṭāʾt* purifies the sanctuary from the contamination that follows from sin so that the sacrificial system as a whole can continue. The most important community *ḥaṭṭāʾt* is offered on Yom Kippur, the Day of Atonement, when the innermost area of the sanctuary is cleansed of the accumulated offenses of the community.[21] In addition, the *ḥaṭṭāʾt* can be used to address unintentional individual sins. For example, someone who has accidentally had contact with a dead corpse is required to perform a *ḥaṭṭāʾt* sacrifice.[22] However, different offerings are required depending on who committed the error: a priest, the entire community, a ruler, or a common man.[23]

The *ḥaṭṭāʾt* is distinctive because it primarily addresses the purity of the sanctuary space, not that of the sacrificer. At the beginning of a sacrificial ritual, the *ḥaṭṭāʾt* rite cleanses the sanctuary on behalf of someone who has contaminated the sanctuary because of his transgression, but it does not

cleanse the individual himself. Rather, it purifies the sanctuary of ritual contamination caused by a person's sin.[24] For example, if an individual sacrifices his child to Molech, that individual must be put to death to pay for his sin. In addition, however, the community must offer a *ḥaṭṭāʾt* to purify the sanctuary so that the community's ritual life can continue. Clearly the offering in this case does not purify the individual involved; he is executed.[25] Rather, the performance of the *ḥaṭṭāʾt* addresses the impurity caused by the individual's behavior. The focus of the *ḥaṭṭāʾt* is the contamination of the sanctuary of YHWH.

The *ʿāšām* is the third type of sacrificial rite. Like the *ḥaṭṭāʾt*, the *ʿāšām* is mandatory and involves an animal offering (Lev. 5:1–19, 7:1–7). The *ʿāšām*, however, differs from the *ḥaṭṭāʾt* rite in several ways. The word *ʿāšām* is most frequently translated as "guilt" offering, although the precise meaning of "guilt" has been interpreted in many different ways.[26] The name emphasizes the fact that the *ʿāšām* is performed when an individual feels guilt for a previous error.[27] Whereas the *ḥaṭṭāʾt* is performed in response to the discovery of an unwitting sin, the *ʿāšām* is performed when an individual feels or internalizes guilt over a past sin. The emphasis in the texts referring to the *ʿāšām* makes this sense of guilt clear: "When a man or woman commits any of the sins that men commit by breaking faith with the Lord, and that person feels guilt, he shall confess his sin which he has committed, and he shall make restitution and add one fifth [for his wrong]."[28] The *ʿāšām* offering is also distinguished from the *ḥaṭṭāʾt* in that it is performed only on behalf of an individual layperson. There is no *ʿāšām* described specifically for the community as a whole or for the priests as representatives of the community.

The fourth sacrificial rite, the *šělāmîm*, or "well-being" ritual, also involves an animal offering. This rite is distinctive in several ways. The plural ending of the term *šělāmîm* has raised questions about its etymology, but the consensus is that it probably comes from the same root as *šalom*, meaning "peace."[29] The *šělāmîm* rite is the only sacrifice in which animal flesh is eaten by the laity. In fact, it may be eaten by the wives of the priests as well as laymen.[30] The *šělāmîm* is also "the only sacrifice which never serves in a *kippur* [or expiatory] role."[31] Instead, it seems to be more clearly a gift or general expression of thanks to YHWH.[32]

The *minḥâ*, or "grain" offering, completes the major categories of sacrificial rites. Cereal or grain offerings appear in two different contexts. First, they appear as substitutes for a preferred animal offering when a common

Israelite cannot afford an animal for the *ḥaṭṭāʾt*. Second, grain offerings are the required substances of *minḥâ* rites. Given the importance of these grain-based offerings, it is unfortunate that most sacrificial theorizing glosses over the *minḥâ* offering rites (along with grain-based rites in other sacrificial traditions).

The Jewish sacrificial system requires the participation of both priests and laity. The male priests, who were chosen on the basis of genealogy and gender, took on distinct responsibilities during individual rites, but there was no permanent differentiation between categories of priests comparable to what we find in Vedic sacrifice. Certain responsibilities were reserved for the high priest alone—such as entering the Holy of Holies on Yom Kippur—and he supervised the sacrifices, but otherwise there was no fixed specialization. The Bible describes the sacrificial space as a series of concentric rectangles. These rectangles circumscribed ritual areas that were increasingly less accessible to laity and priests. The outer courtyard constituted the eastern half of the sanctuary, with a public entrance at the eastern end. Laypeople would bring their offerings to the entrance of the outer courtyard. This term probably refers to the area immediately outside the courtyard up to the altar.[33] The presenter would bring the victim into the eastern entrance and slaughter it. The priests would then manipulate its blood on the altar in the outer courtyard.[34] Afterward, the offering was dismembered and burned on the outer altar. Other laypeople and priests could be present in this outer courtyard area, witnessing the entire sacrificial procedure.[35]

Just west of the outer courtyard was the inner court, with an enclosed area, the shrine. Rabbinic tradition argues that this area was one grade holier than the outer courtyard, although the Bible makes no mention of this.[36] Laypeople and disqualified priests were not allowed access to the inner court. This area contained a table, a menorah, and an altar of incense. To the west of this area, in the center of the inner courtyard, was the Holy of Holies. This area was draped off from the community, laypeople and priests alike, with a large heavy curtain or veil (*pārōket*). Only the high priest entered this area, once a year, on Yom Kippur.

It is immediately apparent that the space of the Tabernacle, and later the Temple in Jerusalem, was divided into increasing levels of sanctity. Fewer and fewer people were admitted to each successive area of the sanctuary. Both priests and laity could enter the outer courtyard, but only the priests could enter the shrine area, encompassing the incense altar and the menorah. Finally, only the high priest could enter the Holy of Holies,

and only on a single day of the year. Each sacrificial area was used to address different categories of sins. The outer, most accessible, area dealt with unintentional individual offenses. The shrine area, where only the priests could go, dealt with only unintentional community offenses—sins that originated with the entire Israelite community and, as a result, generated more serious consequences. Finally, the innermost area dealt with intentional sins, which were considered the most serious. The graver the offense, the more deeply the priest(s) had to go into the sanctuary in order to expiate it.

The stated purpose behind the sacrificial system as a whole was to maintain the Israelites' relationship with YHWH. According to biblical and rabbinic thinking, sin separated the Jews from YHWH, and so sin had to be expiated. The sacrificial system provided the means to expiate individual and communal sin, thus renewing the people's relationship to YHWH. Certain sacrifices were scheduled into the calendar to address impurity on a regular basis. For example, the *tāmîd* was to be performed twice daily. This ritual includes a portion of lamb and an offering from the most readily available agricultural products: wheat, wine, and oil. On a grander scale, the annual Yom Kippur sacrifice includes a *ḥaṭṭā't* and an *'ōlâ* offered on behalf of the high priest and a *ḥaṭṭā't* and an *'ōlâ* offered on behalf of the congregation, each of which requires the appropriate animal offering.[37] Presumably such a sacrifice would cleanse away a year's worth of impurity in the sanctuary and among the people.

In the following pages we will draw upon data from the Vedic and Jewish sacrificial traditions to re-imagine sacrifice from a polythetic perspective. In so doing I want to approach sacrificial events keeping their full spectrum of activity in mind. Each basic activity—selection, association, identification, killing, heating, apportionment, and consumption—will be treated as a provocation, sparking fruitful insights into and numerous questions about the nature of sacrifice. The approach outlined here is expressly designed to complicate rather than simplify our understanding of sacrificial phenomena. Most important, each of the following chapters is meant to be suggestive, not comprehensive. No single chapter can explain fully the significance of any sacrificial procedure. Nor can I fully uncover the dynamic relationship between any single procedure and all the other activities performed with individual sacrificial offerings. Instead, the following chapters will hint at the possibilities of research yet to come.

CHAPTER TWO

Reevaluating the Role of Killing in Sacrifice

> Sacrifice is ritual slaughter.
> —WALTER BURKERT

In the popular imagination, sacrifice is most closely associated with killing. Similarly, scholarly approaches to sacrifice have also tended to emphasize the importance of killing. As a result, research on sacrifice has overlooked the importance of other activities performed during sacrificial ritual.[1] In fact, the theories of sacrifice that dominate religious studies today focus almost exclusively on killing and violence. This chapter addresses these mischaracterizations and attempts to put killing in its proper place in the broader context of sacrificial activity.

Numerous scholars assume that sacrifice is the killing of an animal victim. M. F. C. Bourdillon, in his introduction to the edited volume *Sacrifice*, notes that one contributor to the volume "confines his comments to rituals which involve the immolation by death (at least symbolically) of a living being. Most of the essays presented in this volume presume that this is the principal denotation of 'sacrifice.'"[2] Bourdillon's phrasing suggests that he recognizes that limiting "sacrifice" to the "death . . . of a living being" is somewhat arbitrary. Yet he quickly moves past this potentially fruitful insight, and the traditional fascination with and em-

phasis on death goes unquestioned, not only in his introduction but throughout the entire volume.

Unfortunately, Bourdillon's willingness to associate "sacrifice" with the death of an animal victim is quite common. This problem can be traced back to Henri Hubert and Marcel Mauss. In *Sacrifice: Its Nature and Functions,* Hubert and Mauss describe the death of a sacrificial oblation as "the culminating point of the ceremony."[3] Numerous influential scholars have followed in their footsteps. I have already noted that Frits Staal arbitrarily chooses to limit "sacrifice" to the ritual slaughter of animals within the Vedic system. Walter Burkert, another important scholar of sacrifice, focuses on the death of the animal oblation, arguing that sacrifice is rooted in hunting practices: "The central, practical, and necessary act would be to kill animals for food. Sacrifice is ritual slaughter."[4] Repeatedly scholars have called attention to the death of the animal victim as the singular and defining act in sacrificial ritual.

No scholar is more closely associated with the notion of sacrifice as "violence" than René Girard, so it is important to explain his argument clearly. Girard begins his classic work *Violence and the Sacred* with a critique of Hubert and Mauss, claiming that their argument is circular: "Because the victim is sacred, it is criminal to kill him—but the victim is sacred only because he is to be killed."[5] In response to this apparent problem, Girard asks why sacrifice is so frequently associated with violence. Quickly thereafter he links sacrifice and murder, noting that "sacrifice and murder would not lend themselves to this game of reciprocal substitution if they were not in some way related." Throughout the book Girard develops the argument that sacrifice is centered on notions of substitution and deferred violence: a sacrificial victim receives the deflected violence originally intended for the sacrificer. Thus sacrifice is a violent act, with the death of the victim at its core. Within human society the sacrificial victim acts as a scapegoat, toward which violence has been redirected. In modern contexts, in which "blood sacrifice" no longer occurs, the original violence is transposed into some other form of societal conflict—but it never loses its violent nature. At the heart of Girard's argument is his assumption about religion in general: "[T]here is a common denominator that determines the efficacy of all sacrifices and that becomes increasingly apparent as the institution grows in vigor. This common denominator is internal violence —all the dissensions, rivalries, jealousies, and quarrels within the commu-

nity that the sacrifices are designed to suppress. The purpose of the sacrifice is to restore harmony to the community, to reinforce the social fabric. Everything else derives from that."[6]

Before proceeding too much further, let me emphasize that I do not want to minimize the significant contributions that scholars such as Girard, Burkert, and Staal have made to the study of sacrifice, and I am not denying the important role that killing plays in many sacrificial events. Clearly, sacrifice often involves killing and violence—but it does not *equal* killing or violence. And although it may be appropriate to identify the death of an animal victim as the definitive and culminating sacrificial moment in some religious systems, I find it problematic to characterize Vedic and Jewish sacrifice this way. The texts that present the most detailed descriptions of public sacrifice in both of these traditions do not privilege the killing of the offering substance over other procedures. Rather, they describe elaborate and complex combinations of *all* the sacrificial procedures discussed in the previous chapter. When we focus on the death of a victim to the exclusion of other sacrificial procedures in Jewish and Vedic sacrifice, it is as if we have created a theoretical hall of mirrors that exaggerates one feature of sacrificial practice while minimizing other features, ultimately producing a distorted reflection of the whole.

In the following pages I examine the role that killing plays in the Vedic and Jewish sacrificial traditions and then conclude with some general reflections on the study of sacrifice: (1) sacrificial killing is performed with plant as well as animal offerings, which raises questions about the prominence of animal offerings in sacrificial theorizing; (2) killing is not necessarily about blood or violence; and (3) killing is often *not* a definitive or culminating activity within sacrifice. Rather, the significance of killing within the broader scope of sacrificial activity is inextricably linked to other procedures, procedures that deserve much greater scholarly attention than they have received to date. My hope is that this study will encourage us to view the killing event not as a definitive or independent feature of sacrifice but as one element integrated into a complex cluster of sacrificial activity.

Vedic Soma Offerings: Killing and Vegetal Offerings

The Vedic tradition provides a wealth of data for scholars of sacrifice, particularly in the Śrauta Sūtras, the priestly manuals that provide the

most detailed descriptions of sacrificial ritual (800–300 BCE). As a result, some of the most influential general theoretical work on sacrifice has been based on data from the Vedic tradition.[7] The Vedic system is particularly interesting for the study of sacrificial killing for several reasons, which we will explore in the following pages.

As described in Chapter 1, the Vedic *śrauta* (public) sacrificial system is traditionally divided into three categories: *iṣṭi, paśubhanda*, and soma rites. The *iṣṭi* traditionally focuses on vegetal offerings, usually grain-based. These grain-based offerings are not simply substitutions for animal offerings. Rather, they constitute a distinct category of sacrificial offerings in and of themselves, equal in importance to animal offerings. The *paśubhanda*, or animal sacrifice, is usually more complex than the *iṣṭi* rites. A *paśubhanda* traditionally includes *iṣṭi* rites, but it focuses on the animal offering. Animal rites are performed less frequently than grain-based rites, but they rank higher in the sacrificial hierarchy. Finally, the soma sacrifice, the pinnacle of the sacrificial hierarchy, encompasses both *iṣṭi* and *paśubhanda* rites while focusing on the soma offering.[8] We will examine the *iṣṭi* rites in more detail in a later chapter devoted to vegetal offerings; for now we will focus on soma sacrifices.

Interestingly enough, we find language referring to "killing" (root *han*) in the soma sacrifice, describing what happens to the soma plant. It would be tempting to dismiss the use of this verb as imaginative metaphor, but such a dismissal does not do justice to the general personification of the plant that permeates the sacrifice. Throughout the ritual the plant is addressed directly and honored as a special guest, the god Soma, who is processed into the sacrificial arena. As Charles Malamoud points out, "from the outset, the *soma* plant one presses, as well as the *soma* drink quaffed by the gods and brahmins[,] *is* the god Soma."[9] At certain points in the ritual the participants address or refer to the soma as if it were another human participant. MS 3.9.1:112.8 states, "King Soma has come to his house, it is in his power." The plant is a living entity—and therefore it can be killed.

The priests kill the soma plant on the last day of the soma sacrifice, which typically lasts several days.[10] In the Jyotiṣṭoma (the five-day basic soma ritual), the pounding of the soma occurs on the fifth (final) day.[11] It has been preceded by the public selection of priests and the consecration of the *yajamāna* (Day 1); the mock purchase of soma and a companion "hospitality" rite that pays honor to the soma (Day 2); Pravargya and

Upasad rites (Day 3); and Pravargya, Upasad, Agnipraṇayana, Agnīṣoma-praṇayana, havirdhāna-praṇayana, and the slaughter of a goat as a kind of fore-offering (Day 4). All these activities clearly build toward the culmination of the ritual on Day 5.

The final day of the sacrifice is divided into three pressing (*savana*) sessions, during which the soma stalks are pounded to release their juice. Each pounding or pressing session is performed roughly the same way as the other two, with a few minor variations.[12] First a few stalks are taken from a heap of soma in a cart that has been processed into the sacrificial arena. The *adhvaryu* priest takes a large stone and places it on an animal hide. The stalks will be ground upon this stone (the *upara*). Then the priest places some soma stalks on the stone. Water is poured over the stalks to help loosen the plant fibers, and priests beat the stalks with stones held in their right hand. There are three rounds, or "turns" (*paryāga*), of pounding. The pounded stalks are collected in a trough, stirred with water, washed, and pressed through a woolen strainer so that the potent soma juice that has been extracted can be captured in cups and consumed by ritual participants.

Two points are worth noting about the activities on Day 5. First, the culmination of the ritual is *not* the "killing" of the soma but rather the drinking of it in morning, midday, and evening rites (more on this later). Second, the Vedic sources refer to the pounding of the soma stalks as a kind of killing. TS 6.4.8.1–3 refers directly to the event as the slaying of the soma king. TS 6.6.9.2 states, "[T]hey kill the *soma* when they press it. In the slaying of the *soma* the sacrifice is slain." ŚB 2.2.2.1 asserts, "[I]n pressing out the king [soma], they slay it." Another passage reads, "When one is about to strike [the soma] one must think in one's mind of him whom one hates, saying, "this is the one I strike, it is not you [Soma]. For if one kills a Brahman who is a man, one incurs blame. How much more so if one strikes him [Soma], for Soma is a god. And one kills him when one presses him, one kills him with this [stone]."[13] Clearly, one kills soma in Vedic sacrifice.

Numerous scholars have noted this unexpected language. Malamoud states definitively, "One kills soma."[14] But how is it that one can "kill" a plant stalk? This is most readily understood by recognizing that there is no fundamental qualitative break between plant and animal life in Vedic thought. Rather, animal life and plant life exist on a continuum. The "life essence" (*medha*) of the first human sacrificial victim is understood to

have gone out from him into the horse, then into the ox, into the sheep, and then into the goat, the most common sacrificial animal victim. From the goat this life essence flowed into the earth and entered plant life (ŚB 11.2.3.6f). Consequently, the essence of soma is not qualitatively different from the essence of animal life. And just as animal victims are killed during the sacrifice, so, too, is soma killed.

What is the significance of all this for scholars of sacrifice? The Vedic soma ritual brings to light three important issues. First, we are confronted with the presence of nonanimal oblations within a rich sacrificial system. These nonanimal oblations cannot simply be ignored or dismissed as substitutes for animal offerings. Numerous passages include vegetal substances right alongside animals as appropriate sacrificial oblations. The Yajña Paribhāṣā Sūtras, for example, recognize two general groups of oblation substances, animal and vegetal. BŚS 24.1 lists five types of substances: plants (*auṣadha*), milk (*payas*), animals (*paśu*), soma, and clarified butter (*ājya*). These classificatory systems are by no means standard, but they do indicate that the Vedic system consistently incorporates nonanimal oblations. Most contemporary theorizing about sacrifice, however, draws primarily from discussions about the manipulation of animal substances only. Vegetal substances are generally treated as second-class offerings or substitutes for animal oblations. As a result, the procedures performed with nonanimal substances have been virtually ignored in general theorizing about sacrifice (an issue we will address more extensively in the next chapter). Theoretical approaches to date have tended to limit the term *sacrifice* to rituals that involve an animal victim. The Vedic tradition, however, presents the *iṣṭi,* the *paśubandha,* and the soma sacrifices as integrally connected elements within a single, coherent sacrificial system. To ignore the soma sacrifice simply because the focal offering is not an animal is to skew the data in light of an arbitrary theoretical model when, in fact, the reverse ought to occur: our theoretical approaches to sacrificial activity ought to be adjusted to reflect the realities of the data.

Second, killing in the context of the soma sacrifice challenges dominant assumptions about "death" within sacrifice. Because dominant theories of sacrifice generally associate death with animals, they tend to characterize killing procedures—and sacrifice in general—as violent and bloody. Obviously, however, when a soma plant is killed, no blood is shed, and it would be difficult to characterize the methodical cycle of soma pressings as "violent." How, then, are we to respond? We can either eliminate the soma

rituals from our theorizing about sacrifice or adjust our understanding of sacrifice to incorporate the Vedic soma tradition. An adjustment that reflects the activity involved in the soma sacrifice would require us to accept the fact that killing is not always represented as violent.

Finally, theoretical approaches to sacrifice have tended to accord "killing" a privileged position within a host of sacrificial activity, giving it weight and significance that other activities do not have. The Vedic sources, however, do not indicate that the act of killing the soma stalks is more significant than any other manipulation of the soma plant. Rather, the Vedic sources treat the soma pounding as just one activity in a complex sequence of many actions (instead of as a definitive, climactic act). In this context, killing loses its exotic and privileged status. It is no longer a unique and circumscribed event bookended by insignificant "before" and "after" procedures. Instead, killing becomes linked with the other procedures performed.

If the act of killing is not characterized by uniqueness but rather by integration with other ritual manipulations, then we are prompted to examine how the killing of the soma plant functions in relation to other sacrificial activities. Simply put, what is killing for? A quick overview of the soma ritual suggests that the priests "kill" the plant offering *not* because killing is the be-all and end-all of the rite but because killing makes it possible for subsequent activities to occur. Specifically, killing the soma stalk makes the juice of the plant available for consumption. This juice is considered very potent. Baudhāyana, founder of one of the earliest schools of *śrauta* ritual, seems to have taught that the juice of the first pressed stalk "is capable of destroying the sense-power, virility, progeny, and cattle of the sacrificer."[15] Killing the plant makes it possible to access and then drink this potent juice. Thus killing has little significance in and of itself; it is significant because it makes the soma juice available.

Killing in the context of the Vedic soma ritual, then, challenges common stereotypes. First, it does not involve an animal's death. Second, it is neither dramatic nor bloody. Finally, it is not the culminating or focal point of the sacrificial activity. Rather, it is a necessary prelude to another activity. Killing in the context of the soma sacrifice is best understood in relationship to the activities that follow, the subsequent manipulations it makes possible. On a broader level, these observations suggest that scholars of sacrifice need to rethink some common assumptions about killing that permeate religious studies.

Vedic Animal Offerings: Killing and Violence

Not surprisingly, the Vedic system also includes animal-based sacrifices. Like the Vedic vegetal rites, these animal sacrifices also challenge assumptions about the nature and importance of sacrificial killing. Most important, procedures involved in killing Vedic animal offerings challenge prevailing assumptions that sacrificial killing automatically includes violence and bloodshed. The killing of animal victims (traditionally goats) cannot really be described as bloody or violent, at least as presented in the ritual texts. There is blood, to be sure, but not when the animal is killed. In the Vedic system, animal victims are traditionally suffocated or strangled with a noose.[16]

The verb most frequently used to describe the death of the animal offering in a *paśubhanda* (animal sacrifice) is *śam*, which means "to quiet" rather than "to kill."[17] Consequently, people who kill the animal victim are literally called "quieters" (*śamitra*), not slaughterers. ŚŚS 5.17.1 directs, "You divine quieters as well as you who are human, begin!"[18] Jan Heesterman notes that this kind of death distinguishes ritual activity from common slaughter, "for cutting the victim's head is well known outside the *śrauta* system of ritual as the normal method of immolation."[19] The sacrificial death of an animal victim is markedly different from bloody slaughter performed for mundane purposes. This difference is one reason that, when an animal offering is put to death in the Vedic *paśubhanda*, the tradition directs the priests to stop the animal from breathing, not to draw blood (ĀpŚS 7.16.5).

Several scholars argue that the bloodless killing involved in Vedic animal sacrifice is a change from earlier practices. Jan E. M. Houben notes, for example, that the Ṛg Veda (a textual source that predates the Śrauta Sūtras) suggests that the horse sacrificed in the Aśvamedha was killed with an ax, not strangled.[20] But as the Vedic system developed, it required not only the death of a sacrificial victim but a quiet (nonviolent, *ahiṃsā*) death. As Houben explains, "[W]e see here an earlier period in which there is relatively little embarrassment about violence in ritual, and a subsequent period, reflected in most of the Brāhmanas and Śrauta-sūtras, in which this embarrassment increases."[21]

Several modern Indic scholars (e.g., Houben) as well as classical Indian philosophers (e.g., Kumārila) note that Vedic thought makes a distinction between death and violence, particularly within the sacrificial context. In

his essay "To Kill or Not to Kill," Houben notes that the Vedic sources do not characterize sacrificial killing as violent.[22] In later material, the developing principle of *ahiṃsā* expands to limit killing *outside* a sacrificial context, but this notion seems to be grounded in the assumption that sacrificial slaughter should *not* be viewed as violent or injurious.[23]

For our purposes, the distinction between killing and violence is important because it suggests that we need to rethink how to interpret sacrificial activity. The tendency has been to assume that since sacrifice involves killing, and since killing is violent, then sacrifice must be violent. It would be better to nuance this assumption a bit: since sacrifice *often* involves killing, and since sacrifice *must not include violence* in the Vedic worldview, then sacrificial killing is characterized as nonviolent. In other words, rather than beginning with a general assumption about killing (i.e., that it is inherently violent) and then interpreting sacrifice accordingly, one might begin with each specific sacrificial system's understanding of sacrifice (i.e., that the sacrificial setting nullifies any potential violence) and then characterize killing accordingly.

One of the major issues we confront here is the fact that modern and Western (specifically Christian) notions of sacrifice have largely shaped the field of sacrificial studies. Within Christianity, Jesus's death on the cross is the ultimate—and therefore paradigmatic—sacrifice. Jesus' crucifixion involved a slow, painful, and bloody death, significant in part because it expiated sins through vicarious suffering. Vedic sacrifice, in contrast, is not expiatory and involves no concept of vicarious suffering. Houben notes that, in the Brāhmaṇas and the Śrauta Sūtras, "on the one hand, killing is important, and it is even central in the sacrifice; on the other hand, acts of violence are avoided, concealed, and denied."[24] Ritual killing explicitly does not equal violence.

In light of the Vedic *paśubandha* evidence, then, we must acknowledge that the sacrificial killing of animal victims is not necessarily even dramatic. Heesterman, who asserts that "killing is obviously a *conditio sine qua non* for animal sacrifice," also characterizes Vedic ritual as "an utterly flat, though intricate, sequence of acts and mantras, perfectly regulated and without ups or downs."[25] Animal sacrifice is unarguably complex but not necessarily violent. If this is the case, then any theory of sacrifice that characterizes the *paśubhanda* as a uniquely climactic (and violent) moment misrepresents the Vedic system. We turn now to an alternative understanding of killing within the context of a rich and complex sacrificial system.

Vedic Animal Offerings: Killing and Other Sacrificial Elements

As we explore animal offerings in the Vedic system, we continue to ask, what is the significance of "killing" in this sequence of activity if violence and bloodshed are not the goal? The priestly manuals indicate that the death of the animal victim in Vedic sacrifice is significant not so much because of the death itself but because killing makes the animal ritually available for the elaborate manipulation, division, and distribution that follow. These activities are connected to but distinct from the death of the animal, as indicated by a number of factors. Most significant, the priests who divide the animal into portions and distribute these portions are traditionally *not* the ones who kill the animal. Rather, the priests are instructed to turn their back on the strangling procedure so as not to see the animal die.[26] The strangulation is performed in a place distinctly removed from the priests. Clearly priestly activity (which includes the apportionment, heating, and consumption of the animal victim) is meant to be distanced from (rather than associated with) the killing of the animal.

In addition, Vedic sources suggest that killing carries less ritual "weight" than other procedures. Specifically, the priests' activity suggests that the apportionment of the animal—including its dissection and the distribution of parts to various ritual participants—is far more ritually important than the animal's death. For example, immediately prior to the strangulation, one of the priests (the *hotra*) recites a lengthy chant, which includes directions regarding how the animal's parts are to be divided.[27] The chant says nothing about how the animal should die. In addition, the ritual sources spend much more time discussing the manipulation of the animal carcass than the animal's death. For instance, MS 1.6.11.104.6 specifies that one should not damage the joints of the animal offering (*tasyāḥ pārūṃṣi na hiṃsyuḥ*). ŚŚS 5.17.3–5 describes the way the priests should arrange the animal's body after it has been killed: "Direct its feet to the north. Direct its eye toward the sun, release its breath to the wind, its life to the mid-regions, its hearing to the quarters, and its bones to the earth. Remove its skin in one piece. Before ripping up the navel, remove the omentum, keeping its breath within. Make his breast as a falcon, with his upper forelegs as hatchets, his lower forelegs as spikes, and his shoulder blades as tortoises. Leave his loins unbroken, his thighs as door-leaves, his knees as oleander-leaves. Twenty-six are its ribs; loosen these one after the other. Leave each limb whole."

Numerous other passages explain the complicated and detailed manipulation of the victim's body.[28] The body must be washed and dissected in specific ways. Certain portions are designated for specific ritual participants (e.g., heart and kidneys for the ancestors, the "choice part," or *vara,* for the *brahman*).[29]

In some ways killing the animal victim parallels killing the soma plant. The manipulation of the animal allows access to and proper consumption of various animal parts, just as the killing of the soma plant allows access to and consumption of the plant juice. Malamoud notes this parallel, commenting that "the forcible expulsion of the [soma] juice is explicitly assimilated to the execution of an animal victim."[30] In both the *paśubandha* and the soma sacrifices, then, the death of the offering—whether animal or plant—is significant not primarily for what it accomplishes on its own but for the activity it makes possible later on in the ritual.

What tentative conclusions can we come to based on this brief discussion of Vedic soma and animal sacrifice? It is commonplace to note that the Vedic ritualists characterized sacrifice as work. ŚB 1.1.2.1 declares that "truly, sacrifice is work" (*yajño vai karma*). By "work" the sources mean more than "labor"; they imply the productive manipulation of earthly elements. Sacrifice, then, is constructive; it creates something, generates something that was not present earlier. General theories of sacrifice, however, have interpreted killing as a destructive force. I would suggest that the reason for this interpretation is that killing is usually lifted outside its ritual context and isolated from other sacrificial activities when scholars do their theorizing. We have seen, however, that Vedic sacrificial killing always occurs in combination with other activities, sometimes hundreds of activities. Sacrifice is not simply the killing of an offering; otherwise, every murder would be a sacrifice. When we recognize that no single procedure—including killing—definitively "marks" sacrifice, we are forced to pay attention to *all* the activities that occur in a sacrificial event, as well as the relationships constructed between these activities. Recognizing that sacrificial killing occurs in combination with other activities should encourage us to re-imagine sacrifices as organic complexes of activity rather than as a linear sequence of discrete procedures. Examining these complexes can lead to new lines of inquiry into the nature of sacrifice in general. For example, we have seen that the death of both the soma plant and the animal victim in the Vedic system makes possible the subsequent manipulation of both plant and animal offerings.

Specifically, killing can be viewed as a constructive act because after death both animal and soma offerings are divided into multiple portions. The sacrificial process, which "constructs, integrates, and constitutes the real," transforms a single substance (such as a goat) into multiple distinct offerings (skin, head, heart, entrails, fat, blood, and so forth).[31] Consequently, a single sacrificial victim is able to yield multiple offerings. In response to this observation, scholars of sacrifice might view killing as a constructive activity, the transformation of seemingly monolithic "raw material" selected at the beginning of any given sacrificial ritual. Killing reveals and releases the internal complexity of a seemingly monolithic substance, making it available for subsequent manipulation to generate multiple variegated offerings and providing access to the "life essence" of each offering.

In addition, the fact that slaughter serves different purposes within each sacrificial tradition suggests that there may be broader and more fundamental differences between the religious communities themselves. For example, the absence of bloodshed in Vedic animal killing draws our attention to culturally constructed views of blood. Blood is understood to contain the "life essence" of animals within Western traditions but not in Vedic thought. In the latter, the life essence is found in the juice of the soma plant and in the breath—rather than the blood—of animals. Consequently, control of the breath is of paramount importance in a *paśubandha.* While the animal is being strangled, the priests must ensure that the victim dies without uttering a sound, and if the animal makes a noise while being strangled, specific expiation rites are required.[32] The study of sacrifice, then, might benefit from some sustained comparative attention to various cultural manifestations of life essence, not just blood.

We see from this overview that Vedic sacrificial procedures prompt a reevaluation of the role killing plays—and does not play—in sacrificial activity. Sacrifice needs to be re-imagined as a complex ritual activity that may include, but is not necessarily defined by, killing. In addition, killing needs to be re-imagined as one of many intimately connected sacrificial acts. It must be distinguished from violence, which may or may not accompany the death of an offering. And it must sometimes be viewed as part of a constructive (rather than destructive) process. We turn now to Jewish sacrificial ritual to determine the issues raised by biblical and rabbinic discussions of sacrifice.

Jewish Animal Offerings: Killing and Other Sacrificial Elements

The Jewish sacrificial system is as rich and complex as the Vedic system. Its fundamentals are outlined in the Bible and further elaborated in the Mishnah (ca. 220 CE).[33] The system includes (but is not limited to) a class of offerings called *zĕbāḥîm,* or slain offerings.[34] The preferred offering substance for a slain offering is an animal taken from the flock or the herd.[35] There are several types of slain offerings. The *ʿōlâ*, best translated as "burnt offering," includes an animal offering that is almost entirely consumed on the outer altar fire. The designated *ʿōlâ* animal offering is an unblemished bull, ram, or male goat.[36] A lay person brings the live animal near the outer altar, lays his hands upon the animal's head to identify publicly with the offering, and then slits the animal's throat (*šāḥaṭ*) in a ritually prescribed manner before YHWH.

The fact that lay people are permitted to kill the offering animal suggests that slaughter requires no specific ritual expertise or authority, at least in the context of sacrifice. But after the animal's throat has been cut, the priests take responsibility for presenting the animal's blood by tossing it "against the altar, round about" (*ʿal-hammizbēaḥ sābîb*). Leviticus 1:5 indicates that this activity involves ritual expertise and thus falls to the priests. Then the animal is skinned and cut into pieces.[37] The priests arrange the animal head, body portions, and fat in a prescribed arrangement on the fire. Finally, they burn the animal offering on the altar.

A second type of oblation, the *ḥaṭṭāʾt* (often translated as "sin offering" or, more correctly, "purification offering"), also requires offerings from the herd or the flock, but the specific choice depends upon whom the offering is meant to represent.[38] As in the *ʿōlâ*, the animal victim is selected according to certain criteria and then brought to the outer altar. The presenter identifies with the animal victim by placing his hands on the animal's head, and then the animal is slaughtered. But at this point the procedure begins to differ from the *ʿōlâ*. In the *ḥaṭṭāʾt*, the anointed priest catches some of the blood of the bull in a ritual vessel and brings it to the entrance of the inner shrine. There, "the priest shall dip his finger in the blood and sprinkle some of the blood seven times before the LORD against the veil of the sanctuary. And the priest shall daub some of the blood on the horns of the altar of fragrant incense before the LORD, which is in the tent of meeting, and the rest of the blood of the bull he shall pour out at

the base of the altar of burnt offering, which is at the entrance of the tent of meeting" (Lev. 4:6–7). After this, the fat portions are removed and burned on the outer altar, but the animal's skin, flesh, head, legs, entrails, and dung are carried away to a clean place and burned (Lev. 4:11–12, 19–21, 26, 31, 35).

The *šĕlāmîm* (sacrifice of "well-being"), yet a third type of slain offering, differs procedurally in some ways from both the *ʿōlâ* and the *ḥaṭṭāʾt*. The blood is tossed "against the altar round about" (*ʿal-hammizbēaḥ sābîb*) as in the *ʿōlâ*. But once the animal is dismembered, only certain portions of the *šĕlāmîm* are presented on the altar. The remaining pieces are eaten by the priests and the individual who presented the animal offering: "The priest shall turn the fat into smoke on the altar, but the breast shall belong to Aaron and his sons. And the right thigh from your well-being sacrifices you shall give to the priest as an offering. The one among the sons of Aaron who offers the blood and fat of the well-being offering shall have the right thigh for his portion. For I have taken the breast of the heave offering, and the thigh that is offered from the people of Israel, from their well-being sacrifices, and I have given them to Aaron the priest and to his sons, as a perpetual due from the people of Israel" (Lev. 7:31–34). Even this early on in our discussion of Jewish slain offerings, several factors seem to indicate that the killing of the animal is not the culminating moment in Jewish animal sacrifice. Rather, other elements of the ritual are, particularly the application of the blood. Blood manipulation is significant in Jewish sacrifice for several reasons. First, blood is one of the few elements of the animal offering that may not be consumed by the ritual participants. According to biblical teaching, blood contains the life force of an animal: "[T]he life of the flesh is in the blood" (Lev. 17:11). Consequently, no one—priest or lay person, Israelite or non-Israelite—is permitted to consume blood. Leviticus 17:10 declares, "I will set my face against the one who eats blood, and will cut that person off from the people." Blood manipulation is carefully regulated so that the blood is returned to YHWH. This part of the sacrifice is viewed as an acknowledgment that all life comes from YHWH.

Blood is also significant because blood manipulation distinguishes certain animal sacrifices from others. For example, Leviticus explains that when an *ʿōlâ* is offered the blood is tossed against the sides of the outer altar: "Aaron's sons, the priests, shall toss its blood against the altar round about" (Lev. 1:11). This procedure differs from either of the two *ḥaṭṭāʾt*

procedures. In one *ḥaṭṭāʾt* rite the priest dips his finger in the blood and sprinkles it seven times against (or toward) the veil in the inner sanctum. Then the priest daubs (*nātan*) blood on the horns of the inner altar, and he pours out the rest of the blood at the base of the outer altar (Lev. 4:6–7, 18). In another *ḥaṭṭāʾt* procedure the blood is daubed on the outer or sacrificial altar, and the remaining blood is poured out at the base of the altar (Lev. 4:25, 30). For our purposes these distinctions are important because they demonstrate that the manipulation of the blood—rather than the slaughtering procedure—signals the purpose and personality of each sacrifice.

In addition to blood manipulation, other sacrificial procedures seem to be more ritually significant than the killing of the animal offering, particularly the apportionment of the animal victims. The animal must be dismembered according to a prescribed procedure, and its parts must be distributed appropriately. For example, in the *ʿōlâ* the animal skin is given to the priest. The carcass is dismembered, arranged on the outer altar, and burned entirely. None of the animal is eaten by any of the ritual participants. The animal portions must be arranged on the altar in a specific sequence: head first, then the fat, then the body sections, and finally the washed entrails and legs. In the *šĕlāmîm*, in contrast, only a few parts of the animal are burned on the altar (such as the suet and the kidneys; Lev. 3:3–11); other portions of the flesh are reserved for the ritual participants to eat (Lev. 7:20, 31–36). Mary Douglas has suggested that this attention to the precise distribution and arrangement of the body portions distinguishes sacrificial killing from mundane killing because it involves treating the animal carcass with respect.[39]

The biblical discussions of the slain offerings, therefore, indicate that killing an animal victim is relatively meaningless when it is divorced from other sacrificial procedures. In relationship with other prescribed activities, however, killing functions in a variety of meaningful ways. Later mishnaic discussions of the slain offerings indicate an increasingly complex characterization of sacrifice. For example, M. Zebāḥîm explores when a sacrifice is—and is not—invalidated. M. Zeb. 1.1 explains that certain offerings are invalid when not offered under their proper name: "All slain offerings that are not slain under their own name are valid, but they are not accredited to the owner in fulfillment of his obligation, except for those from the Pesach or from the *ḥaṭṭāʾt*, the Pesach at its appointed time, and the *ḥaṭṭāʾt* at anytime." Another discussion focuses on the priests'

intentions concerning the place and time of sacrifice. For example, M. Zeb. 2.3 states a general principle: "This is the general principle: if anyone slaughtered or received or conveyed or splashed [the blood] intending to eat something that is meant to be eaten, or intending to burn something that is meant to be burned, outside its proper place, it is invalid, but there is no extirpation [*kārēt*]. [But if he intended to eat something] outside its proper time it is as refuse [*piggûl*], and they are liable for extirpation on its account." In countless cases, M. Zeb. focuses on the procedures that occur *after* the animal has been killed, emphasizing their importance in determining the validity of a sacrifice. Such discussions are significant because they indicate that the act of killing a sacrificial victim never stands alone. Rather, the act of killing is always linked with (and often secondary to) other procedures performed during the sacrifice, procedures that receive great attention from the rabbis.

We have learned several important things by this brief glance at killing in the Jewish sacrificial system. First, the manipulation of the blood and the distribution of various portions of the body are the distinguishing features of individual sacrifices. One distinguishes an *ʿōlâ* from a *ḥaṭṭāʾt* based on blood manipulation and apportionment, not the slaughter procedures. In addition, killing procedures work with other procedures—particularly the manipulation of the blood and the distribution of offering portions—to shape the distinctive identity of any sacrificial rite.[40] These procedures *taken together* constitute Jewish sacrificial events. The slaughter of the animal victim helps accomplish the overall objectives of particular sacrifices only insofar as it is performed correctly along with earlier procedures, such as the offering's selection, and subsequent procedures, such as the proper distribution of portions. In other words, killing in the context of Jewish sacrifice—as in Vedic sacrifice—is important not for what it accomplishes on its own but for what is accomplishes in relationship with other actions. In the cases of the slain offerings, the *selection* of the appropriate offerings and the appropriate *apportionment* of elements of the animals, including the blood, indicate the personality and purpose of each sacrifice.

A review of biblical and rabbinic discussions of sacrifice leads us to rethink stereotypic—and often emotionally charged—notions of killing. For example, in contrast with a seeming obsession with violence in modern theorizing, the rabbinic references to animal slaughter are relatively matter of fact. They do not characterize animal slaughter as particularly

violent or distasteful. The absence of detailed instructions in the biblical and mishnaic texts, and the fact that lay people performed the slaughtering, seem to imply that any (adult male) Israelite worth his salt knew how to cut an animal's throat correctly. In addition, the slaughter was performed publicly, in the outer courtyard area, so presumably it was not tremendously traumatic to onlookers. Subsequent kashrut laws require that animals slaughtered for food be killed painlessly, suggesting that Judaism has consistently been concerned with *avoiding* pain and violence in animal slaughter.[41] Given this expression of concern, it is hard to argue that the sacrifice of an animal victim should be interpreted as a violent or even dramatic moment.

In addition, the focus of the mishnaic discussions suggests that the rabbis were much more interested in what happened *after* an animal was slaughtered than with the slaughter itself. Blood had to be carried and applied properly to the altar (M. Zeb. 8.6–12). The carcass had to be apportioned appropriately between the altar, the priests, and the ritual patron. The meat had to be eaten in ritually prescribed places and at ritually prescribed times (M. Zeb. 10.5–7). Even the *intention* to violate these guidelines could invalidate a sacrifice (M. Zeb. 3.3–5). Clearly, the slaughter of an animal could be understood as "sacrifice" only when accompanied by other procedures. As in the Vedic system, Jewish sacrifice involves complicated manipulations that must all be performed correctly for a sacrificial event to be performed successfully.

Concluding Thoughts

Having touched on some basic elements of Jewish and Vedic sacrifice, we conclude now with several general observations and comments. We begin with the assumptions commonly held concerning killing in sacrificial practice. First, scholars generally assume that sacrificial theory should focus on the treatment of animal victims. Hubert and Mauss allude briefly to nonanimal offerings in *Sacrifice: Its Nature and Functions*, but their theorizing is driven by the treatment of animal offerings: "[W]e must designate as sacrifice any oblation, even of vegetable matter, whenever the offering or part of it is destroyed, although usage seems to limit the word sacrifice to designate only sacrifices where blood is shed."[42] When sacrificial theorists discuss vegetal substances at all, they tend to treat them as substitutes for animal offerings, not as preferred offerings themselves. The

assumption seems to be that the death of animal offerings is what is *really* important in sacrificial activity. Our study of Vedic soma sacrifice, however, highlights the problems with this assumption. The Vedic tradition places the soma ritual—not the *paśubandha*—at the summit of the sacrificial system. In addition, vegetal and liquid offerings are used far more frequently than animal offerings. The Jewish system also includes vegetal offerings, both as substitutes for primary offerings and as the preferred substance in a *minḥâ,* or grain-cake offering. A comprehensive approach to sacrifice has to incorporate *all* the offering substances employed in a sacrificial system.

Second, it is common to view killing as a violent and dramatic element of sacrifice. Clearly, however, within the sacrificial arena, killing need not involve violence, at least as viewed through the eyes of the traditional sources. In fact, sacrificial killing may be contrasted with mundane killing specifically because it provides a sacred (= nonviolent) death as opposed to a worldly (= violent) death. Many of us tend to think of killing as a violent act, but we have seen that the Vedic and Jewish ritual texts do not always describe it that way. The fact is that, for the most part, the authors of these ritual texts present ritual slaughter in a matter-of-fact way, and we must at least consider this characterization, not just dismiss it as unrealistic or euphemistic. Most theoretical approaches to sacrifice have assumed that the slaughter of an animal victim is violent because it is bloody, assuming that these go hand in hand. But a quick review of Vedic sacrifice shows us that killing does not always involve bloodshed. In fact, the traditional *paśubandha,* or animal sacrifice, explicitly forbids bloodshed while the animal is being killed (KŚS 6.5.17–18). The language used to describe this procedure doesn't even refer to it as killing; rather, it is referred to as "quieting." One possible explanation for this characterization is that it is an elaborate deception, an attempt to describe sacrifice one way (the way it "ought to be") in order to deflect attention away from the way it really is. But another possible explanation is that the Vedic ritualists did not, in fact, view ritual killing as violence.

It is clear that both the brahmanical Hindu and the biblical and rabbinic Jewish traditions distinguished between death and violence. Death within a sacrificial context was permitted, but the procedures were intended to cause as little pain to the victim as possible. Thus, brahmanical Hindu and biblical and rabbinical Jewish sacrifice direct our attention away from the fact of the death of a victim to questions about how that

death transpired. Killing, then, in certain sacrificial systems, is significant not because it leads to death but because of how one's sacrificial death differs from a "natural" death. The opposition is not life versus death but natural (violent, painful) death versus sacrificial (nonviolent, nonpainful) death. Sacrificial death is generally intended to be nonviolent. I would suggest that the *absence* of language referring to violence in sacrificial texts, rather than being explained away, deserves more thoughtful attention than it has received to date.

The final assumption scholars seem to make is that killing is a definitive and essential element of sacrifice. We have seen, however, that in certain instances killing plays a supporting role, facilitating more important activities, such as the manipulation and distribution of the oblation. In the Vedic soma sacrifice, one kills the soma plant to gain access to the juice. One kills the *paśu* (animal victim) in order to divide and distribute its internal organs. In the Jewish system, one kills the animal to gain access to its blood and to manipulate its body in specifically prescribed ways, ways that explicitly distinguish sacrifice from mundane activity. The act of killing is sacrificial only in concert with other activities.

These insights are helpful when we turn to other sacrificial traditions as well. Mary Douglas refers to a Dinka ceremony performed when incest has occurred. The "victim is cut in half *alive*, longitudinally through the sexual organs."[43] The victim dies, but the cut through the sexual organs is the focus of the sacrifice. The cut is not primarily made to kill but rather to inscribe, to mark the body in a specific way. As Douglas notes, by making the longitudinal cut "the common origin of the incestuous pair is symbolically negated."[44] In this particular sacrifice, the prescribed division of the body is what is crucial to the efficacy of this sacrifice, at least as much as the death of the victim. I would argue that in many sacrificial events the division or apportionment of the offering is more significant than its death.

The absence of language referring to killing is significant also. We have already drawn attention to the verb *śam* in Vedic animal sacrifice. Although we recognize, of course, that the animal does in fact die, we should think about the significance of the language that the ritualists themselves choose to use. In fact, some scholars have concluded that *śam* and other related verbs, combined with descriptions of the strangling procedure, signal the importance of breath in the Vedic tradition. Breath (not blood) is the "life essence" of the animal. Thus, the "capture" or "containment" of

breath is critical to the value of an animal oblation. We know that brahmanical Hindus were not the only ones to practice suffocation. Douglas notes that the Dinka sometimes suffocated a victim, depending upon the sacrifice's purpose.[45] Consequently, a truly comprehensive approach to sacrifice explores connections between blood, breath, and other manifestations of "life essence" in both animal and plant oblations, drawing attention to other aspects of sacrificial practice.

Finally, we should note that certain sacrifices do not involve killing at all. One of the classic examples is the Vedic *agnihotra*, the twice-daily offering of cow's milk that a single officiant (or the householder himself) ought to perform. It is tempting simply not to classify the *agnihotra* as a sacrifice—but the Vedic ritualists themselves don't allow this: "Those who offer the agnihotra truly inaugurate a long sacrificial session" (ŚB 12.4.1.1). The *agnihotra* is categorized as the simplest form of *śrauta* sacrifice. Although the *agnihotra* does not involve killing, it does incorporate other activities associated with sacrificial practice: the selection of the appropriate oblation substance (generally cow's milk, inaugurated by calf suckling, not by pressing the cow's udders), its distribution in specific amounts (e.g., "the fullest ladle for the most favorite son of the sacrificer . . . and the later ones less and less") at appropriate times (sunrise and sunset), and its consumption by fire.[46] It is these activities, I contend, that make the *agnihotra* a sacrifice.

Similarly, the Jewish sacrificial system does not privilege killing. As explained in the previous chapter, Jewish sacrifices involve animal, vegetal, and liquid oblations, and only the animal victims die. However, there are several contexts in which an animal used in the ritual is released rather than executed, often in combination with an animal victim that is slaughtered. For example, Leviticus 14:1–7 describes the sacrifice performed to cleanse a leper. In this ritual, one bird is slaughtered while the other is dipped "in the blood of the bird that was slaughtered" (14:6) and then released.

One ritual that has drawn considerable attention is the Yom Kippur (Day of Atonement) rite. During the course of the ritual, two goats are presented as a purification offering. One goat (traditionally called the "scapegoat") is led into the wilderness to "Azazel" while another goat is slaughtered (Lev. 16). The passage reads: "And from the Israelites he [Aaron] shall take two male goats for a purification offering. . . . Aaron shall place lots upon the two goats, one marked 'for YHWH' and the other

'for Azazel.' Aaron shall bring forward the goat designated by lot 'for YHWH' to sacrifice it as a purification offering, while the goat designated by lot 'for Azazel' shall be placed alive before YHWH to perform expiation upon it by sending it away into the wilderness to Azazel" (Lev. 16:5, 8–10). What are we to make of this second goat? Considerable debate surrounds this passage, but scholars traditionally argue that the goat left alive is not sacrificed. Milgrom, for example, states categorically, "The he-goat for Azazel was not a sacrifice."[47] However, the passage indicates that this goat "performs expiation" in some way. It is more precise to say that the he-goat is not killed. Yet the language of the passage suggests that this second goat is included in the general sacrificial activity. I would argue that the he-goat is, in fact, part of the sacrifice, not killed but manipulated in a different way. A theoretical approach that views killing as only one of many possible sacrificial manipulations allows us to consider other ways of understanding this act as "sacrificial."

Close study of the Vedic and Jewish sacrificial systems leads us to several important conclusions about killing and sacrifice. First, we are led to a more focused and nuanced understanding of the act of killing *in relation to other activities performed.* As Douglas notes about ritual in general, "Events which come in regular sequences acquire a meaning from relation with others in the sequence. Without the full sequence individual elements become lost, imperceivable."[48] Instead of seeing killing as an independent and definitive feature of sacrifice, we need to approach killing as only one of many important—and interdependent—elements in a complex ritual. Second, we are led to the realization that animals are not the only sacrificial oblations worth paying attention to. As we have seen, both the Vedic and Jewish sacrificial systems involve vegetal and liquid offerings as well as animal offerings. How would sacrificial theorizing benefit from a close study of these nonanimal oblations? We turn to vegetal offerings in our next chapter.

CHAPTER THREE

Vegetal Offerings as Sacrifice

When theorizing about sacrifice, scholars automatically think animal victims. Vegetal offerings are, if anything, merely an afterthought. The dominant theorists—Hubert, Mauss, Burkert, and Girard—virtually ignore vegetal sacrifice in their work, literally reducing vegetal offerings to footnotes.[1] Consequently, the manipulation of vegetal substances (grain cakes, porridges, rice balls, and the like) has played a very small role in theorizing about sacrifice. However, vegetal oblations appear prominently in the ritual literature of many sacrificial traditions, including the Vedic and Jewish traditions, and it is important to emphasize that these vegetal offerings are not just substitutes for animal offerings but act as distinct offerings in their own right. Yet vegetal offerings have received very little attention within ritual studies, routinely taking a back seat to animal offerings.

Rather than attempting to review the full range of vegetal offerings that appear in Vedic and Jewish sacrificial rites (an impossible task), this chapter focuses on several key principal vegetal rites with an eye toward discerning the contributions that vegetal offerings make to sacrificial activity. As many people are aware, vegetal-based offerings are often used as sub-

stitutes for animal offerings. For example, it is widely known that in the Jewish tradition, Leviticus 5:11 allows a poor man to offer grain when he cannot afford birds for the sin offering: "But if you cannot afford two turtledoves or two pigeons, you shall bring one-tenth of an *ephah* of choice flour as a sin-offering, as your offering for the sin that you committed."[2] It is less commonly known that grain offerings were substituted for animal offerings in a relatively recent performance of the Vedic *agnicayana* sacrifice in Kerala: "[T]he animals would be represented by cakes made of a paste of rice flour (*aṭa*)" folded into a banana leaf.[3] Clearly, vegetal offerings can substitute for animal offerings.

In addition, vegetal offerings frequently accompany animal offerings. For example, the original Pentecost sacrifice was supposed to include two loaves of bread along with several animal offerings (Lev. 23:17–20); the first-fruits festival required a one-year-old lamb for the whole burnt offering, accompanied by a grain offering made with "two-tenths of an *ephah* of fine flour mixed with oil" (Lev. 23:13). Similarly, the various Vedic *paśubandha* (animal) and soma (soma juice) sacrifices all involve multiple grain-based offerings. Clearly, vegetal offerings permeate both sacrificial systems.

Most important for our purposes, however, vegetal-based offerings often serve as the principal offering in both Vedic and Jewish sacrificial rites. In this role they are the focus of the ritual activity, not simply substitutes for a preferred animal victim. Throughout this chapter, we will focus on vegetal substances that function in this capacity, as principal offerings. First, we shall see that vegetal offerings, typically grain cakes prepared in various ways, serve as principal offerings in the Vedic and Jewish sacrificial systems just as frequently as animal offerings do. Having observed that vegetal offerings are an integral part of Vedic and Jewish sacrifice, we will examine how these offerings resemble and differ from animal sacrifice. Although vegetal offerings are manipulated in many of the same ways that animal offerings are, there are some significant variations. The most obvious variation is that the sacrificial procedures (selection, association, identification, killing, heating, apportionment, and consumption) usually occur in a different order in vegetal sacrifice than in animal sacrifice. This difference is significant because changes in sequence affect how the procedures relate to one another in each rite. More important, we will see that killing (though it does occur in some vegetal rites) is not the focal point of vegetal sacrifice. Rather, apportionment—the divi-

sion and distribution of the offering—is. The changes in sequence and the ritual significance of apportionment both deserve further attention in general sacrificial theorizing.

Vegetal Offerings within the Vedic Tradition

As explained in the Introduction, the Vedic *śrauta* (public) sacrificial tradition is commonly divided into three broad classes of rituals: *iṣṭi* (vegetal offering), *paśubandha* (animal offering), and soma (juice of the soma plant) rituals.[4] The Vedic *śrauta* sacrificial system can best be imagined as a complex hierarchy, in which increasingly elaborate rituals incorporate and build upon more basic rituals. The *iṣṭi* (vegetal sacrifice) constitutes the lowest rung of the Vedic sacrificial hierarchy. As one moves up the hierarchy, *iṣṭi* rites are encompassed within the *paśubandha* rites. Finally, *iṣṭi* and *paśubandha* rites are incorporated within soma sacrifices. In other words, vegetal offerings stand as independent sacrificial rituals, *and* they are incorporated into animal and soma sacrifices as secondary offerings. Vegetal rites pervade the entire Vedic system, from the most basic *iṣṭi* to the most complex soma sacrifice.

Iṣṭi sacrifices are performed for various reasons, "on the occurrence of certain events or for the purpose of securing some desired object."[5] That is, they are presented regularly on traditionally prescribed occasions as required offerings, and they are presented as optional offerings when the *yajamāna* (ritual patron) desires certain worldly goods. For example, "one who desires offspring should offer a cake on eleven potsherds to Indra" (TS 2.2.1.1), and someone who wants "land or kinsmen should offer a cake on eleven potsherds to Indra-Agni" (TS 2.2.1.2). The *darśapūrṇamāsa* (new- and full-moon sacrifice) is the model (*prakṛti*) for all *iṣṭi* sacrifices, so we will base our discussion on this rite.[6] The *darśapūrṇamāsa* is a two-part sacrifice, performed in accordance with the moon's cycle, as the name implies (*darśa* refers to new moon; *pūrṇa* refers to full moon). The sacrifice should begin on the first full-moon day after *agnyādheya*, the establishment of the three sacrificial fires by a householder. Āpastamba Śrauta Sūtra 3.14.11–13 explains that a householder, after he establishes the three sacrificial fires, should perform the *darśapūrṇamāsa* for thirty years or until he becomes an ascetic or until he is unable to perform the ritual because of old age. The ritual requires the participation of the sacrificer, his wife, and four priests—the *āgnīdhra*, the *adhvaryu*, the *hotṛ*, and the *brahman*.

The *iṣṭi* incorporates several grain-based oblations, but the principal offering is the *puroḍāśa,* or grain cake. As with animal sacrifices, the *iṣṭi* begins with the selection of grains according to specific criteria laid down in the priestly traditions. Vedic sacrifice generally requires the use of unblemished rice or barley (KŚS 1.9.1), both of which are domesticated grains, paralleling the use of unblemished domesticated animals in the *paśubandha.*[7] In fact, the Śrauta Sūtras make explicit parallels between the grain and an animal victim's body: "The chaff is the hairs, the bran is the skin, the bright side is the blood, the ground grain is the flesh, the more solid grain is the bones" (AitBr 6.9). The rice and barley used in the sacrifice are obtained and kept at the place of the sacrifice "in the number and amount" prescribed (KŚS 1.10.3). At the beginning of the *darśapūrṇamāsa* the grain is contained in a cart. Baudhāyana Śrauta Sūtra 1.4–6 specifically states that the grain cake, or *puroḍāśa,* should be made from the stock of grain contained in this cart. The *adhvaryu* priest approaches the cart and mounts it, taking ritually prescribed steps. While pronouncing appropriate mantras, the *adhvaryu* takes up four handfuls of grain—no more and no less. Once he has finished winnowing the grain, separating out any grass or pebbles, the *adhvaryu* removes this grain from the cart in a very specific manner (KŚS 2.3.14–16). He then "throws on them [the handfuls of grain] some more grains with his hand."[8] The ritualized "taking" of a specific amount of rice establishes the fact that *these* grains—and no others—are intended for sacrificial, rather than mundane, use. The grains are placed near the *gārhapatya* fire and purified with water. Only the grain that is measured out in this manner is used in the actual sacrifice.

After the appropriate amount of rice or barley has been selected, the grain is processed to generate fine, purified flour for the grain-cake dough. As in animal sacrifice, certain portions of the vegetal offering are more valuable than others: "The omentum is the chief part of cattle; the strew [is] the chief part of plants" (TS 6.3.9.5). Threshing and winnowing procedures are performed to yield the best part of the grain. The husks are removed, leaving polished grains. Once the polished grains have been separated from their husks, the grains are pounded and winnowed further using ritual implements fashioned specifically for these activities.

At this point in the ritual sequence, the manipulation of grains differs from that of animal offerings. As we have seen, shortly after animal offerings are selected, they are associated with the appropriate god(s), identified with the appropriate ritual patron, and then killed. Grain offerings,

however, have to be fully constituted as ritually appropriate offerings before they can be associated with deities or identified with a sacrificer. The grain is ground into fine flour by the *patnī* (the ritual sponsor's wife), mixed with water (and sometimes other ingredients) to form a dough, and finally shaped into grain cakes. Consequently, grain offerings are heated shortly after the prescribed grains have been selected. This heating process completes the constitution of a ritually fit offering, a procedure we will examine more closely later on in this chapter.

Each *puroḍāśa* is baked on a clay potsherd *(kapāla)* or on several potsherds arranged in a precise order and configuration.[9] The potsherd arrangement is preheated with embers from the *gārhapatya,* or primary cooking fire.[10] The grain cake is shaped by rolling the dough into a ball, flattening the ball, and then forming it into the shape of a tortoise: "He [the *adhvaryu*] makes the cake assume the shape of a tortoise, but its back should be neither too high nor too low like an *apūpa* and the cake should be as large as the hoof of a horse."[11] Then the *adhvaryu* flattens the dough onto the *kapāla*: "He should then flatten the ball so that it extends over all the potsherds" (TS 2.6.3.4). When the grain cake is cooked, the *adhvaryu* removes the cake from the potsherds and puts it in another container.

Once the grain cakes have been formed, they continue to be manipulated much like animal victims. First, they must be associated with specific deities. "When several *puroḍāśa*s are made, the portions separated one by one are taken to be assigned to the deities according to the sequence of the principal offerings. When the last two portions are separated from each other . . . the Adhvaryu touches each of the portions and mentions the deity to whom he assigns it."[12] In this manner the grain-cake offerings are associated with the appropriate deities.

Like an animal victim, the *puroḍāśa*s are identified with the sacrificial patron in various ways throughout the ritual. No single activity in and of itself directly identifies the vegetal offering with the *yajamāna*; rather, a combination of activities links the two. First, certain *sūtra*s identify the *yajamāna* with specific tasks throughout the ritual: "The *yajamāna* is the one who is said to be giving gifts, pronouncing words, touching, giving more gifts, selecting priests, fasting, and [establishing] measurements" (KŚS 1.10.12). Note that the *yajamāna* is credited with these activities even when he is not the actual agent. In addition, during the course of the ritual, the *yajamāna* gives verbal permission for other ritual participants—particularly the *adhvaryu*—to perform certain activities. For example, the

yajamāna authorizes the *adhvaryu* to begin pouring out the grains: "The adhvaryu asks the permission of the sacrificer in the words 'sacrificer! shall I take out the sacrificial material' and the sacrificer replies 'yes, do take out.' "[13] Immediately after the grains have been removed from the cart, the sacrificer recites mantras over them. By requiring the *adhvaryu* to obtain the *yajamāna*'s permission before he pours out the grains, the ritual identifies the *yajamāna* with the grain in preparation for its formation into cakes.

As in the animal sacrifice, the *yajamāna* does not make direct contact with the offering substance. Rather, the *yajamāna*'s representatives make contact with and manipulate the offering substance on his behalf in several ways. First, the *adhvaryu* gazes at the *āhavanīya* fire, the fire that will receive (and destroy) the offering substance later in the ritual. The *adhvaryu* then looks toward the *yajamāna*'s home, nonverbally directing the offering (with his gaze) to benefit the *yajamāna*'s household. More significant, shortly after the grains have been selected, the *adhvaryu* touches them, muttering the phrase "*idam devānām*" over the grains that have been poured out and "*ida u naḥ sada*" over the grains that have remained.[14] Direct physical contact between the *adhvaryu* and the grain functions as indirect mediated contact between the sacrificer and the offering substance.[15] The *adhvaryu*'s actions generate the most obvious identification between the *puroḍāśa* and the sacrificer.

As in animal sacrifice, the *yajamāna*'s wife also plays a limited role; the most significant parts of her involvement are when she threshes (*ava* + *han*), winnows (*phalī* + *kṛ*), and grinds (*piṣ*) the grain. Then she pounds the grain three times.[16] In this work the *patnī* acts as her husband's representative. Thus in the vegetal sacrifice, as in the animal sacrifice, the activities of all the *yajamāna*'s representatives—the priests and his wife—identify him with the sacrificial offering and, consequently, with the benefits of the sacrifice.

The two basic grain offerings of the Vedic *iṣṭi* are cooked in different ways. The *puroḍāśa* (the principal offering), a mixture of pounded grain flour and water, is baked on a clay potsherd (*kapāla*) or on several potsherds arranged in a precise order, as discussed previously.

Rice grains are also prepared as *caru,* or boiled rice. Typically, the container used to cook the rice is surrounded with embers from the *gārhapatya* fire, which heats the vessel. When the container is hot, rice grains are thrown into the vessel. Then water is heated to a boil and added

to the rice. Finally, when the rice and water combine into a kind of porridge, the vessel containing the rice grains is removed from the fire and placed on the *vedi* (ĀpŚS 24.3.28).

The preparation of both the grain cake and the rice porridge is explicitly distinguished from mundane cooking in several ways. First, the *adhvaryu* (rather than the *patnī*, who cooks food at home) performs the ritual cooking. The *adhvaryu* broadcasts this fact lest anyone confuse the two. He addresses the *gārhapatya* fire with "O Fire! Dash aside the fire that eats (cooks) raw food (not cooked in accordance with śāstra); and forbid that fire that eats flesh (cooks ordinary meat food)."[17] Finally, ritual heating is distinguished by the tortoise-shaped form made by the *adhvaryu*. The combined result of these actions is that sacrificial cooking is viewed as qualitatively different from the cooking that occurs in day-to-day-life.

Once the grain cake has been heated, associated with various gods, and identified with the *yajamāna*, it is broken into pieces and distributed among the various ritual participants, including the deities. As in animal sacrifice, the priests direct this process of apportionment, dividing, renaming, and distributing sections of the grain offering just as they would with an animal victim.

Clearly, information from the Vedic texts indicates that vegetal rites are just as much a part of the Vedic sacrificial system as animal rites are. In terms of sheer quantity, vegetal offering substances overwhelm animal offering substances. Vegetal offerings constitute an independent category of sacrifices, and they also occur in both the *paśu* and the soma sacrifices as secondary offerings. Two factors explain why vegetal offerings are accepted with such ease into the Vedic sacrificial system. First, vegetal offerings, like animal offerings, are linked to Prajāpati's act of creation. Prajāpati himself is said to have prepared the first batch of *caru*: "The *caru* that Prajāpati, first-born of righteousness, cooked with fervor [*tapas*] for Brahman . . . by that *caru* let me overcome death" (AV 4.35.1). Just as Prajāpati established animal sacrifice at the time of creation, he also established vegetal sacrifice with his offering of *caru* to Brahman. By this act, Vedic mythology places vegetal offerings on par with animal offerings within the Vedic sacrificial system.

Second, as discussed in the previous chapter, the Vedic worldview does not recognize the same definitive break between animal and vegetal substances which scholars in the modern West take for granted. Rather, in the Vedic imagination both flora and fauna are located on a single spectrum

that includes all living things. In this context animal life is not qualitatively distinct from vegetal life. In fact, according to the Brāhmana mythology, vegetal life contains the same essence (*rasa* or *medha*) of life that runs through all living creatures, including humanity: "[The gods] pushed upward the sap of the waters; it became the plants and the trees. They pushed upward the sap of the plants and the trees; it became fruit. They pushed upward the sap of fruit; it became food. They pushed upward the sap of food; it became seed. They pushed upward the sap of seed; it became man."[18] The "sap" of life runs through all living creatures. In a related passage, the Aitareya Brāhmaṇa states, "The one who sacrifices with the rice cake sacrifices with the quality of all sacrificial animals [*paśus*]" (2.8–9). With reference to this passage Brian K. Smith comments, "[T]he primary intention of the culminating portion of this myth is to extol the merits of the vegetable offering by equating it to an animal sacrifice."[19] The vegetal offering therefore ranks as equivalent with the animal offering based on the fact that it, too, contains the essential "sacrificial quality" that permeates all sacrificial offerings.[20]

Vegetal Offerings within The Jewish Tradition

If the Vedic system were unique in its elaborate incorporation of vegetal offerings, perhaps it would not be so important to include vegetal sacrifice in general sacrificial theorizing. The Vedic system, however, is not unique. The Jewish sacrificial tradition as laid out in the biblical and mishnaic literature also incorporates vegetal offerings—particularly grain cakes—as part of its complex sacrificial system.

The Jewish sacrificial system is built on five main sacrificial rites, including one general vegetal rite, the *minḥâ*.[21] Some texts characterize the *minḥâ* as a single, independent offering; others present it in combination with an animal offering. Most scholars argue that Leviticus, a relatively early text, presents the *minḥâ* as an independent rite. W. Robertson Smith argued that the animal or "slain" (*zebaḥ*) offerings preceded the *minḥâ* offerings historically because slain offerings were part of nomadic culture and *minḥâ,* or tribute, offerings were part of settled culture.[22] Modern anthropological theory rejects Smith's clear break between nomadic and settled culture. As a result, most scholars now argue that animal sacrifice and vegetal sacrifice coexisted in the Israelite sacrificial system.[23] According to biblical requirements, the grain used for the *minḥâ* is always wheat

or barley, the primary grain products of the region inhabited by the Israelites. Specifically, the *minḥâ* is composed of the coarsely ground flour or "groats" of the wheat.[24] M. Abot explains that the groats are obtained through "a sieve [that] lets through the flour but retains the *sōlet* [wheat grains]."[25] Whereas the priestly literature provides a taxonomical rationale for choosing some animals for sacrifice, the grains seem to be chosen solely on the basis of their availability. "All the [grain] offerings of the congregation or of the individual may be brought from within the land [of Israel] or from outside the land [of Israel], from the new [produce] or from the old [produce]."[26]

As in the Vedic system, grain is measured out in precise amounts as the first step toward forming a grain cake. The utensils used to measure the grain for a *minḥâ* are unique to ritual use, and the measurements themselves are not used in any other context. A passage from M. Men. (9.1) makes the importance of measuring very clear. It describes two dry measures, the "tenth" and the "half-tenth," each of which is used in measuring out precise amounts of grain for the various offerings. For example, the *ʿōmer* offering presented on the 16th of Nisan required a tenth of an *ephah*; the two loaves presented at Pentecost required two-tenths, and the showbread in the Temple required twenty-four-tenths (M. Men. 6.6). Later passages in the tractate further specify whether measures can be "heaped up" or "level."[27] The act of measuring grain in these precise amounts distinguishes food grain from ritual grain.

Although the general act of measuring initiates the constitution of a *minḥâ* offering, it is the particular amounts of grain that indicate the specific purposes of specific types of *minḥâ* offerings. For example, the *minḥâ* in the twice-daily offering (*tāmîd*) requires "a tenth of an *ephah* of fine flour for a grain offering."[28] Other offerings, however, require two-tenths of an *ephah* of grain.[29] Thus, not only does the measurement of the grain distinguish a general *minḥâ* offering from grain cakes being prepared for food use, but it also differentiates between types of *minḥâ* offerings before any other procedure is performed.

Once the grain has been measured out and sifted into fine flour, the layperson presenting the sacrifice prepares the *minḥâ*.[30] Animal victims are associated with YHWH publicly, in the outer courtyard itself, by orienting the animals in certain cardinal directions. Vegetal offerings also have to be associated with YHWH in some public manner. This association is primarily accomplished by mixing the grain for the offering with

other substances: oil, salt, and frankincense.[31] The addition of these substances is strictly governed; quantities for specific combinations are precisely prescribed. For example, Philip Blackman notes, "*Three logs* of oil were mixed with *one-tenth* of an *ephah* of flour for the High Priest's meal-offering; in the case of the *meal-offering* offered with a *libation, one-tenth* of an *ephah* of flour was mixed with *three logs* of oil for a lamb, *two-tenths* of an *ephah* of flour and *four logs* of oil were mixed for a ram, and for a bullock *three-tenths* of an *ephah* of flour and *six logs* of oil were mixed."[32] In addition, certain passages state emphatically that including oil or frankincense inappropriately will invalidate an offering. For example, "One is liable [for transgressing a negative commandment] on account of the oil alone or on account of the frankincense alone. If he puts oil on it, he renders it invalid, but if he puts frankincense, he should pick it off [and the grain offering will be valid]" (M. Men. 5.4). Numerous passages lay out specific directions for the inclusion of oil, salt, and frankincense.

The ground flour is first mixed with oil. The presenter adds olive oil (*šemen*) to the grain, either mixing it in or spreading it on grain cakes. The procedure is explained in M. Men. 6.3: "All the grain offerings that are prepared in a ritual vessel require three operations [with oil]: pouring in, mixing in, and adding [more] oil into the vessel before [the offering] is ready."[33] Oil was considered a luxury item in biblical times, and its use had certain ritual connotations. Adding oil to a grain mixture marks the final product as intended for the altar rather than the household table.

Salt is also added to the *minḥâ* offerings. In fact, Leviticus 2:13 expressly commands that salt be included in the offering: "You shall season all your grain offerings with salt; you shall not let the salt of the covenant [*melaḥ berît*] with your God be lacking from your grain offerings; with all your offerings you shall offer salt." The language could not be stronger. Throughout the Torah, the presence of salt in ritual offerings represents the everlasting covenant established between YHWH and the Israelites.

Most important, frankincense (*lebōnâ*) is added to the uncooked *minḥâ* offerings.[34] Frankincense, a fragrant gum resin found in several species of trees native to southern Arabia, was very rare and therefore also very expensive. Martin Noth argues that the addition of frankincense was intended "to lend additional solemnity to the meal-offering procedure."[35] I would argue that frankincense "lends solemnity" specifically because it associates portions of individual grain cakes with YHWH. This association becomes clear when the layperson brings the *minḥâ* to the priest.

Leviticus 2:2 and 6:14 indicate that only a part of the grain and oil is presented into the altar fire but that *all* the frankincense is put into the fire, as an offering to YHWH. Clearly participants distinguish between the offering portion to be consumed by the priests and that portion given over to YHWH—YHWH's portion is marked by frankincense.

Minḥâ offerings are also associated with YHWH by the *absence* of certain ingredients. In particular, both leaven (*ḥāmēṣ*) and honey (*dĕbaš*) are prohibited in sacrificial grain cakes. The prohibition against leaven goes back to the Exodus, when the Hebrew slaves had to leave Egypt quickly, without allowing their bread to rise. As the subsequent sacrificial cult became established, Noth explains, "[a]ll grain-cakes were kneaded with lukewarm water and they were kept from becoming leavened."[36] The biblical guidelines dictate that "cakes prepared with leavened dough and honey may only be offered as 'first fruits,' i.e. as a gift to the holy place or priests, and not as a sacrifice" (M. Men. 5.2). Honey is prohibited because it ferments easily but also because it was regularly used in Greek, Hittite, and Mesopotamian offerings. By omitting honey, the Israelites made it clear that they were *not* worshiping foreign gods. To summarize, the presence of oil, salt, and frankincense and the absence of leaven and honey mark the *minḥâ* as a sacrificial offering intended specifically for YHWH.

After the specified grains have been selected, ground into flour, and mixed with oil, salt, and/or frankincense, the *minḥâ* offerings need to be heated. Here we begin to see dramatic differences between Jewish animal and vegetal sacrifice. Grain cakes can be cooked in three different ways, either in an oven (*battanûr*), on a griddle (*'al-maḥabat*), or in a pan (*bammarḥešet*). The biblical texts and subsequent midrashic literature explain that these different cooking styles yield different results. The dough for a baked *minḥâ* is placed in a clay pot or cylinder, which has probably been preheated. The warm clay pot in turn gradually heats the grain mixture. Because there is no leaven, the cooked cakes do not rise; they remain flat. In contrast, a *minḥâ* prepared on a griddle (probably iron) is flatter and more brittle than that baked in an oven. It is broken into pieces after it has been cooked.[37] Finally, Leviticus Rabbah 3.7 says that the *minḥâ* prepared in a pan (stewing pan, *marḥešet*) shakes or trembles (*rôḥăšîn*), in contrast to the *minḥâ* made on a griddle. The "pan" differs from a "griddle" in that it is earthenware and probably has taller sides and a lid, thus yielding a different result.[38]

The various grain offerings that result from these different cooking

styles serve distinct ritual needs. Some festivals required one specific type of *minḥâ*, prepared as appropriate in an oven, on a griddle, or in a pan. Other festivals require combinations of multiple grain offerings. The thank offering, for example, requires "unleavened cakes mixed with oil, unleavened wafers spread with oil, and cakes of fine flour well-mixed with oil . . . [as well as] cakes of leavened bread" (Lev. 7:12, 13). Unlike animal offerings, which are all cooked in the same way on the altar, grain-cake offerings are prepared in various ways to address a wide variety of cultic concerns. As a result, there can be numerous permutations of *minḥâ* offerings, yielding multiple distinctive rites.

Individuals present their cooked *minḥâ* offerings to the priests, and from that time forward the priests are responsible for its ritual manipulation. However, each *minḥâ* continues to be identified with the layperson who presents it. The sacrificer presents the prepared offering to the priest, presumably in his hands or in a container held in his hands. This minimal physical contact identifies a vegetal offering with the sacrificer. How can the simple act of bringing a grain-cake offering be enough in and of itself to identify an offering with a particular sacrificer? It may be helpful to think back to the principles of identification in Jewish animal sacrifice to see whether they are instructive here. We noted earlier that animal victims were identified with particular sacrificers through physical contact, specifically physical contact with the hands. An individual presenter places his hands on the animal's head between its horns or holds a bird in his hands to mark the offering as his. Assuming that there is some consistency in the sacrificial system as a whole, we would expect to find some kind of physical contact between the sacrificer and vegetal offerings—and we do. In addition to transporting the *minḥâ* to the priest (which may or may not involve direct handling of the grain cakes), we know that the sacrificer handles the grain cakes in their preparation because the sacrificer himself is supposed to prepare them: "When someone presents a grain offering to the Lord, his offering shall be of semolina; *he* shall pour oil upon it, lay frankincense on it, and present it to Aaron's sons, the priests" (Lev. 1:1; my emphasis). Even if the presenter does not touch the grain cakes directly when he hands them to the priest (which would be highly unlikely), we can assume that there was direct physical contact between the sacrificer and the offering when the *minḥâ* cakes were being prepared.

Another piece of evidence that supports the idea that direct physical contact, particularly with the hands, identifies a sacrificer with a grain

offering is found in the trial for adultery described in Numbers 5. In this ritual procedure any woman suspected of adultery is required to hold a barley offering (which is called a *minḥâ*) in her hands as she takes an oath. The texts indicate that her husband provides the *minḥâ* (Num. 5:15), so we cannot assume that the wife has had any prior physical contact with the offering. But the wife does come into direct contact with the offering during the ritual: she is required to handle the *minḥâ* in the course of the ceremony itself (Num. 5:18). In fact, the ritual explicitly requires contact at the time when the woman takes the oath that tests her faithfulness. Direct physical contact is clearly considered necessary.[39]

Finally, in the descriptions of the *tāmîd* we find that the priest makes the grain cakes for the daily offering (M. Tamid 1.3). Since the daily offering was meant as a general tribute to YHWH from all of Israel, the priest, as the Israelites' representative, makes physical contact with the grain, both in its preparation and in its presentation. The contact between the grain and the priests' hands identifies the *minḥâ* offering with Israel via its ritual representative. It is clear, then, that the *minḥâ* offerings are identified with the sacrificer through direct physical contact, specifically with the hands. In this aspect, of course, the *minḥâ* parallels Israelite animal sacrifice. We can conclude, then, that Jewish sacrifice in general requires physical contact between the sacrificer and the prescribed offering substance in order for a sacrifice to be valid.

It is important to note that the *minḥâ* is an equal partner with the four animal-based rites in the Jewish sacrificial system. The *minḥâ* functions primarily as an independent rite, which has its own identity and serves a different purpose than the animal rites—though the purpose of the *minḥâ* is equally important. Independent grain-cake rites are required for the thanksgiving oblation, the ordination of priests, the Nazirite's vow, the trial for adultery, the daily *tāmîd,* the showbread offering, and the first-fruits offering.[40] The biblical and rabbinic texts move fluidly from discussions of one ritual to another without any suggestion that vegetal-based rites are inferior to or categorized separately from animal rites.[41] In addition, most festivals incorporate both animal- and vegetal-based offerings. For example, the very first dedication oblations for the Tent of Meeting altar included grain as well as animal oblations (Num. 7:12f). The Mishnah includes discussions of the *minḥâ* along with animal rituals in tractate Kodashim.

Given this overwhelming evidence that vegetal offerings act as full and

equal partners with animal oblations, why have grain oblations been treated as second-class sacrificial rituals? Various factors have contributed to this problem, but probably the most important fact is that grain offerings serve as substitutes for animal offerings in certain instances.[42] As mentioned earlier, Leviticus 5:5–13 describes a "graduated" *ḥaṭṭā't* system in which a grain offering substitutes for an animal offering. A poor man who cannot afford a female animal is permitted to offer two birds, and if he cannot afford this, he can present an *ephah* of flour.[43] Thus, by virtue of its seamless shift from an animal offering to a vegetal offering, the graduated system makes it possible for virtually anyone to fulfill one of the most basic sacrificial requirements.[44]

Clearly, vegetal offerings—particularly grain cakes—figure heavily in both the Vedic and the Jewish sacrificial systems. Yet they have received relatively little respect in terms of what they have to contribute to sacrificial studies broadly speaking. In the following pages I would like to draw attention to two key aspects of vegetal sacrifice that have implications for our understanding of sacrifice. First, heating grain cakes involves far more than cooking. In fact, heating procedures are the culmination of a protracted process that ultimately yields a fully constituted, ritually appropriate vegetal offering. Second, the procedures involved in vegetal-based sacrifice highlight the often overlooked importance of apportionment activities and the relative *un*importance of killing.

Heating and the Constitution of Vegetal Offerings

In both the Vedic and the Jewish vegetal sacrificial traditions, grain mixtures are heated relatively early on compared with the sequence of sacrificial procedures in animal sacrifice. Specifically, vegetal substances are usually heated *before* they are associated with the appropriate god(s), identified with a specific sacrificer, or apportioned to the ritual participants. This obvious procedural shift highlights a less obvious (but no less important) fact: raw grains have to be formed into a sacrificial whole before they can be accurately identified as ritual offerings. Here we find a marked difference between animal and vegetal sacrifice. Animal offerings are consecrated or "set apart" for sacrifice precisely because their physical form is *recognized* as being appropriate for the ritual manipulation. They are ready for ritual slaughter, dismemberment, and distribution in their natural form. Because of this, sacrificial heating is primarily about cook-

ing in animal sacrifice. Heating makes an animal victim fit for human consumption, or it conveys various animal portions to the god(s), but it doesn't help constitute the offering itself. In contrast, no real oblation exists in vegetal sacrifice until the grain cake has been heated. The grains, even once they have been pounded, winnowed, ground, and mixed with other ingredients, are still not suitable offerings; only after the grain cake has been cooked is a fully constituted, valid oblation truly present. The sacrificial terminology itself indicates that a transformation has taken place: cooked grain cakes have distinctly different names (*puroḍāśa, minḥâ*) from the raw materials that constitute them. Similarly, the biblical and mishnaic literature uses different words for the grains (*sōlet*) than for the grain cake (*minḥâ*). Thus, in vegetal sacrifice heating is primarily about transformation—it is a constructive activity in that it completes the creation of a suitable oblation substance.

The process of creating a complex, differentiated whole from a simple, undifferentiated substance resonates with both the Vedic and the Jewish creation stories. For example, in the Vedic cosmogony Prajāpati emits undifferentiated substance from his own person before he then divides and orders that substance into the structured universe.[45] Vedic vegetal rituals thus replicate Prajāpati's cosmogonic activity. Brian K. Smith, in fact, has argued that Vedic creation should be understood as a two-step process, involving first the creation of undifferentiated substance and only second the ordering and differentiation of that substance.[46] Similarly, the biblical creation story is largely a story about division. YHWH creates distinction after distinction from undifferentiated substance. He separates light from darkness, day from night, water from earth, and earth from firmament. In the act of creating and then apportioning the vegetal offering, ritual participants imitate YHWH's creative activity. We will discuss the importance of the apportionment process in some detail later on, but at this point it is sufficient to note that before the Vedic or Jewish priests divide vegetal offerings, the ritual community has to create this offering from raw materials. Specifically, they make them by, among other things, heating them.

The fact that vegetal oblations have to be "made" rather than "found" raises broader issues for sacrificial theorists. It suggests that there is a place for human agency and creativity in obtaining a suitable offering. In fact, I would argue that the focus of vegetal sacrifice is the creation of a complex whole (usually a grain cake) out of an undifferentiated substance (grains)

in such a way that differentiated parts (pieces cut or pinched from the grain cake) can subsequently be distributed to multiple recipients. This insight is significant because it suggests that sacrificial offerings are not received passively in toto as gifts from the divine realm; rather, they require active cooperation between the divine creator and humanity.

Not all grain offerings, however, are heated—at least not in the traditional sense. For example, we noted earlier that in the biblical discussions frankincense is required for the uncooked *minḥâ* offerings but not for the cooked (Lev. 1:1–3, 14–16). Milgrom underscores this point: "No frankincense, it seems, is required for these cooked cereal offerings. Its presence cannot be assumed."[47] It could well be argued that the addition of frankincense replaces heating (and vice versa) in these voluntary offerings. In these situations, the addition of frankincense *rather than* cooking transforms the grain offering into a ritually acceptable substance in the Temple cult. Charles Malamoud has discerned a similar dynamic in Vedic practice. He notes that soma is not heated: "The real problem lies with *soma*. . . . it is never cooked."[48] Malamoud then resolves this apparent procedural problem by arguing that the person who consumes soma has already been cooked;[49] hence cooking occurs, albeit metaphorically rather than literally. The fact that heating can occur *without* fire opens the door to broader interpretations of "heating" specifically and "sacrifice" more broadly. Metaphoric understandings of "heating" become increasingly popular as both Hinduism and Judaism develop. We will return to this in our concluding chapter.

To summarize: in the heating of vegetal offerings, we note humanity's active participation in the production of a suitable sacrificial offering. This means that sacrificial offerings are not just discovered—they are sometimes made. Individuals and communities labor according to divinely prescribed guidelines to create ritually suitable offerings.

Killing and Apportionment

Just as vegetal-based sacrifice incorporates heating in distinctive ways, vegetal offerings also require us to reconsider how killing factors into the Vedic and Jewish sacrificial systems. First, surprisingly, in some rites vegetal offerings are said to be killed, and we will elaborate upon this point in a moment. Second, even when vegetal substances *are* killed, killing is never the focus of vegetal-based sacrifice. Rather, apportionment—the division

of an offering into discrete parts and the subsequent distribution of these parts to appropriate ritual participants—carries more significance in vegetal sacrifice. Let us take each of these points in turn.

Killing

As we have discussed previously, sacrifice in general has long been associated with killing, specifically the death of an animal victim. Part of what makes the study of vegetal offerings intriguing is the fact that, at least in the Vedic tradition, vegetal offerings are themselves said to be killed. As noted earlier, grains used within the Vedic *iṣṭi* are pounded after they have been gathered and winnowed and before they are formed into grain cakes. The vegetal grain-cake offering is said to be destroyed or "killed" when the *patnī* (the ritual sponsor's wife) pounds the rice or barley grains. The pounding of the grains parallels the strangling of the *paśubandha* animal victim, and this pounding is explicitly referred to as killing: "The victim that is slaughtered, this is the *puroḍāśa*" (AitBr 6.9). The verb used to describe the pounding of the grain is *han*, "to kill," the same verb used to describe the killing of the soma plant. Whereas explicit language referring to killing is minimized in the *paśubandha*, it is used repeatedly throughout the *iṣṭi*. Heesterman comments, "[T]he pounding of the grain and the pressing of the soma—explicitly called a killing—are still performed within the enclosure. Although subdued by the ritual, sacrificial death is still residually present."[50] In examining the Vedic tradition, we are forced to acknowledge that, in some sacrificial systems, vegetal substances can be killed.

In sharp contrast to Vedic practice, Jewish vegetal sacrifice seems to have nothing to do with violence or killing. None of the language found in the biblical material suggests that one should interpret any of the manipulation of the grains or grain cakes as killing. The Mishnah, which discusses the preparation of *minḥâ* grain cakes extensively, never characterizes the preparation of the grain or offering of the *minḥâ* as violent. Consequently, we have no reason to believe that Jewish vegetal sacrifice was considered violent in any way.

This observation leads us to two key points. First, there is a radical difference between the Vedic and Jewish understandings of vegetal sacrifice. Why? The contrast probably arises from radically differing worldviews. The Vedic tradition posits a "metaphysics of resemblance," whereas the Jewish tradition posits a "metaphysics of difference."[51] In other words,

Vedic thought begins with an assumption of similarity or resemblance between different elements in the microcosmic and macrocosmic realms. The Vedic sacrificial system is primarily built upon this principle of similarity. Judaism, in contrast, assumes a fundamental difference between the creator deity (and the divine realm as a whole) and the created world. The Jewish sacrificial system is thus primarily built upon a principle of difference.

Second, since the Vedic and Jewish ritual views of plant life derive from these broader views of the created world in each tradition, they are reflected in the manipulation of vegetal offerings. As discussed earlier, in Vedic thought, plants exist on a continuum with all living things, including animals. Plants, animals, and humans all have the same essence of life flowing through them (*rasa* or *medha*). Human life, in fact, derives its "life essence" from plants. All in all, there is no radical distinction between animal and vegetal life. As a result, it is not awkward within the Vedic worldview to think of plants being killed, like other living things. The Jewish worldview is dramatically different. According to the Bible, YHWH created the vegetal realm completely separately from the animal realm.[52] The Bible describes no commonality between vegetation and animals. As a result, the rabbis had no reason to consider a vegetal substance "alive" in the same way that animals (or humans) are alive. Consequently, if plants are not alive in the same way that animals and humans are, they cannot be killed. Hence, vegetal sacrifice in the Jewish sacrificial system is nonviolent.

The implication for sacrificial theorizing is inescapable. If we hope to develop general theories of sacrifice, these theories must address *all* types of sacrifice, including vegetal sacrifice. Given the evidence from the Vedic and Jewish systems, we must accept the fact that sacrifice does not necessarily involve violence. Unfortunately, Western theorizing about sacrifice has largely been influenced by Protestant Christian thought, which has led to a heavy emphasis on the crucifixion of Jesus of Nazareth and, consequently, on killing. Western scholarship seems to have simply eliminated vegetal rites altogether from general discussions of sacrifice. We have therefore tended not to address the glaring absence of killing in vegetal rites. I would argue that the opposite needs to occur. If general theorizing does not incorporate vegetal sacrificial activity, then that theory—rather than the data—must be set aside.

What significance does the *absence* of killing have for the study of sacrifice? Killing and violence serve as the foundation for most of the

dominant theorizing about sacrifice. So if killing is not the driving force behind vegetal sacrificial activity, then what is? I believe that close study leads us to recognize that *several* types of sacrificial manipulation are important and that the apportionment of the vegetal offerings in particular deserves more scholarly attention than it has received to date. We turn to those apportionment procedures now.

Apportionment

Both the Vedic and Jewish systems include detailed instructions regarding the apportionment of grain cakes after they have been shaped and cooked. In the Vedic *iṣṭi*, the *adhvaryu* removes the cooked *puroḍāśa* from the potsherds with tongs and places it in a pan smeared with clarified butter. Then the *adhvaryu* begins to divide the grain cake. He breaks away two portions of the *puroḍāśa* with his thumb and two forefingers (without using his fingernails), one from the eastern part of the grain cake and the second from the western portion of the cake.[53] (The *adhvaryu* is actually prohibited from touching the grain cakes directly "until the time of their cutting into portions" [KŚS 2.6.31].) The sizes of these portions are specifically prescribed in the texts; the portions for the deities are to be the size of the phalanx of the thumb (KŚS 1.9.6). All the oblation portions should be offered to the east of the first offering, "each succeeding oblation to the east of the preceding one and touching it."[54] These offerings, considered the principal offerings (*āhuti*) of the *darśapūrṇamāsa*, are offered into the *āhavanīya* fire in the name of the appropriate deities.

At the moment that the *adhvaryu* begins dividing the cakes, he starts making distinctions between the portions intended for the gods and the portions intended for human participants. The portions consigned to the *āhavanīya* fire for consumption by the gods are considered the principal offerings (*āhutis*) of the sacrifice. For example, the first cake at both the new- and full-moon offerings is always dedicated to Agni. "At the sacrifice of full moon the second cake is destined for Agni-Soma and at the sacrifice of new moon for Indra-Agni [or] for Indra" (YV 1.3.14.17).[55]

Once a grain cake has been prepared appropriately, vegetal sacrificial ritual centers on the division and distribution of portions of the oblation to various ritual participants, including the gods. The procedures applied to the grain cake resonate with those applied to an animal victim, since animal victims are also apportioned. As noted earlier, the primary texts make explicit connections between portions of the grain cake and an

animal's body. By constructing these parallels, the texts explicitly link vegetal sacrifice with animal sacrifice in a broader sacrificial system. Links to animal sacrifice are generated through the differentiated portions of the grain cake, which are distributed to ritual participants and the gods just as the animal victim's organs would be. Thus the ritual language is explicitly designed to link vegetal sacrifice with animal sacrifice, suggesting that the offering substances, though different in nature, are equivalent.

Even *caru*, the boiled rice porridge, is separated into distinct portions. "He [the *brahman* priest] should look at the boiled rice. . . . He should smell it . . . without touching it, and *having them remove a portion from it*, [he should] place [this serving] on the part of the *iḍā* designated for the brahman priest" (ĀśvŚS 1.13.3–4; my emphasis). Note that a serving of the rice porridge is set aside from the rest and manipulated to fulfill a specific purpose. The grains are subsequently associated with the appropriate deities by the *adhvaryu* with specific gestures and mantras. Both grain cakes and grain porridges, then, are apportioned in some fashion.

The biblical story of creation, although markedly different from the Vedic version, also includes a process of apportionment. Genesis 1 describes a six-day process in which the Creator alternately generates a substance and then separates it from another substance. Light is separated from darkness, the firmament from the waters, the greater light from the lesser light. The entire process of creation is a process of differentiating one substance from another and setting those substances in orderly relation to one another. Similarly, grain cakes are divided into multiple parts and distributed in different ways. After the appropriate ingredients for the *minḥâ* have been assembled and the grain offering has been prepared in one of several possible ways, the *minḥâ* is brought to the priest. He takes a handful of the offering, puts it in a ritual vessel, and consigns it to the fire. The priest cannot simply remove any portion at random; the handful he removes must include all the frankincense, leaving none behind. As a result, the portion of the *minḥâ* placed on the fire conveys a fragrant aroma to YHWH. If the entire *minḥâ* were thrown onto the altar fire, there would be, in effect, no apportionment. But this is not the case. The bulk of the *minḥâ* is distributed to the priests to be consumed by them. Thus all *minḥâ* offerings are apportioned into parts for YHWH and the priests.[56]

The apportionment of a vegetal offering is much simpler than that of an animal offering. But in both cases the division of the offering into distinct segments is designed to make it possible for one offering substance

—animal or vegetal—to fulfill multiple purposes. The "handful," although a vague term to our ears, came to designate a specific amount by the time of the rabbis. Blackman, in his notes to a translation of M. Men. 1.2, comments, "He [the priest] dips his closed outstretched fingers into the meal and scoops up a handful; with the small finger he levels off the meal on that side, and with the thumb he evens it off on that side also, so that none drops off on either side. This was deemed a most difficult operation to ensure that there was neither excess nor deficiency in quantity."[57] Clearly the "handful" was a specified amount. The mishnaic tractate Menāḥôt discusses at great length the potential danger to the sacrifice if an inadequate amount is removed. For example, M. Men. 3.5 states, "[Even] the smallest portion [missing] from the handful impairs [the validity] of the greater portion." In other words, if the priest removes too small a handful, the entire offering is invalidated.[58] A "handful" became standardized enough as a unit of measurement that the Mishnah could refer to a shortfall without having to justify or explain the reference.

In addition, the "handful" cannot be removed randomly from any portion of the *minḥâ*. If frankincense has been included in the *minḥâ*, the handful given to YHWH must include all of it; otherwise the offering is invalid (*pasul*). In the animal offering procedures, certain parts of the animal victim are manipulated differently than others, and certain portions were reserved for YHWH. In a similar—although simpler—way, certain portions of the *minḥâ* are also manipulated in distinct ways.

The selection, association, and apportionment procedures are designed to work together in vegetal sacrifice. Specific amounts of grain are measured out initially *in order that* smaller amounts (a handful) can be removed at a later time. A specific substance (frankincense) is added to the grain cake *in order that* apportioning can proceed in a specific manner based on the presence or absence of that substance. Difference is constructed *in order that* apportionment can take place. Without the processes involved in the selection and association steps, the apportionment of the *minḥâ* could not take place.

In addition, note that the priests (rather than the laity) must apportion the *minḥâ*. "This is the law of the grain offering. The sons of Aaron shall offer it before the Lord, in front of the altar. One shall take from it a handful of the fine flour of the grain offering with its oil and all the frankincense that is on the grain offering and burn this as a token portion" (Lev. 6:14–15). Why would it be necessary for the priests—rather than a

layperson—to divide and distribute a grain cake? Although one could argue that ritual expertise and training would require priests alone to supervise animal dismemberment, simply because of the complexity involved, it hardly seems necessary to have trained ritual personnel to simply pinch off a portion of a grain cake. Yet the texts emphasize that the priests, and only the priests, are permitted to remove the token portion. In Chapter 2 we saw that, by reserving certain activities for the priests, the tradition underscores the fact that apportionment is a ritually significant activity. This holds true in vegetal sacrifice as well. Priestly activity at the altar is choreographed in just as detailed a fashion for vegetal sacrifice as it is for animal sacrifice. The fact that the priests—rather than the laity—divide and distribute portions of the *minḥâ* emphasizes the importance of both the vegetal offering in general and the apportionment procedure in particular. In fact, the apportionment of a vegetal offering is particularly important precisely because there is no killing involved; apportionment takes on greater significance as a sacrificial procedure.

In both the Vedic and the Jewish sacrificial systems, vegetal offerings are divided into multiple portions in a manner similar to the division of an animal offering, and for similar purposes. Apportionment distinguishes one segment of a vegetal offering from another—in fact, it creates distinct portions where they did not exist before. This differentiation makes it possible for one simple grain cake to yield multiple offerings, addressing multiple purposes. For example, the Vedic *puroḍāśa* yields a principal offering, a separate *sviṣṭakṛt* offering (a kind of expiatory offering), and an edible portion for the ritual participants. Each of these different portions has its own value in the ritual economy, and these values are roughly equivalent to sections of an animal offering. The principal offering is equivalent to the omentum of the animal sacrifice; it is the most valuable, and so it is offered entirely to the deities. Other portions of the grain cake are less valuable, and therefore they are given to the priests and the sacrificer. Apportionment, then, generates hierarchy as well as multiplicity. It also helps reinforce the equivalence between a vegetal offering and an animal offering.

Just as important, the process of apportionment is rooted in Vedic and Jewish cosmogony. According to Vedic mythology, Prajāpati created the world by dividing himself. Thus by dividing any offering substance (no matter what that substance is), the ritual participants, specifically the

priests, replicate Prajāpati's creative activity. This replication of Prajāpati's self-dissolution is thus a constructive activity, not destructive, because it regenerates and sustains the cosmos. In this ritualized activity, participants are more than reminded of Prajāpati's work; they participate in the continued creation of the cosmos through their own apportionment of offering substances. In Vedic thought activities that divide and distribute substances, activities that might initially appear destructive, are actually creative and regenerative. Similarly, within the Jewish sacrificial system a single, undifferentiated offering (e.g., a grain cake) is manipulated to yield multiple distinct offerings, which reflect the hierarchical relationships between YHWH, priests, and laity as they are distributed. Generating an integrated whole (*minḥâ*) from relatively undifferentiated grain parallels the biblical creation story, in which YHWH creates an ordered and highly differentiated cosmos out of formlessness. In the act of apportionment, then, both Vedic and Jewish sacrificial participants are imitating the divine. The division of the grain cake and the distribution of the portions take on a constructive—rather than destructive—dimension.

Concluding Thoughts

Procedures applied to vegetal offerings parallel procedures applied to animal offerings in several important ways. Vegetal offerings are selected from the domesticated realm of plant life, just as animal victims are selected from the domesticated realm of animal life. Physical criteria (including the absence of blemishes) play a role in distinguishing suitable from unsuitable vegetation. Other procedures, however, are distinctive to the selection of vegetal offerings, the most notable of which is the act of measurement. In Vedic sacrifice the *adhvaryu* measures out a particular amount of grain (four handfuls, plus some more "heaped over") for the ritual. Similarly, Temple sacrifice employs specific dry measures for grain offerings. The selection process involves conscious, deliberate, creative activity on the part of the ritual participants, not just passive recognition of physical characteristics.

Vegetal offerings are also apportioned in a manner similar to that for animal offerings, and for similar purposes. The act of division distinguishes one portion of a vegetal offering from another—in fact, it creates distinct portions where they did not exist before. Apportionment makes it

possible for one grain cake to yield multiple offerings playing multiple roles: the principal offering, expiatory rites, and edible portions for the ritual participants. Each of these different portions has its own value in the ritual economy. The principal grain-cake offering is equivalent to the omentum of the animal sacrifice; as the most valuable portion, it is offered entirely to the deities. The other, less valuable portions are consumed by the priests and the sacrificer. Apportionment, then, accomplishes multiple goals. It reinforces the ritual similarity between vegetal and animal offerings. It also produces multiple ritual portions out of a single offering. Finally, it generates hierarchical distinctions between ritual portions that reflect sociocultic distinctions between the ritual participants.

Because the process of apportionment (which is crucial to both animal and vegetal sacrifice) is rooted in cosmogony, it should be viewed as a creative rather than a destructive act. Within the Vedic system, the ritual participants mimic Prajāpati's creative activity when they divide the offering substance (no matter what that substance is). In the sacrifice the ritual participants cooperate in the continued creation of the cosmos through the apportionment of the oblation—a foundational concept in Vedic thought. Similarly, the Jewish priestly activity parallels YHWH's division and organization of the primordial chaos into an ordered cosmos. Thus, activities that at first glance appear destructive—the dismemberment of an animal, the breaking apart of grain cakes—are actually constructive and regenerative when situated in the context of sacrifice.

However, although vegetal sacrifice parallels animal sacrifice in important ways, significant differences exist between the manipulation of vegetal sacrificial offerings and that of animal sacrificial offerings. First, the sequence of sacrificial procedures differs significantly. Since vegetal oblations must be formed to constitute a ritually acceptable offering, heating frequently occurs earlier in the ritual than it does in animal sacrifice. In addition, the process of heating actually helps to produce a suitable vegetal offering, rather than simply cooking a fully constituted offering. Also, vegetal oblations, for the most part, do not involve violent activity; rather, the focus of the ritual activity is apportionment. However, rather than using these differences as an excuse to eliminate vegetal oblations from sacrificial studies, these differences should challenge long-held assumptions about the nature of sacrificial activity.

Perhaps most important, vegetal sacrifice should force us to rethink the

relationship between sacrifice and killing. Surprisingly, we noted that Vedic vegetal sacrifice sometimes involves killing—or at least, the indigenous vocabulary used refers to the killing of grain substances. We can conclude that, at least in some sacrificial systems, killing is not a privilege reserved for animal victims alone. In contrast, we noted that Jewish vegetal sacrifice involves no killing at all. The texts describing the manipulations of vegetal offerings do not reference killing or any kind of violence. These two observations lead to some remarkable conclusions. First, we must accept the fact that one can "kill" vegetal substances, unless we ignore the native descriptions of Vedic sacrifice. Consequently, theorizing about sacrificial killing must be expanded to include vegetal offerings; to omit them is to impose arbitrary modern Western distinctions upon another culture. Just as important, we must accept the fact that some sacrificial rituals—animal and vegetal—do not include killing at all. Consequently, any adequate model of sacrifice must allow for the possibility that killing does not always occur and certainly is often not the focal point of sacrificial activity.

In general, we become aware of how little attention has been paid to vegetal ritual, both in textual and fieldwork studies of individual traditions and in general theoretical discussions of sacrifice. Whereas it is relatively easy to find textual and ethnographic work on animal sacrifice across numerous religious traditions, it is relatively difficult to find extended discussions of vegetal sacrifice. Research on vegetal offerings tends to be restricted to "area studies" conversations, rather than extended into general or comparative thinking about sacrifice. Why are vegetal offerings so easily set aside? There are several potential answers to this question. First, vegetal substances are used so often that they may, in fact, be too common. Their very frequency makes them less likely to attract attention: they are not exotic enough to merit scholarly rumination. In addition, as we have noted, vegetal offerings frequently stand in for animal offerings; consequently, they are often imagined solely as substitute offerings when, in fact, they function as preferred principal offerings as well. Most important, relatively little drama accompanies vegetal offerings, whether they are grain cakes or porridges. Even though rhetorically the language of the Vedic *iṣṭi* asserts that a vegetal offering is being killed, the ritual performance itself involves no procedure similar to an animal's strangulation or a throat slitting. For sheer drama, there's nothing like an animal dying, preferably violently. Our scholarly fascination with death and violence in

sacrifice may be largely due to Western intellectual roots in Christianity, in which the defining moment is Jesus' agonizing death on the cross. Dramatically speaking, no vegetal sacrifice can compete with the crucifixion. But our review of vegetal ritual in the Vedic and Israelite sacrificial systems has shown that sacrifice is about far more than drama or a single climactic moment. Rather, sacrifice involves a rich and dynamic matrix of activities.

In the first chapter of his classic work *Violence and the Sacred*, Girard comments: "Without ever expressly excluding the subject of human sacrifice from their research—and indeed, on what grounds could they do so?—modern scholars, notably Hubert and Mauss, mention it but rarely in their theoretical discussions. . . . All reduction into categories, whether implicit or explicit, must be avoided; all victims, animal or human, must be treated in the same fashion if we wish to apprehend the criteria by which victims are selected."[59] Girard was partially right. We, as scholars, have tended to limit the types of sacrificial "victims" we observe, with no real justification for doing so. To do so is to play havoc with the traditions themselves and to limit our own understanding of sacrifice. But Girard did not expand the category of sacrifice broadly enough; he still restricted sacrifice to animal-like victims. If we are to be true to the Vedic and Jewish (and countless other) sacrificial systems, we must take vegetal offerings into account as well. I would propose that we expand on Girard's comments and begin to take vegetal offerings seriously as integral elements of sacrifice, not just as substitutes for or inferior versions of animal offerings but as significant and efficacious offerings in and of themselves. Once we include vegetal offerings, then we must generate theoretical approaches that reflect and explain their presence as partners with animal offerings within the general sacrificial system.

We are, of course, not the first to notice the presence of vegetal offerings in the Vedic and Jewish sacrificial systems. Deep within their footnotes, Hubert and Mauss acknowledge that vegetal oblations constitute a major part of Vedic sacrifice: "Even the creation of the sacred thing during the course of the ceremony is much more evident in the case of the [vegetal] oblation than in any other case, since it is often made entirely on the very place of [animal] sacrifice."[60] For some reason, however, Hubert and Mauss chose to privilege animal "sacrifices" over vegetal "oblations" in their theorizing, ignoring the fact that the traditions themselves fail to do so. As vegetal substances become acknowledged as equal partners with animal substances in the Vedic and Jewish sacrificial systems, any theoret-

ical approach that claims to help illuminate sacrifice as a religious phenomenon must "fit" them both well. The polythetic approach does just that, both by highlighting similarities between animal and vegetal sacrificial ritual and by accommodating variations between the two sacrificial procedures, variations that broaden and enrich our understanding of sacrifice as a religious phenomenon.

CHAPTER FOUR

Liquid Sacrificial Offerings

If vegetal offerings have been relegated to the fringes of sacrificial theorizing, then liquid offerings have been swept completely aside. Scholars of sacrifice virtually ignore the manipulation of liquid substances in their general theorizing, even though liquid substances permeate most of the world's great sacrificial systems, including the Vedic and Jewish traditions. In this chapter I identify several liquid offerings that permeate the Vedic and Jewish sacrificial systems, both as companion or secondary offerings and as principal offerings. Then I examine the manipulation of the dominant principal liquid offering substances—milk, soma juice, and animal blood—in each of the two traditions. I conclude with some thoughts on how the presence and distinctive manipulation of liquid offerings might reshape theorizing about sacrifice in general.

Fair warning: this discussion is a lengthy one, involving detailed descriptions of several liquid sacrifices. Detailed description is necessary because we are examining sacrificial rites that have largely been ignored in the past. Consequently, it seems appropriate to include extensive discussion as I argue that (1) liquid substances are integral elements of the Vedic

and Jewish sacrificial systems in various ways and (2) liquid offerings yield unique insights into the complexity of sacrificial practice in general.

Liquid Offerings in the Vedic and Jewish Sacrificial Systems

Both the Vedic and the Jewish sacrificial systems incorporate several distinct liquid substances in various roles. Certain liquids appear frequently in sacrificial activity but do not function as offerings, and it is important to distinguish between liquids that are simply used in sacrifice and those that function as true liquid offerings. Water, for example, is required in both Vedic and Jewish sacrifice. In the Vedic system, water is used to purify ritual utensils (BŚS 25.14–16) and ritual personnel and to cleanse (KŚS 6.3.21) and to anoint the sacrificial offering (KŚS 6.4.1; 9.5.2).[1] In the Jewish system the priests use water to wash animal parts,[2] to purify priests (Lev. 16:23–24), to cleanse the sanctuary from sin,[3] and to cleanse individuals who have had contact with a corpse (Num. 19:11–13). Water, then, is generally a cleansing or purifying agent, and it should not be viewed as an offering substance in either the Vedic or the Jewish sacrificial systems.[4]

However, several liquid substances do function as sacrificial offerings. Some liquids serve as the principal or focal offerings in specific Vedic and Jewish rituals. For example, within the Vedic tradition, milk is the principal offering in the twice-daily *agnihotra*, and soma juice is used in the elaborate soma rituals. In the Jewish tradition, blood is manipulated in various ways at the altar. We will examine the manipulations of all three of these substances in some detail in the following pages.

Liquid substances also often function as "companion" offerings, substances that accompany principal offerings. Companion offerings may be combined with another substance (e.g., oil mixed in with pounded grain to form a *minḥâ*, ghee (clarified butter) incorporated in many Vedic animal, grain-based, and soma rituals). Companion offerings may also be presented independently before or after the principal offering (e.g., offerings of milk during the *agniṣṭoma* rite). These companion offerings do not carry the same ritual weight that the principal offering does, but they are necessary for the rite to be performed correctly. Yet virtually all sacrificial theorizing fails to review the manipulation and significance of these companion offerings. Such an omission radically oversimplifies and misrepre-

sents what actually occurs in many sacrificial situations. Consequently, we will begin our discussion by noting several companion offerings that appear in Vedic and Jewish sacrifices.

Liquid offerings permeate the Vedic sacrificial system. Ghee, in particular, appears in virtually every Vedic *śrauta* sacrifice. Christopher Minkowski comments, "Ghee (clarified butter) is ubiquitous in the rite, offered sometimes independently and sometimes as a basting for another oblation. Statistically the most offerings in the *yajña*s are made with ghee. . . . [I]t makes a good fuel for a fire, and smells good when burning."[5] The *darśāpurṇamāsa* (the new- and full-moon sacrifice) requires multiple oblations of heated ghee to Viṣṇu or Agnīsoma. In the *paśubandha*, a ghee offering is made into the *āhavanīya* fire for the *yūpa* (sacrificial stake to which the ritual animal offering is tied; KŚS 6.1.4). In the soma sacrifice, the hospitality rite (*ātithya*) ends with an offering of ghee, and the *tānūnaptra*, the rite that binds the priests to the *yajamāna* (the ritual patron), involves the remains of the *ātithya* ceremony. In most cases ghee appears as a secondary or supplementary oblation, a fore- or after-offering accompanying the principal offering. However, the Śrauta Sūtras provide just as detailed instructions for these secondary offerings as they do for the principal offering.[6]

Milk, like ghee, appears in almost every Vedic sacrifice.[7] An oblation of milk to Indra constitutes the *sānnāyya* rite, an optional component of the *darśapurṇamāsa*. In this rite two calves are separated from their mother as they are suckling, and the milk the calves would be drinking is collected. The goal is to obtain milk that has been induced not by human hands but rather by the natural suckling of the calves. This milk is then offered to Indra or Mahendra (KŚS 4.2.7–10). In other rituals milk is mixed with other substances. For example, in the *pravargya* rite (an element of the soma sacrifice), ghee is heated in one pot (the *mahāvīra* pot) and then mixed with milk from a she-goat and a cow. This rite is performed multiple times throughout the soma sacrifice.[8] The addition of the milk to the heated ghee is supposed to create a flash of light.[9] In the soma sacrifice milk is also added to soma juice for the *maitravaruṇa* cup. Jamison notes that the Ṛg Veda portrays this blending of milk and soma as a kind of erotic meeting: "The Rig Veda soma hymns continually treat the meeting of soma with the milk, usually couched in erotic terms: the virile bull soma racing eagerly to the equally desirous cows."[10]

Similarly, certain liquids appear frequently as companion offerings in

Jewish sacrifice, particularly oil and wine. Oil is used in various ways in Jewish sacrifice. In some cases, oil simply aids in cooking. At another level, oil is used to anoint, specifically ritual personnel or utensils. In addition, we noted in the previous chapter that oil is frequently mixed in with grain offerings. "If your offering is a grain offering baked on a griddle, it shall be of fine unleavened flour *mixed with oil*. You shall break it [the grain cake] into pieces *and pour oil on it* because it is a grain offering" (Lev. 2:5–6; my emphasis). The grain cake prepared in a pan is also mixed with oil (Lev. 2:7). Oil is a required element in these rituals; in fact, the absence of oil can invalidate a grain offering (M. Men. 3.5). The specific manipulation discussed in the texts suggests that oil is more than a cooking aid; adding oil to a ritual offering may be a kind of anointing similar to the anointing of ritual priests and utensils. Adding oil may be a way to associate the grain cake offering with YHWH. We can generalize from the numerous examples given in the biblical and mishnaic texts and posit that including oil as an ingredient indicates and even contributes to the ritual status of an offering.

Wine is also an element of Jewish sacrifice. W. Robertson Smith argued long ago that wine was primarily used as a substitute for blood, and this view has become a commonly held interpretation. It does not seem to hold up, however, upon closer examination. First, wine offerings frequently accompany animal offerings, in which case there is no need for a blood substitute, since animal blood is readily available. Second, other research has shown that wine as a preferred offering goes back to antiquity. Wine offerings were offered in Mesopotamia, in Ugarit, and among the Hittites and the Greeks.[11] Certain passages indicate that wine libations offered in concert with *minḥâ* offerings are said to generate a *reaḥ niḥoaḥ*, a fragrant offering for YHWH. "You shall present as a grain offering two-tenths of a measure of choice flour, along with a third of a *hin* of oil mixed in and a third of a *hin* of wine as a libation, as a fragrant offering for the Lord" (Num. 15:6–7) The rabbis interpret this last phrase to mean that the wine offering gave particular pleasure to YHWH.

Wine intended for cultic—rather than mundane—use had to meet certain requirements. Wine that a non-Jew had dedicated for any religious purpose was forbidden, as was any wine that was produced by non-Jews. The Mishnah goes so far as to rate the quality of wine procured from various regions and lists other restrictions: "They may not bring old wine —this is the view of Rabbi; but the sages declare it [old wine] valid. They

may not bring sweet wine or wine that has been smoked or has been cooked, and if they brought any such wine it was declared invalid. Neither may they bring wine made from grapes grown on espaliers, but only wine made from grapes grown on trailing vines or in cultivated vineyards" (M. Men. 8.6). Cultic wine was stored in special containers, libation jugs (*qeśôt hannāsekh*; Lev. 4:7). According to the rabbis, the wine was used specifically for libations of the outer altar. Milgrom describes the procedure: "According to rabbinic tradition, the wine was placed in perforated bowls atop the altar from which the wine drained into the ground underneath. Most likely the wine originally was poured upon the base of the altar and not burnt upon its hearth, the flames of which might be extinguished, in violation of Leviticus 6:6."[12] The rabbinic literature develops more specific guidelines for storing and manipulating wine. According to M. Men. 8.7, sacrificial wine should be stored in small containers, and the priests should use only wine "from the third part down" of the container, so that no froth (from the top) or sediment (from the bottom) will be used. Specific amounts of wine are designated to accompany other offerings: "half of a *hin* of wine for a bull, a third of a *hin* for a ram, and a quarter of a *hin* for a lamb" (Num. 28:14). Specifically prescribed quantities of wine help to distinguish one sacrifice from another, much as the different animal species do. It seems reasonable to conclude that wine libations functioned independently as regular accompaniments to grain and animal offerings.

The pervasive presence of these companion offerings suggests that our discussions of sacrificial offerings need to become more nuanced and sophisticated. Just as we have tended to focus on a single kind of offering (animal), we have tended to focus on a single type of offering (principal). But even a cursory examination of Vedic and Jewish sacrifice reveals that both traditions often include multiple substances within individual rituals. The complex interplay of principal and companion offerings is required for many rituals to be performed correctly. Sacrificial theorizing needs to recognize and incorporate this dynamic in order to interpret complex sacrificial traditions correctly. We will come back to this important point in the next chapter, but first we need to complete our review of liquid offerings by examining several key principal liquid sacrifices.

Liquid Substances as Principal Offerings

Most important for our purposes, liquid substances frequently serve as the principal offerings in various sacrificial rites. In the following pages we will examine three liquid offerings: milk and soma juice in the Vedic system and blood in the Jewish system. After exploring the rituals that focus on the manipulation of these substances, we will note how the procedures involved resonate with and differ from animal and vegetal sacrifice.

In the Vedic tradition, every twice-born householder is required to perform the *agnihotra* ritual, commonly classified among the seven *havir-yajñas*.[13] This simple ritual involves pouring cow's milk into the *gārhapatya* fire twice daily, once in the morning and once in the evening.[14] The milk is heated over the fire's embers, cooled, and then offered to the deities. In the morning, milk is poured from a ladle into the fire for Sūrya and then to Prajāpati; in the evening the milk is first offered to Agni, then to Prajāpati. The *yajamāna* (or the *adhvaryu*, if the *yajamāna* has engaged a priest to perform the *agnihotra* on his behalf) drinks what remains in the ladle. This ritual is obligatory, required throughout one's lifetime: "[I]ndeed, the *agnihotra* is a *sattra* that ends with old age or death, for he is released from it only by old age or death" (ŚB 12.4.1.1).

Even this seemingly simple sacrifice involves many procedural elements. Portions from Kane's summary of the manipulation are worth quoting at length here:

> The adhvaryu takes from the gārhapatya fire some burning coals for boiling the milk and keeps them to the north of the gārhapatya in a separate spot. Then he goes near the cow, holds the vessel in which the cow has been milked, brings it towards the east of the āhavanīya, sits to the west of the gārhapatya and heats the vessel on the burning coals mentioned above. He takes a darbha blade . . . kindles it and holding it over the milk illuminates the milk with its light. He then takes water in a sruva and sprinkles one drop or some drops into the boiling milk (Āśv. II. 3. 3 and 5). He should then again hold a burning blade (the same blade used before) over the hot milk and light it up. He does this thrice and then casts away the blade to the north. . . . Then the pot of milk is slowly lifted with three mantras and drawn down to the north from the burning coals (Āśv. II.3 8, Tai. Br. II. 1. 3 "vartma karoti"). Then the burning coals on which the milk was boiled or heated are thrown back in the gārhapatya fire. Then a *sruva*

and *sruc* both made of vikankata wood are cleaned with the hand (to remove dust) and are heated on the gārhapatya (or āhavanīya according to Āp. VI. 7. 1). He then again heats the *sruc* and *sruva* on the gārhapatya, asks the yajamāna "shall I take out milk from the pot with sruva)" and the yajamāna replies standing "Yes, do take out." Then the adhvaryu holds in his right hand the *sruva* ladle and in his left hand the agnihotra-havanī with its mouth turned upwards, pours out into the agnihotra-havanī milk from the milk pot (already heated) with the *sruva* four times and keeps the *sruva* in the milk pot. In Āp. VI. 7. 7–8 and Āśv. II. 3. 13–14 it is said that the adhvaryu knowing the mind of the householder should draw the fullest ladle for the most favorite son of the sacrificer or if the latter desires that the eldest son should be most prosperous and the later ones less and less, then the first ladle is filled to the fullest; on the other hand if he wishes the youngest to be prosperous then the last ladle drawing is the fullest. Then the adhvaryu . . . carries the *sruc* towards the āhavanīya holding it as high as his nose. . . . [H]e reaches the āhavanīya and places the *sruc* and *samidh* on darbha blades (on the *kūrca*, says Baud. III.5) to the west of the āhavanīya. He [the adhvaryu] himself sits to the northwest of the āhavanīya facing the east, bends his knees, holds the sruc in his left hand and with the right hand offers the *samidh* in the midst of the āhavaniya fire. . . . When the samidh has caught fire and is burning brightly, he offers the first oblation (of milk) on the *samidh* about two finger breadths from its root. . . . Then he places the *sruc* on the kuśa blades and looks at the gārhapatya with the thought "bestow on me cattle." Then he again takes up the *sruc*, makes a second offering (of milk) which is larger in measure than the first one, but this is offered silently, while he contemplates upon Prajāpati in his mind. This second offering is made to the east or north of the first in such a way that the two will not come in contact. He keeps more milk in the *sruc* than what is taken up in making the second offering. He then raises the *sruc* twice . . . in such a way that the flames of the fire turn north-wards and places the *sruc* on the kūrca. He scours with his hand turned downwards the spout of the ladle and then rubs his hand to which some drops of the milk stick on the north side of the *kūrca* . . . with the words "salutation to the gods" . . . or "to you for securing cattle." . . . He then sits down to the northwest of the gārhapatya with his face turned towards the east, bends his knee, offers the *samidh* in the gārhapatya fire, then drawing out in the *sruva* milk from the pot offers it into the fire with a mantra. . . . He offers a second oblation of milk by the *sruva*. . . . Then he

> offers one oblation of milk with the sruva ladle in to the dakṣiṇāgni. . . . He then touches water, turns northwards and with one of his fingers . . . he takes out what remains in the *sruc* and licks it noiselessly without allowing it to come in contact with his teeth.[15]

Even in this basic ritual, milk functions as a sacrificial offering. The milk is poured into the sacrificial offering fires (the *gārhapatya* and *āhavanīya* fires) at specifically designated times, and the oblation is clearly intended to yield specific results (e.g., the relative prosperity of one's sons; cattle). In addition, the manipulation of the milk includes several procedures common to animal and vegetal sacrifice, beginning with the selection of a particular substance. Specific liquid substances are chosen depending upon the intended result of the rite. Kane explains, "The homa is performed with cow's milk for him who performs agnihotra as a sacred duty and not for any particular reward in view, but one who desires to secure a village or plenty of food, or strength or brilliance may employ respectively yavāgū (gruel), cooked rice, curds or clarified butter (Āśv. II.3.1–2)."[16] Thus the selection of milk (rather than gruel, rice, curds, or ghee)—our initial sacrificial activity—in the *agnihotra* indicates the ritual's intended effect from the outset.

In addition, the milk for this rite must be acquired in a specific manner. Kane explains,

> [A]n order is issued to the person engaged to milk the agnihotra cow that stands to the south of the sacrificial ground with her face to the east or north and that has a male calf. At the time of milking, the calf is to the south of the cow, and first sucks milk and then the calf is removed and the milking is done. The person to milk the cow should not be a śūdra (Kāt. IV. 14. 1), but Āp. (VI. 3. 11–14) allows even a śūdra to milk the cow, while Baud. (III.4) says that he must be a brāhmaṇa. Rules are laid down about the udders from which milk is to be drawn. . . . The milking is not to be begun by pressing the udders, but by making the calf suck them first.[17]

Specific instructions are given regarding who may obtain the milk, how the milk should be expressed from the udders (ĀpŚS 6.4.2), when the milking should occur (ĀpŚS 6.4.5), the vessel in which the milk should be contained (KŚS 4. 14.1; ĀpŚS 6.3.7), and the preparation of the milk. Thus the liquid offering substance to be obtained and the manner in which it is to be obtained are strictly governed, just as in animal and vegetal sacrifice.

Milk is also heated like many animal and vegetal offerings. The milk is usually heated over coals from the *gārhapatya* fire.[18] In addition, a burning blade of grass is held above the heated milk to illuminate it. A few drops of water are added to the milk, and then a burning blade of grass is held above the watery milk three times. Then the *adhvaryu* pours out the heated milk onto the sacrificial fires.[19] When the offerings to the gods have been completed, the *adhvaryu* "holds the sruc [sacrificial ladling spoon] in such a way that its rod is turned east or north, and licks the sruc itself twice."[20] Thus the milk offering is consumed by the fires (and thus, ostensibly by the deities) as well as by the *adhvaryu.*

There are some important distinctive elements to the milk manipulation in the *agnihotra*. For example, the *yajamāna* regularly acts ritually on his own behalf. Unlike the *paśubandha* and the *iṣṭi* rituals, in which the *yajamāna* is explicitly removed from contact with the offering, the *agnihotra* is a more intimate activity, which the *yajamāna* can perform himself throughout his lifetime. I would argue that the *yajamāna*'s actions identify him with his offering. When an *adhvaryu* does act on the *yajamāna*'s behalf, the *adhvaryu* ritually asks the *yajamāna* whether he should draw milk from out of the pot, and the *yajamāna* gives his permission. This public request, made before the milk is poured out into the sacrificial fires, is an acknowledgment that the *adhvaryu* is about to do something the *yajamāna* properly has the right to do. In addition, the *agnihotra* is performed on sacrificial fires that have been established in the *yajamāna*'s name, on his behalf, and on his own property. These elements reinforce the understanding that the twice-daily offering is to be identified with the *yajamāna*.

In addition, there is a significant *absence* of activity: the *agnihotra* does not involve killing. In his discussion of the *agnihotra,* Heesterman makes two important observations: "[T]he agnihotra, being a milk offering, does not require sacrificial killing. But this does not seem to have been a consideration with the ritualistic and speculative thinkers. At least this point does not come up in the ample discussions in the brāhmaṇas and Upaniṣads. Rather it is the agnihotra's concern with fire and food."[21] Heesterman, referencing the major interpretive Vedic works, notes that killing is not the focal activity in the *agnihotra*. In addition, much like Malamoud, he emphasizes the importance of the heating of the milk and its consumption by ritual participants and the sacrificial fires. Once again, killing is not the dominant or defining procedure in sacrificial activity. This observation is

most intriguing when we note how frequently the *agnihotra* is supposed to be performed—twice daily.

Soma

The *agnihotra* is a relatively simple sacrificial ritual. At the other end of the Vedic sacrificial spectrum lies the complex soma ritual, to which we have already referred several times in this work. The word *soma* has multiple referents: the deity Soma, the plant called soma, and the juice of the soma plant. The term can, and often does, suggest all these referents simultaneously. The primary goal of the soma sacrifice is the attainment of heaven for the *yajamāna*, although there may be other mundane goals as well. As noted earlier, there are said to be seven forms of soma sacrifices-Agniṣṭoma, Atyagniṣṭoma, Ukthya, Soḍaśin, Vājapeya, Atirātra, and Aptoryāma—and the Agniṣṭoma (or Jyotisṭoma) is the *prakṛti,* or model, of the soma ritual. The most impressive soma ceremonies (the *rājasūya*, the *vājapeya*, and the *aśvamedha*) are restricted to princes. Soma sacrifices require at least sixteen priests, and they incorporate many rites, including multiple *iṣṭi* rites and at least one *paśubandha* rite, as well as practices unique to the soma sacrifice itself.

It is impossible to provide more than a bare-bones outline of the soma ritual here.[22] Before a soma sacrifice begins, soma stalks are selected and gathered. As the eastern ritual space (the *mahāvedī*) is constructed during the course of the sacrifice, a cart is placed in the center of the *mahāvedī*, heaped with stalks of the soma plant. After the formal selection of the priests, the consecration of the *yajamāna*, and an opening *iṣṭi*, certain soma stalks are formally selected for use later in the ritual. A mock "purchase" of soma (*somakrayaṇa*) is dramatized in the ritual. Someone other than the priests pretends to be the soma "vendor" (JaiŚS 3.7.31). The vendor is asked to remove any weeds from the soma stalks (the *adhvaryu* priest actually turns his back while this is being done). The *adhvaryu* then engages the vendor in a scripted haggling session, upping the "bid" five times. Eventually the vendor sells the soma for an entire cow. At this point soma stalks are placed on the southern side of a bull's hide, near the *pratiprasthātṛ* (the *adhvaryu*'s assistant). Ultimately, however, the cow is taken back—the soma is, in effect, acquired for nothing.[23]

The purchase of the soma stalks makes explicit the priest's (and thus the sacrificer's) right to manipulate (including kill) the soma later in the ritual. At this point it is important to make two observations. First, the

true offering substance—the soma juice—is not actually selected; rather, the stalks that will subsequently yield this juice are. This distinction may seem to be a fine one, but we will return to this point later. Second, since the period of the Brāhmaṇas, the soma ritual has not used soma plants. In fact, scholars are not even completely certain what the soma plant was. R. Gordon Wasson has argued that the original soma was the hallucinogenic mushroom "fly agaric" (*Amanita muscaria*).[24] D. S. Flattery argues that it was the hallucinogenic plant "wild rue" (*Peganum harmala*).[25] Because of the absence of the soma plant, a variety of replacements has been used consistently in Vedic rituals. Staal lists a number of potential replacements, including "Ephedra, Sarcostemma, and other creepers and plants without particularly remarkable properties."[26] The Śrauta Sūtras even describe a procedure for tuning milk into soma: the bark of the *parṇa* tree is added to the milk, ritually converting it into soma (ĀpŚS 1.6.8). Whatever the replacement, the disappearance of the soma plant did not lead to the disappearance of a rite entirely focused upon it. Instead, acceptable substitutes were found, and the soma sacrifice continued.[27] Even the name stayed the same; the sacrifice has never been renamed to acknowledge the absence of soma, and the plant being used—whatever it is—continues to be called "soma" both in the manuscript traditions and in ritual performances.

Now, substitutions are employed frequently in virtually every sacrificial tradition, and the Vedic tradition regularly provides for substitutes on a one-time basis under many different circumstances. But it is noteworthy that this particular substitution has been universally employed for hundreds, if not thousands, of years. Brian K. Smith has gone so far as to suggest that there may never have been a true soma plant: "That an 'original' soma never existed at all is a speculation that has not been put forward by Indologists and perhaps deserves consideration."[28]

Accepting the fact that the soma offering is not, in fact, soma, we move on to subsequent procedures. We find that the process of association occurs somewhat differently in the soma sacrifice than in Vedic animal- and grain-based sacrifice. In other sacrifices an association between the principal offering substance and the appropriate deity is generated *during the course of the ritual*. The soma plant, however, is by its very nature already linked with the deity Soma. The plant is considered "the earthly form of the god Soma."[29] A number of elements included in the ritual reflect soma's perceived status. For example, immediately after the soma has been purchased, it is offered hospitality as an honored guest (*ātithye-*

ṣṭi). The soma plant is addressed directly throughout the sacrifice as if it were a human participant, and the plant is constantly referred to as "King Soma" (*soma rājan*) throughout the ritual and in the ritual texts describing the preparations for the pressing.[30] The bundle of soma is treated like an honorable personage, like Soma himself. For example, early in the ritual the soma stalks are processed into the *havirdhāna* (the ritual arena where the stalks will be pressed), politely escorted from the cart, seated on a chair indicating rank, and offered refreshment. The sacrificer's servant removes some soma stalks (*aṃśu*) from the cart, ties them in a cloth, and covers them with a turban (ĀpŚS 10.24.7–14; KŚS 7.7.12–21). At this point the *yajamāna* "pays homage to soma and waits upon Aditi."[31]

Soma's desirability as an offering substance is based primarily upon the fact that soma is seen simultaneously as the plant and the god. As a result, there is no need for specific actions to associate the offering substance with a deity, since the offering substance *is* the deity. Instead, the sacrifice includes activities that publicly *recognize*—rather than create—a connection between the soma plant and Soma the god. The element of "recognition" is important because it implies that the process of association need not take place within the context of sacrifice. Instead, the preexistent connection between an offering substance and a specific deity (which is often more fully developed in the mythological or theological strands of a tradition) may be what qualifies a substance for selection. This circumstance leads to a change in the sequence of the selection and association procedures from those we find in Vedic animal and vegetal offerings: soma offerings are first recognized as having an association with a deity and subsequently selected for sacrifice.

The soma sacrifice continues with the identification of the offering with the *yajamāna*. At first glance the identification of the soma offering with the *yajamāna* appears markedly different from identification in animal and vegetal sacrifice because the *yajamāna* makes direct physical contact with the soma stalk. After the soma has been purchased, the *adhvaryu*, carrying the soma wrapped in cloth, approaches the *yajamāna*. The priest places the cloth containing the soma directly on the right thigh of the sacrificer. Shortly thereafter the *yajamāna* takes the cloth bundle into his hands and places it on his head. Carrying the soma, he approaches a cart. The *adhvaryu* places the soma bundle on this cart, and the ritual continues.

The *yajamāna* makes even more direct contact with the soma plant a short time later. The cart is wheeled into place in the *mahāvedī* for the

pressing that is to follow. The *adhvaryu* or *hotṛ* priest touches the soma or the cloth covering it. Then the *yajamāna* touches the soma stalks.[32] One of the Śrauta Sūtras directs, "The *yajamāna* then breaks contact with the *soma* stalk," clearly implying that the *yajamāna* has previously made direct contact with the plant (KŚS 9.1.6).

This direct contact is markedly different from what we have seen in other types of Vedic sacrifice. In animal and vegetal sacrifice the *yajamāna* scrupulously avoids direct contact with the principal offering. Yet in the soma sacrifice there appears to be no such restriction. How do we explain this apparent contradiction? I believe that the problem can be resolved by recognizing that the soma stalk that the *yajamāna* touches is not actually the sacrificial offering. Rather, the soma stalk acts as a kind of vessel or host for the true offering substance, the soma juice. Consequently, contact with the plant stalk does not present the same dangers that contact with the actual sacrificial substance would. In this interpretation the *yajamāna*'s behavior is consistent with what we have observed in other Vedic sacrifices.

The sacrificer also identifies with the soma offering in more indirect ways, indicating that the encased plant juice (and not the plant stalk) is the sacrificial offering. After the soma juice has been extracted, the *adhvaryu* directs the *yajamāna*'s gaze in a number of directions, first to the filled cups, then to the *upāṃśu* (pressing) stone, then to the cups again, and then to the *droṇakalaśa* (a trough that receives the juice pressed from the stalks; KŚS 9.7.8–11). We have already seen that gazing effects a kind of indirect contact in Vedic animal sacrifice. In addition, Mānava Śrauta Sūtra states that the woolen strainer used to strain the soma juice is to be "woven by those living with the sacrificer," forging another kind of mediated contact.[33] Each of these procedural elements forges an identification between the offering and the *yajamāna*, and each of the identification procedures underscores the fact that the soma juice, not the soma plant, is the principal offering.

The high point of the soma sacrifice is the pressing of the soma stalks. The *sūtya* (from root *su*, meaning to press out or extract) day is divided into three pressing sessions: morning (*prātaḥ savana*—this pressing includes the *mahābhiṣavaṇa*, the great pressing), midday or afternoon (*mādhyandina savana*), and evening (*tṛtīya savana*—this pressing occurs immediately after sunset; ŚŚS 2.7.1–2). Malamoud explains, "There are two outflows (*dhārā*) of *soma* from the morning pressing, three from the

midday pressing and four from the evening pressing."[34] Each pressing session is performed roughly the same way as the other two (as described below), with a few minor variations.[35] Most important, a larger portion of the soma is used in the morning pressing and a smaller portion for the midday pressing (ĀpŚS 12.9.7).

First, a few stalks are taken from the heap of soma in the cart. Water is poured into the *ādhavanīya* trough. The *adhvaryu* takes the *upara* (the stone on which the stalks are ground), places it on an animal hide, and then places some soma stalks on the stone. Water is poured over the stalks, and priests pound them with stones held in their right hand. This pounding is called the first "turn" or "round" (*paryāga*). In a second turn the soma stalks that were scattered in the first round are collected and pounded again. Finally, there is a third turn. The Śrauta Sūtras direct how many times the stalks are to be pounded in each turn: "He strikes eight, eleven, and twelve times respectively for the first, second, and third striking."[36] The pounded stalks are collected and placed in the *ādhavanīya* trough, stirred with water, washed, and pressed through a woolen strainer so that the soma juice, which has been extracted by the pressing and mixed with the water, can be captured in cups.

We have already noted that numerous scholars understand this pounding as a kind of killing. This characterization is important to our present discussion for several reasons. We have seen previously that the principal animal and vegetal offerings are killed in the Vedic tradition. Thus there is a kind of continuity between the Vedic animal-based, grain-based, and soma sacrifices: they all involve killing. The soma plant is killed to release its "life essence," its *medha*, the soma juice. The priestly traditions make it clear that this "life essence" is powerful. Baudhāyana, founder of one of the earliest schools of *śrauta* ritual, states that the first stalk that has been pressed, releasing juice, "is capable of destroying the sense-power, virility, progeny, and cattle of the sacrificer; one should recite a formula over it."[37] The plant stalks themselves are not dangerous or powerful, but the juice in the plants can help or harm an individual, depending upon the priests' manipulation.[38]

Perhaps most significant, although killing occurs in the soma ritual, the principal offering itself is not killed. The stalks are killed, but though the stalks and juice are, of course, related, they are not identical or interchangeable. The stalks are killed in order to release the principal offering, the soma juice, at the appropriate ritual moment. Thus killing the soma

stalks makes the soma juice available for further ritual manipulation. The fact that the stalks—and not the juice—are killed implies that killing serves primarily to release or make accessible the principal offering substance, to make it available for ritual manipulation. Killing brings the principal offering to the sacrifice; it is not the primary manipulation of that offering (or of the ritual). Consequently, the killing of the soma plant is a means to an end, not an end in itself.

As in other sacrificial rituals, apportionment is a key element of the soma rite, and the process is quite elaborate. The juice extracted by the pressing process is divided into different cups that have distinct designations and significations. The soma juice that runs freely (*dhārā*) through the woolen strainer fills several wooden cups. The first is called *antaryāma*; the *adhvaryu* offers this cup when the sun rises: "At the sunrise [he pours the offering], when it has dawned or [immediately] after sunrise."[39] Subsequently, several cups are filled: *aindravāyava, maitravāruṇa, sukra, manthin, āgrayaṇa, ukthya*, and *dhruva*. These cups of juice are placed at designated points on a four-cornered mound (*khara*) in the pressing area, a mound that was prepared earlier in the ritual specifically for this purpose. Each cup of soma juice is distinguished from the others in various ways. First, the cups themselves look different. For example, "the cup belonging to Indra-Vāyu has a cord on it and the cup for the Mitravaruṇa has a protuberance like an udder at the throat of a goat."[40] In addition, each cup must be fashioned from a specific type of wood. For example, "the Ṛtu-cups . . . are made either of Kārṣmarya or Āāvatha-wood" (KŚS 9.2.13). Each cup is placed in a specific location in the ritual arena; the *āgrayaṇa* cup, for instance, is placed in the middle of the mound (KŚS 9.2.10). Finally, some cups are used only at certain pressings. For example, the *sāvitra, pānīvata*, and *hāriyojana* cups are used only in the evening pressing.

In addition to the cups, other factors distinguish certain discrete amounts of soma juice from other amounts. Some forms of the juice have distinct names. For instance, the soma that falls into the *droṇakalaśa* is called *śukra*, "shining" (KŚS 9.5.15). In addition, the juice that is placed in each cup is subsequently manipulated in its own distinct way. Certain cups—the *āgrayaṇa, ukthya,* and *dhruva* cups—are filled to the brim with pure soma juice. Other cups are mixed with boiled, then cooled, milk; the juice in the *manthin* cup is mixed with barley flour. In the evening pressing, the Āditya cup is mixed with sour milk or curds. In this same session

soma is mixed with milk to make *aśir*. Discrete portions of soma, then, are distinguished from others by being mixed with other substances.

After all the cups have been filled, the remaining soma juice is poured to fill half the *droṇakalaśa* trough. At this point the stream of juice is stopped.[41] All the fluid in the woolen strainer is wrung into the *droṇakalaśa* trough, and the strainer is set over the *pūtabhṛt* trough. A portion of soma juice from the *ādhavanīya* trough is poured through the strainer. Following this, the priests and the sacrificer perform a complex series of chants. The liquid offering of soma, therefore, is apportioned in several ways after it has been extracted from the pressed soma stalks. The division of the liquid into multiple cups and the manipulation of the juice in various ways generate multiple offerings from one offering substance, similar to the generation of multiple offerings in Vedic animal and vegetal sacrifice.

Scholars have noted that the soma offering is the one Vedic offering that is not heated over a fire. Malamoud, for example, comments, "While it is the case that *soma* is subjected to all kinds of procedures . . . it is never cooked."[42] In this way the soma juice seems to differ from other Vedic offering substances. Malamoud, however, argues that the soma is in fact "heated" differently—not over fire but in the milk with which it is mixed: " 'He [Indra] decided to make an offering. Agni said, "You should not offer by pouring into me that which is raw." He mixed it with parched grains and when it became cooked, he offered it.' Mixed together with a cooked substance—including milk—*soma* is thus considered to be cooked."[43] Malamoud explains that soma is said to be ritually cooked because "all milk products and derivate substances in which milk is blended are, as far as Indian physiology is concerned, cooked in advance."[44] The classic proof text of this view is the phrase "Therefore the raw yields the cooked," implying that the cow (considered "raw") produces milk (considered "cooked"; TS 6.5.6.4). Malamoud explains that milk is considered cooked because the milk is really Agni's sperm, and everything that comes from Agni, by definition, is cooked.[45] In another context Staal argues that the hot milk of the *pravargya* rite is associated with all kinds of heat—including *tapas* (internal heat generated by ritual physical disciplines) and sexual excitement—not just cooking. Consequently, ritual substances can be cooked in a variety of ways that may or may not include fire.

What implications does this view of heating have for our understanding of ritual heating? Just as we have seen that not all heating involves cooking, we now see that not all cooking requires heating by fire. The Vedic world-

view contains a broader concept of heating that draws on connections between elements in the microcosmic and macrocosmic realms. Consequently, cooking may be caused by sexual excitement, ritual self-discipline, or contact with specific material substances. For example, the Śrauta Sūtras list alternative activities one can perform if a *śrauta* fire goes out: "One may, in that case, use an ordinary (*laukika*) fire, or offer in the right ear of a female goat (because, according to ŚB 7.5.2.6, Prajāpati created the goat from his ear?), in the right hand of Brahmin (where the 'oblations' of sacrificial gifts, *dakṣiṇās*, are also placed), on a cluster of *darbha* grass, or in water."[46] The ritual fires are important to the sacrifice, but they are not absolutely essential—obviously, the substitutes listed can be used instead. Thus, heating can be transposed, recast in a different form that does not involve fire. This possibility is important because it demonstrates that, even within the strict directives of the Vedic period, one can find the seeds of later practices that reinterpret "heating," practices that do not involve a literal fire at all. I discuss this further in the concluding remarks to this chapter. Although the sacrificial fires are not used to heat soma juice, the priests offer some of the juice into the sacrificial fires near the conclusion of the ritual. The appropriate god(s) consume specific cups of the juice at specific moments in the ritual. For example, the *adhvaryu* is directed to take soma juice in the *antaryāma* cup (the first cup that is filled) and make an offering. "He should sit down toward the north of the fire, carry over the cup along the northern joint of the enclosing sticks, and then make the offering in the northern half of the fire."[47] Later, the priest offers soma juice from the *upāṃśu* cup into the *āhavanīya* fire and the gods receive the sacrificial offerings. In the soma sacrifice the dispensation of the soma liquid into the sacrificial fire for the gods is accompanied by lengthy chants and recitations. These verbal accompaniments are crucial to the sacrifice. Many of these chants encourage the gods to drink the juice, reminding the deities how the juice has been specially prepared for them.

> Beneficent one, drink the noble and full juice of this plant—
> we bestow it upon you fearlessly.
> It has been cleansed by the priests, pressed by the rocks,
> purified by the strainer, and washed in the rivers like a valiant horse.
> Mixing it with milk, like barley, we have sweetened it for you.
> Indra, we call you to this fellowship. (RV 8.2.1–3)

The gods, then, are seen as the primary consumers of the soma juice as it is offered into the sacrificial fire.

In addition, some of the juice is consumed by various ritual participants. After the appropriate cups of soma juice have been offered into the fires, the priests drink the remnants.[48] When the participants in the sacrifice consume the soma juice, it is as if they are consuming the god Soma himself. Each time a priest drinks, an appropriate mantra is spoken. The mantras that are recited characterize soma as the drink of the gods, the elixir of immortality, a drink that confers health, wealth, and progeny on the *yajamāna*. Thus the consumption of the soma juice transforms the *yajamāna*, ultimately making it possible for him to attain his earthly as well as his divine goals.

What have we learned by reviewing the basic procedures of the soma sacrifice? We noted that the selection of the soma stalk does not depend primarily on the passive recognition of certain physical characteristics. Rather, the selection of the soma juice is based largely on its perceived inherent association with the god Soma. Association precedes selection, both logically and chronologically, in soma sacrifice.

At first glance, the soma sacrifice seems to identify the *yajamāna* with the offering substance in a more direct manner than in Vedic animal or vegetal sacrifice. We noted, however, that the *yajamāna* actually makes contact with the soma stalk, not the juice, so his contact with the actual substance of sacrifice (*dravya*) is mediated. The fact that the plant acts as a sheath or vessel for the actual offering substance, the juice, prompts us to ask whether similar situations arise with other liquid offerings. Is the liquid conveyed to the sacrifice in a container—natural or human-made—that limits or mediates contact with human participants? How is this "container" viewed within the tradition? In the soma sacrifice, for example, the stalks are considered rubbish after all the juice has been extracted from them; they serve no ritual purpose. Do we find a similar situation in other liquid sacrifices, or are there sacrifices in which the "vessel" is also put to ritual use?

We have also seen that the Vedic tradition characterizes the pounding of the soma stalks as a kind of killing. Taittirīya Saṃhitā 6.6.9 states, "They kill the *soma* when they press it. In the killing of the *soma* the sacrifice is killed." The fact that liquid sacrifices can include a procedure that the tradition itself characterizes as killing suggests that modern Western con-

ceptions of "killing" and "life" need to be adjusted when examining a cross-cultural phenomenon such as sacrifice.

The soma sacrifice also involves apportionment, which is somewhat unexpected in liquid sacrifice. The soma juice is divided in a number of ways after it has been extracted from the plant stalks. It is poured into distinctive cups, mixed with other substances, and manipulated in different ways. Each of these procedures distinguishes one portion of juice from other portions of juice, generating a multiplicity of offerings from one whole. We have observed similar activity in animal and vegetal offerings, and we can begin to generalize that the process of division accomplishes two purposes in the context of sacrifice. First, it generates many offerings out of a single offering substance. Second, it imposes a new kind of order upon the offering substance, an order created by humans rather than by creation and thus an order that reflects the substance's inferior ritual-cultic status in relationship to humans and the gods. Division is an act that publicizes humanity's ability—and right—to dominate and control other elements of creation, albeit according to divine or cosmic directive. We will return to this issue later in this study.

We have also seen that soma is not heated in the same way that animal or vegetal offerings are. Soma is never heated over a fire. However, it is heated ritually when it is mixed with milk during the course of the sacrifice. Thus soma is considered "cooked" within the context of the sacrifice. Such a transposition of the concept of heating is helpful in that it suggests how later Indian traditions internalize "heating" in the form of *tapas*. Such recasting of heating opens up the possibility that more expansive views of heating may exist in other sacrificial systems as well.[49] It may be helpful to distinguish between cooking and the broader concept of heating, both in discussions of the manipulation of material offering substances and in discussions of postsacrificial ritual practices. Based on the information presented here, we can conclude that the sacrifice of liquid offering substances—specifically milk, ghee, and soma—involves a series of variations on procedures we have observed in animal and vegetal sacrifice.

Neither the model developed by Hubert and Mauss nor the model proposed by Girard adequately addresses the complex procedures applied to liquid offering substances. A polythetic approach, on the other hand, responds to all the major activities of the soma sacrifice, as well as the relative simplicity of the *agnihotra*. Vedic liquid sacrifice across the spec-

trum can be characterized as a dynamic matrix of several activities that interact in various distinctive combinations. As we turn to the Jewish material, we will determine whether a polythetic approach can also be helpful in interpreting Jewish liquid sacrifice.

Blood

In the Jewish sacrificial tradition, blood is the predominant liquid offering.[50] Prohibitions against its consumption and restrictions governing its handling reflect the potency of this substance. Unlike soma, which constitutes its own subcategory of sacrifices within the Vedic system, blood offerings are not categorized separately from animal offerings in the Jewish system. Rather, blood offerings generally accompany animal (flesh) offerings. However, the blood offerings fulfill distinct ritual functions that are often different from those of the flesh offerings. For example, in the *šĕlāmîm* ("well-being") ritual, the animal flesh is characterized specifically as a thank offering. The blood manipulation that accompanies the *šĕlāmîm*, however, is described as expiatory, apparently accomplishing a different ritual objective than that accomplished by the animal flesh.[51] In the following pages we will note the procedural elements involved specifically in blood manipulation within the Jewish sacrificial system. We will see that blood's distinctive handling should be incorporated in general theorizing about sacrificial practice.

Blood is subjected to many of the same procedures that animal and vegetal substances undergo, beginning with the process of selection. But how is blood selected for sacrificial use? Clearly, the blood is contained, so it cannot be selected on the basis of any visible characteristics. Two possible responses come to mind. First, in the Jewish sacrificial system, sacrificial blood must come from a limited number of animals: domesticated beasts of the flock, beasts of the herd, and certain birds, as specified for each particular sacrifice. Thus, blood is selected in part on the basis of its "host" animal. Second, blood in general has a theological association with YHWH, the creator of life, as indicated in the phrase "the life is in the blood" or "the life is the blood."[52] Therefore, I would argue that blood is inherently associated with YHWH. In this sense, Jewish blood selection resonates with Vedic soma selection: just as soma juice has an inherent connection with the god Soma in Vedic thought, blood has an inherent association with YHWH in Jewish thought. Consequently, blood's asso-

ciation with YHWH, established prior to any ritual manipulation, is *recognized* rather than generated. On the basis of this preexisting association, blood is selected for specific sacrificial rites.

Once the blood has been selected (through a specific animal host), we would expect to find some activity that identifies the sacrificer with the blood offering. However, no such activity occurs. There could be several reasons for this lack of activity. We have seen that the sacrificer explicitly identifies himself with an individual animal victim by placing his hands on the animal's head. "He shall lay his hand upon the head of the whole burnt offering and it shall be accepted for him to purge on his behalf."[53] Since the blood comes from the animal, and since the animal and blood offerings are presented in chronological proximity with each other, it would seem reasonable to conclude that the sacrificer, in his contact with the animal victim, also identifies himself with the blood that is inside the animal host as well. Consequently, we could argue that the sacrificer identifies himself with the animal's blood indirectly by making physical contact with the animal's body prior to its slaughter.

There is, however, a problem with this assumption. We cannot simply assume that contact with the animal automatically generates contact with its blood unless other factors support such an assumption. In fact, evidence from other cultures provides examples of ritual participants who clearly distinguish between animal flesh and animal blood and who make direct contact with both. For example, in one of the Greek sacrifices (*sphagia temnein*), the Greek army captains dipped their hands into the blood of an offering animal as they took their oath to defeat an enemy.[54] Therefore we need to see whether there is another way to explain why the sacrificer in Jewish sacrifice does not make direct contact with the blood offering.

One possible explanation is that blood offerings should not be considered sacrificial offerings at all. If this is the case, the issue of association (either directly or indirectly) is moot for our present discussion. August Dillman, Martin Noth, Rolf Knierim, and Rolf Rendtorff, for example, argue that blood is not, in fact, a sacrificial offering.[55] If these scholars are correct, there is no need for a procedure that identifies the sacrificer with the offering. This view is plausible, but I would like to explore yet another possibility.

An explanation can be found which supports the idea that blood is, in fact, a sacrificial offering even though it is not specifically identified with

the sacrificer. Following Milgrom's lead, I would argue that the principal function of the blood sacrifice is not to purify any individual sacrificer, which might require some process of identification. Rather, the blood is sacrificed to purge the sanctuary of contamination. Unlike the animal and grain offerings, the blood offering is primarily directed at ritual *objects* within the sanctuary and the sanctuary itself, not ritual participants. Consequently, although a blood sacrifice purges *on behalf of* an individual or the congregation, it is actually purging ritual space, not people. Given this purpose, it is unnecessary for any particular sacrificer to identify directly with a blood libation because he or she is not the direct object of its cleansing work. In this particular context the direct object of the ritual activity is the ritual space.[56]

If we recognize that the ritual objects and ritual arena are the objects of the blood's work, then we might expect to see some physical contact between these spaces and the blood—and we do. Blood is applied to the ritual arena in several locations by various methods, which we will explore in more detail below. These direct applications link the blood with the objects requiring purgation. Sacrificial offerings such as blood offerings can be understood as objective sacrifices (in Hubert and Mauss's sense of the term) and still share many of the same procedural elements that personal sacrifices include.[57]

After a particular sacrificial animal has been selected and presented at the appropriate ritual space and time, its blood needs to be accessed. Animals have their throat cut, and birds have their neck wrung and then slit open so their blood can flow more freely. I reviewed the specific procedures involved in killing animal victims in Chapter 2, so I will not rehearse them here. Two aspects of animal slaughter, however, deserve further attention. First, the methods used to kill animal victims in Jewish sacrifice facilitate the acquisition of the animal's blood. In other words, killing is not the only—or ultimate—ritual concern. If the animal's death were the sole point of the manipulation, the animal could be strangled, bludgeoned, or executed in numerous other ways. But the method described in Jewish texts makes both the animal flesh and blood available for subsequent ritual manipulation as distinct ritual offering substances. Such an understanding views killing as a transitional element of sacrifice rather than a culminating moment. Animal slaughter is performed with an eye toward providing access to the animal's blood, not simply wreaking violence upon the animal's body.

Second, as soon as an animal victim's throat is cut or a bird's neck is broken, the victim's blood begins to flow. Several factors indicate that the manipulation of this blood is an important—and distinctive—sacrificial activity. The blood must be distributed entirely within the sanctuary, on or near the altar. That is, blood must be handled within the sacred ritual space. In addition, the priests, as the recognized ritual specialists, take responsibility for the distribution of the blood: "All sacrifices are invalid if their blood is received by a non-priest" (M. Zeb. 2.1). This distribution of blood by the priests is one of several ways in which the blood manipulation is distinguished from the handling of the flesh. For example, while one priest dismembers the victim's body, another priest is responsible for manipulating the blood, underscoring the fact that these actions are two different operations. In an earlier chapter we noted that the priests' participation in the apportionment of an animal victim indicated the relative importance of that procedure. Similarly, I would argue that the priests' control over blood indicates the importance of blood manipulation within the rite. The ritual texts' detailed discussions of blood manipulation, along with the priests' supervision and participation, suggest not only that the distribution of the blood important but that it may be the most important procedure involving the blood.[58]

Before we describe the significance of the different blood manipulations, we must note the various ways in which blood is handled. There is not adequate space here to provide a thorough overview of the significance and development of blood manipulation in the Jewish sacrificial system. Numerous authors (especially Jacob Milgrom and Baruch Levine) have written authoritatively on this topic.[59] I also recommend William Gilders's recent work, "Representation and Interpretation: Blood Manipulation in Ancient Israel and Early Judaism."[60] In this work Gilders provides an overview of blood manipulation as discussed in many biblical passages and in certain key extrabiblical texts. Gilders's discussion provides a thoughtful and thorough overview of blood manipulation in the priestly texts, and the following pages draw heavily on his work.

In general, animal blood is captured in cultic basins after which one priest distributes it in the appropriate manner. Gilders discusses four distinct verbs that refer to specific types of manipulation. First, blood may be daubed (Hebrew root *ntn*) on the horns of the altar. Second, it may be tossed (Hebrew root *zrq*) against the altar. Third, it is sometimes sprinkled (Hebrew root *nzh*) on the priests during their ordination and toward the

veil of the sanctuary (*pārôket*). Finally, some blood may be poured out (Hebrew root *špk*) at the base of the altar. Each of these verbs indicates a specific type of blood manipulation appropriate to the specific rite in which it is found.

The specific blood manipulation employed is determined by a number of factors. First, bird blood is handled differently than other animal blood, for obvious logistical reasons. For example, in the *ʿōlâ*, if the offering is an animal other than a bird, "the priests present the blood and toss it [*zrq*] round about the altar" (Lev. 1:5). If, however, the *ʿōlâ* offering is a bird, then the bird's blood "shall be drained beside the altar on the east side, in the place for the ashes."[61] The bird's blood is drained directly from its neck by pressing the bird against the side of the altar (Lev. 1:15).

In addition, blood manipulation varies according to the type of sacrifice being performed. For example, in the first-fruits offering, the blood is tossed on the altar (Num. 18:17). In the Yom Kippur sacrifice, blood is daubed on the horns of the altar and then tossed on the altar seven times. Different rites, therefore, incorporate the distribution of blood differently and, conversely, the different manipulation of the blood is one of the identifying characteristics of each sacrificial rite. In addition, in certain contexts, blood will be manipulated in several different ways, depending upon the intended result. In the *ḥaṭṭāʾt* sacrifice, for example, the manipulation is quite complex: "The priest *shall dip his finger in the blood* and sprinkle part of the blood seven times before the Lord in front of the veil of the sanctuary. Then the priest *shall daub some blood on the horns of the altar* of incense before the Lord, which is in the tent of meeting, and the rest of the blood of the bull he *shall pour out at the base of the altar* of the burnt offering, which is at the door of the tent of meeting."[62] Note that the blood in this ritual is manipulated in at least three distinct ways. In each sacrificial context, the different manipulation of the blood reflects the degree of contamination (and thus purgation) being addressed in the ritual.[63] Blood tossed on the altar purges the altar alone; blood flung on or toward the veil of the sanctuary (the *pārôket*) purges the inner shrine area.

In addition, blood is handled differently depending upon whose contamination is being addressed. For example, the passage quoted above describes the *ḥaṭṭāʾt* performed on behalf of an anointed priest, "thus bringing guilt on the people [of Israel]" (Lev. 4:3). The same procedure is included in a *ḥaṭṭāʾt* performed for the whole congregation. The *ḥaṭṭāʾt* performed for a tribal ruler, however, does not require that the blood be

tossed "seven times before YHWH in front of the veil." Neither is this required if the same ritual is performed for a common person. Purgation on behalf of a priest or on behalf of the whole congregation requires a more extensive procedure than that for any lay individual. Thus the socio-cultic rank of the individual is sometimes reflected in the distribution of the blood.

Later rabbinic writings reflect concerns that developed about the possibility of improper blood manipulation, which can invalidate a ritual. For example, the rabbis describe a "red line" about one cubit above the ground which divided the upper portion of the altar from the lower portion in the Temple. The Mishnah reference to the red line marked around the altar reflects concerns that the blood offerings be manipulated correctly. "The *ʿōlâ* of a bird [has its blood] tossed above [this red line] but the *ʿōlâ* of an animal [has its blood tossed] below [this red line]. If [the priest] alters the procedure in either case, the offering is invalid" (M. Kin. 1.1). Thus the proper placement of the blood in relationship to the altar is very important to the validity of the sacrifice.

We have seen that the blood of an offering is apportioned in several ways: tossed against or "round about" (*ʿal sābîb*) the altar, poured at the base of the sacrificial altar, daubed onto the horns of the incense altar, and sprinkled against or towards the veil (*pārôket*) of the shrine.[64] We have noted that these different manipulations reflect several issues surrounding the nature of the offering. But what does the apportionment of the blood on discrete portions of the altars actually accomplish? The verbs used to express what the blood offerings accomplish are *ṭiher* (cleanse), *ḥiṭṭē* (purify), and *kippēr* (expunge, purge).[65] Milgrom characterizes the sacrificial blood as a "ritual detergent."[66] In several publications he describes the purpose of the blood manipulation colorfully. For instance, "On the analogy of Oscar Wilde's novel [*Picture of Dorian Gray*], the Priestly writers would claim that sin may not leave its mark on the face of the sinner, but it is certain to mark the face of the sanctuary; and unless it is quickly expunged, God's presence will depart."[67] According to Milgrom, blood expunges sin from the "face of the sanctuary." Levine presents a similar interpretation: "[T]he blood was placed on those areas and objects [in the sanctuary] so as to protect the deity and his immediate surroundings from the incursion of impurity which would penetrate the sanctuary through a route leading from the courtyard, outside the tent, through the entrance of the tent, past the altar of incense, and through the *pārôket*, opened to let

the priest in, and into the very spot where the deity sat, astride the cherubim."[68] H. C. Brichto points out, "[T]he verb *kipper* in the sense 'to purge' normally governs inanimate objects directly; a person is never governed directly by this verb, hence is never the object which is purged by the blood of the *ḥaṭṭāʾt*-offering."[69] Thus the biblical texts seem to indicate that the blood will "purify [the altar] from the contamination of the Israelites and consecrate it" (Lev. 16:19). The blood expunges contamination of a ritual space; it does not refer primarily to the cleansing of a person.[70]

Blood is at its most powerful—and its most dangerous—when it makes contact either with holy personnel or with holy objects. Contact with blood is paramount to contact with YHWH and effects a kind of communion between YHWH and the object or individual the blood has touched. This concept is most explicit in the generation of the covenant between YHWH and the Israelites at Sinai described in Exodus 24. Half of the blood from the sacrificial animals is sprinkled on the altar; the other half is sprinkled on the Israelites. In this narrative, the sprinkling of blood binds the Israelites to YHWH and vice versa. The fact that blood effects contact between YHWH and an object or individual creates a problem if blood makes contact with something it should not. For example, if a garment is accidentally spattered with blood in the course of a sacrifice, it has to be washed in a holy place (Lev. 6:27). Blood must be distributed only as directed by YHWH, in appropriate times within the confines of the sanctuary.

Jewish blood manipulation, then, includes several procedures we have identified with sacrificial activity. It is performed by ritual elite within controlled space and time restrictions. It involves some of the procedures we have identified in Jewish animal and vegetal sacrifice: association, identification, and apportionment. However, it is also of interest to note the sacrificial activities that are conspicuously *absent* in blood sacrifice.

For example, blood is never measured out into specific quantities, unlike grains used for grain cakes and other liquid substances. The Mishnah notes that there were seven wet measures used in the sanctuary.[71] These measurements were used in the handling of oil, water, and wine but never blood. The absence of this operation can probably be explained logistically. First, the general quantity of blood is predetermined by the animal's size and species, so quantities are determined somewhat indirectly. Second, blood has to be distributed in the sanctuary relatively quickly after it has been caught in the basin, before it begins to congeal, since congealed

blood is considered inappropriate for cultic use.[72] Consequently, the blood is drained into a basin and then dashed against the altar as soon as possible after the animal has been slaughtered, before any other part of the animal is offered.[73]

Blood is also distinctive in that it is never heated during Jewish sacrificial ritual.[74] One reason may simply be practical: since the blood has to be handled before it congeals, it is best to manipulate blood as soon as it is released from the animal victim. In addition, we have already observed that heating in Jewish animal sacrifice generally serves one of two functions: it either prepares flesh portions for consumption by the ritual participants or conveys specific portions to YHWH. Unlike animal portions, blood is never consumed by the ritual participants; therefore it does not need to be cooked. Blood does, however, need to be conveyed to YHWH, but this step is achieved by applying blood directly to the altar. Once the blood has been applied to the altar, YHWH has received the offering—nothing more is required.[75]

The most striking aspect of blood offerings is the prohibition *against* human consumption. It should be noted that this is not a universal prohibition; many cultures consume blood under sacred and mundane circumstances. But biblical teaching states that humans may never, under any circumstances, consume blood. This prohibition goes back to the Noachide law, applicable to all humanity: "You shall not eat flesh with its life, that is, its blood" (Gen. 9:4). The Holiness source (H) in Leviticus emphasizes the prohibition for the Israelites: "It shall be a perpetual statue throughout your generations, in all your dwelling places. You shall eat neither fat nor blood" (Lev. 3:17). This prohibition comes with a stiff penalty: "[M]oreover you shall eat no blood whatsoever, either of bird or of animal, in any of your dwelling places. Whoever eats any blood, he shall be cut off [*krt*] from his people" (Lev. 7:26–7). Another passage is more expansive:

> If any man of the house of Israel or any of the strangers that live among them consumes any blood, I will set my face against the person who consumes blood and will cut him off from among his people. For the life of the flesh is the blood, and I have given it for you upon the altar to purge on behalf of your lives; for it is the blood that expunges, by [means of] the life. Therefore I said to the people of Israel, no person among you shall consume blood, neither shall any stranger who lives among you consume

> blood. Any man also of the people of Israel, or of the strangers that lives among them, who acquires through hunting any beast or bird that may be eaten, shall pour out its blood and cover it [the blood] with dirt. For the life of every creature is its blood. Therefore I said to the people of Israel, you shall not eat the blood of any creature, for the life of every creature is its blood. Whoever consumes it shall be cut off.[76]

The verb *kārēt*, translated here as "cut off," demands that the individual be cut off from participation in the Israelite community. Some have interpreted this phrase as a euphemism for death.[77] Others have argued that *kārēt* refers to exile from the community and exile for one's descendants. Whatever the term implies, being cut off is presented as one of the most severe penalties YHWH imposes.

The word translated as "eat" here is *ʾākal*, also translated as "consume" or "ingest." This verb is used in every discussion of the prohibition of blood consumption. This prohibition (like the prohibition against consuming fat) is absolute: the blood, which is understood to be the essence of life, belongs to YHWH alone. This prohibition extends beyond the sacrificial arena. The blood of wild animals is also prohibited. It must be drained correctly and covered. The Mishnah specifies that if an animal is slaughtered in the wild, its blood must be drained in certain ways and not others. For example, "No one may slaughter in such a way that the blood flows into any kind of hole. Instead he may make a hole in his house to let the blood flow into it, but he must not do so in the street in such a way as to appear to imitate the heretics" (M. Ḥullin 2.9).

This prohibition against blood consumption has been explained in several ways. Some argue on the basis of internal evidence that YHWH, as the creator of life, demands that blood, the essence of life, be returned to him. Others use comparative evidence to argue that the prohibition against ingesting blood distinguished Israelites from surrounding communities. For example, Martin S. Bergmann notes that the blood manipulation prescribed in the biblical literature counters contemporary non-Israelite practices: "In pre-Yhwhistic times the god was eaten raw and his blood was drunk while still hot. The Jewish religion is an elaborate reaction-formation against this practice."[78] Jehoshua M. Grintz lists several ways in which Israelite blood manipulation differs from sacrifice "to the satyrs 'on the face of the field.'"[79] Grintz argues that these are self-conscious differences, designed to set worship of YHWH apart from the worship of chthonic

deities. These differences include the prohibition against human consumption of blood. The Israelites publicized their allegiance to their god by consigning the most vital part of the animal, its blood, to him.

Thus we see that the manipulation of blood involves two complementary elements, a general prohibition and a more restricted instruction. First, animal blood is prohibited for general human consumption: "You shall not eat flesh with its life, that is, with its blood" (Gen. 9:3–4). To state it positively, the blood is reserved for YHWH. Second, the restriction imposed on the Israelites instructs them to dispose of animal blood properly. One who does not do this is guilty of murder (Lev. 17:3–4). Individuals who slaughter wild animals have to pour the blood into the ground, and sacrificial (= domesticated) animals must have their blood drained upon the altar. These procedures return the life of the animal to its creator, YHWH. They also benefit the community by addressing ritual impurity. Milgrom comments, "[T]he Priestly source propounds a notion of impurity as a dynamic force, magnetic and malefic to the sphere of the sacred, attacking it not just by direct contact but from a distance."[80] The manipulation of blood in particular purifies the sanctuary so that the community can continue to worship YHWH there, so that his presence will not depart from the sanctuary.

Note that the prohibition against consumption, which appears first in Genesis 9, applies to all humanity. The instruction to bring blood to the altar, however, applies only to Israel. The manipulation of blood on the altar affects the Israelite community in a particular way because the blood on the altar expunges Israelite sin. Thus the manipulation of blood, while returning what is YHWH's to YHWH, also distinguishes YHWH's people from other communities. As in Jewish animal and vegetal sacrifice, the manipulation of the principal offering substance highlights and publicizes Israel's special relationship with YHWH.

The application of the polythetic model to Jewish blood manipulation yields several interesting observations. We noted that several elements commonly associated with sacrifice do not occur in blood sacrifice. The blood is not selected explicitly, it is not identified with the sacrificer, it is not consumed by any of the ritual participants, and it is not heated, either literally or symbolically. Instead, the blood is conveyed directly from the slaughtered victim to the altar. Yet, for other reasons, I still characterize blood manipulation as sacrificial. I am reluctant to exclude certain rituals from the category of sacrifice simply because they do not involve all the

procedures traditionally associated with sacrifice. Instead, I suggest that we need (1) to rethink our assumption that certain procedures are essential to sacrifice and (2) to examine how functions commonly fulfilled by one process (e.g., heating) may be accomplished by other procedures (e.g., direct contact).

Also, for the first time we have seen a specific procedural *prohibition*: humans are universally prohibited from ingesting blood. This prohibition suggests that human consumption need not be a defining characteristic of sacrifice. Generally, it suggests that prohibitions *against* certain procedures are as much a part of sacrificial ritual as instructions *for* certain procedures.

In addition, we have noted that the sacrificial procedures that do occur in blood manipulation (e.g., killing, apportionment) take on a slightly different form than in Jewish animal or vegetal sacrifice. For example, no specific procedure explicitly identifies the sacrificer(s) with the blood offerings manipulated in Jewish sacrifice. The blood is identified with a ritual space or object rather than a ritual participant. Further, the offering substance itself is not killed; rather, killing makes this offering substance available for subsequent ritual manipulation. Moreover, blood is apportioned in the course of its application to the altar. The precise placement of the blood in various ways (daubing, tossing, sprinkling, and pouring out) constitutes specific types of sacrifices and effect specific ritual results. Most important, these results affect the ritual *space* rather than the ritual *participants*. This ritual consequence is distinct from the results accomplished by the flesh offerings and is specifically dependent upon the correct manipulation of the blood.

In the Introduction I argued that no single element or procedure is essential to sacrificial ritual. Rather, several activities work together to generate sacrificial rituals. In this chapter, we have seen that liquid sacrifices often lack several of the elements of the sacrificial matrix, forcing us to consider how this affects our understanding of sacrifice, with the conclusion that some rituals are more sacrificial than others. We turn now to a comparative analysis of Vedic and Jewish liquid sacrifice and to a discussion of their broader implications for the general study of sacrifice.

Concluding Thoughts

In the previous pages we reviewed the principal liquid offerings in Vedic and Jewish sacrifice: milk, soma juice, and blood. By "refracting" the

manipulation of these substances into multiple distinct procedures, we are led to several conclusions. Liquid offerings are as integral to the Vedic and Jewish sacrificial systems as animal and vegetal offerings. The primary liquid offerings are subjected to many of the same procedures that animal and vegetal substances are subjected to, albeit sometimes in slightly different forms, suggesting that liquid offerings should be taken just as seriously as sacrificial substances as animal and vegetal offerings. As a result, I argue that liquid substances should be taken into account in any general model of sacrifice used to characterize these traditions and that their manipulation should influence generic characterizations of sacrifice that theorists develop. I have made preliminary observations regarding the presence of, absence of, and variations on each elemental sacrificial procedure within milk, soma, and blood sacrifice. Now it is time to explore the implications of these observations for the study of sacrifice more broadly.

One of the first important observations we have made regarding liquid offerings concerns the selection of liquid offering substances. In animal and vegetal sacrifice the offering substances are chosen, at least in part, on the basis of visible physical characteristics. Liquid sacrifice, however, is different. In Vedic sacrifice, for example, the soma juice—the actual offering substance—is chosen indirectly through the selection of the soma plant. It would be logical to assume that this plant is selected on the basis of its physical characteristics, its species identity as the plant "*soma*" required by the tradition. However, since the late brahmanic period, the plant used in soma sacrifices has not actually been the soma plant but rather a substitute. Primary texts themselves and contemporary performances make no mention of this substitute. The occasional use of substitutes is not unusual in Vedic sacrifice (or in many other sacrificial traditions), but in the soma sacrifice a substitute for the principal offering appears as a permanent feature of the ritual. The principal offering substance is thus completely and permanently replaced without any concomitant change in the description, actions, or recitations that characterize soma sacrifice. It is as if one replaced the bread and wine of Christian communion with crackers and milk, permanently, in every performance, without making any alteration to the words or actions of the liturgy.

The implications of consistent substitution in the soma sacrifice are twofold. First, the alteration demonstrates that one principal offering substance can replace another principal offering substance permanently with-

out generating any significant change in the ritual tradition that describes and directs the sacrificial procedure. Such a change may be noted or explained in other interpretive (theological, mythological) texts, but the ritual tradition itself in effect turns a blind eye to the substitution and continues as if nothing had changed at all. There is no discussion of the permanent substitute in the detailed discussions regarding the soma sacrifice in the primary texts. This absence of discussion should give those of us who focus on ritual texts pause because we cannot rely upon the primary ritual textual or oral traditions to reflect every significant change that develops in ritual practice. Second, the general process of selection in the soma sacrifice demonstrates that the selection of a principal offering may be done on the basis of its "host" or "container"—such as the soma plant—rather than on characteristics of the offering substance itself. The soma plant is selected, not the soma juice. We find a parallel situation in Jewish sacrifice in the selection of blood "contained" in its animal host. The blood used in Jewish sacrifice is brought to the sacrifice through the animal that is slaughtered. The blood is not chosen on the basis of its own physical characteristics; instead it is a by-product of the selection of the animal victim. Should we conclude, then, that the selection of blood is entirely haphazard? No. Blood, like soma juice, is by its very nature inherently qualified for sacrifice because of its physical connection to its host but, more important, because of its prior association with the appropriate god. In both the soma ritual and the Jewish blood rituals, the selection of an offering follows from a preexisting inherent association with the appropriate deity. We see, then, that in both Vedic and Jewish liquid sacrifice the offering substance is chosen primarily on the basis of theologically imagined connections between the micro- and macrocosmic realms, not physical characteristics. The tendency has been to assume that material sacrificial offerings are selected solely on the basis of physical characteristics or their prior relationship with the sacrificer. Our investigation of Vedic and Jewish liquid sacrifice, however, demonstrates that material sacrifices can be selected on the basis of other factors. The fact that liquid offerings, at least in a number of traditions, are selected on the basis of something other than their physical traits encourages us to consider alternative standards of selection that may be used to choose material offerings.

We also noted some striking differences between our two traditions in the procedures employed to identify a liquid offering with the sacrificer. In Vedic animal sacrifice the identification between offering and sacrificer

was very pronounced and constituted one of the most dramatic moments of the ritual. In Vedic vegetal sacrifice identification was less pronounced but still relatively easy to locate in the ritual procedure. In liquid sacrifice the identification of the *yajamāna* with the soma juice is even more subtle. I argued earlier that when the *yajamāna* touches the soma stalks and has them placed against his body he makes contact with the "host" of the soma juice, not the offering itself. This is consistent with the indirect, mediated contact required between offerings and the *yajamāna* in other Vedic sacrifices, albeit much more restrained. The implication of this observation is that a sacrificer need not make direct contact with a liquid offering substance in order for the offering to accomplish ritual goals on his behalf. Indirect, mediated contact may be just as effective.

In Jewish sacrifice, however, the procedure is markedly different. In contrast to animal- and grain-based sacrifice, there is no discernible moment in the ritual when the blood is identified with the sacrificer. We concluded that identification with the sacrificer is unnecessary in this case because the ritual space (rather than the sacrificer) is the direct beneficiary of the sacrifice. I argued that the blood ultimately purges a sacrificial object (the altar, the holy of holies), *not* the sacrificer himself. I reiterate this point because it has widely been assumed that sacrificial offerings stand in or substitute for a sacrificer and that this substitution is a large part of why sacrifice works. The substitution is often generated and made evident to the ritual participants and observers through direct or indirect contact between the sacrificer and the offering. Hubert and Mauss note, "This association of the victim and the sacrifier is *brought about by a physical contact* between the sacrifier (sometimes the priest) and the victim. . . . *Through this proximity* the victim, who already represents the gods, comes to represent the sacrifier also."[81] Our study of liquid sacrifice, however, forces us to ask the question, *is* an offering always identified with an individual or collective sacrificer via some kind of contact? Is the identification, in fact, always an element of sacrifice?

We are also forced to rethink the significance of killing by its limited role in Vedic and Jewish liquid sacrifices. In the brahmanical, biblical, and rabbinic traditions, liquid offering substances are not killed. They are, however, extracted from their hosts through the death of that host. Other traditions also kill an offering host in order to extract an offering substance. The ancient Greeks, for example, slit the throat of an animal victim so that the blood could be poured out over the altar (*bōmos*) and flow into

the ground, thus linking the realm of humans, manifest in the altar, with the realm of the gods, manifest in the earth.

This observation has several implications. First, not all sacrificial substances are killed. Thus, once again, we see that the death of the primary offering substance cannot be put forward as an essential or defining element of sacrifice in general. More interesting, even when a sacrifice involves killing, it does not necessarily mean that the principal offering itself is killed. In other words, a sacrifice may involve killing something that is *not* the principal offering. Consequently we cannot always assume that the substance that is being killed in a sacrifice is, in fact, the principal offering of that particular ritual. This point is important because scholars have frequently assumed that killing is the focal activity of sacrifice and that it is always applied to the principal offering. Jan van Baal, for example, states: "I call an offering any act of presenting something to a supernatural being, a sacrifice an offering *accompanied by the ritual killing of the object* of the offering."[82] The Vedic and Jewish sacrificial systems indicate that this need not be the case. Finally, the fact that killing in the Vedic soma and the Jewish blood sacrifices makes the principal offering accessible for ritual use forces us to revisit the execution process and to rethink its significance in sacrificial ritual. Killing has largely been understood as a common element of sacrifice, and the interpretation of killing has been focused on the theological, mythological, or ritual significance of the animal victim's death. The act of execution, however, is sometimes important not for these reasons but because of how it relates to other sacrificial activities at a more functional level. Specifically, killing often facilitates subsequent sacrificial procedures. For example, we have seen that killing the soma plant actually has very little to do with the plant stalk itself; its primary purpose is to release the soma juice, the true offering substance. Thus the primary goal of the plant's "death" may be to provide ritual access to the principal offering, not the death of the soma plant itself. Theoretical approaches predicated on death and violence as an inherent element of sacrifice may easily miss alternative reasons underlying the method of killing employed. Based on these observations, we need to acknowledge the varying degrees to which killing is incorporated into sacrifice, the multiple meanings killing may have in sacrifice, and the very real possibility that killing may not be an element of sacrifice at all in some traditions. At this stage in our work, we need to do more than simply note how a sacrificial victim is killed; we need to ask how the killing relates to other sacrificial procedures.

Such observations should provoke more nuanced and sophisticated understandings of sacrificial killing and its role in sacrifice.

We also noted that some liquid offerings are apportioned in discrete amounts just as animal and vegetal offerings are. Soma juice is poured into different cups and distributed between various deities and ritual participants. Similarly, the blood in Jewish sacrifice is distributed by being manipulated in various ways at various locations in the sanctuary, such as the base of the altar, the horns of the altar, and the veil covering the inner shrine. Liquid offerings in other traditions are also divided into distinct portions. For example, blood is manipulated in a similar fashion in Greek sacrifice. The blood from the animal victim is captured in goblets (*sphageion*) and then presented on the altar (*bōmos*). Great care is taken to assure that the blood falls only in appropriate places. Speaking generally, the culmination of most liquid sacrifices occurs when the liquid offering substance is apportioned to the appropriate parties.

Other traditions also use the process of apportionment to convey a liquid offering to the appropriate god(s). W. Robertson Smith notes that in virtually all the Arabian sacrifices the blood offering "flows over the sacred symbol, or gathers in a pit (*ghabghab*) at the foot of the altar idol. . . . What enters the *ghabghab* is held to be conveyed to the deity."[83] In some traditions blood was dabbed directly onto a representation of the face of a deity.[84] In light of this data, we may propose a tentative generalization: liquid offerings may be conveyed to the god(s) by heating, but they may also be conveyed via direct contact with the altar or other objects in the ritual space. In the latter situations, the distribution procedure conveys the offering and concludes the sacrifice.

Apportionment is also important because it displays the offering substance to ritual participants and to the public at large. Ron Grimes has commented, "The power to display another, as 'other,' is considerable. To display is not merely to show or to make visible but to create. A display, particularly when it is effective, is a performance; it is active rather than inert. . . . An effective displaying of cultures is an enactment, a putting into force."[85] Display of the principal offering reinforces cosmogonic, ritual, and social hierarchies. Thus it is necessary to make the soma juice or the animal blood visible because the principal offerings must be exposed to public view, subject to the power and expertise of the ritual elite, who are themselves subject to the ritual system itself.

Thus the apportionment phase of liquid sacrifice functions in several

ways. First, apportionment can convey the offering to the appropriate god(s) via contact with the sacrificial space. Second, apportionment may conclude a sacrifice, making heating and consumption unnecessary (and thus nonessential elements of sacrifice). Finally, the activities involved in the distribution of liquid offerings frequently display the liquid offering substance to the public (lay community, outsiders) as well as to ritual participants, reinforcing cosmogonic and sociocultic hierarchies.

Liquid sacrificial offerings are also intriguing because of the actions to which they are *not* subjected. I noted earlier that offering substances are frequently heated over a fire. Sometimes that fire cooks the offering, that is, prepares it for consumption by human ritual participants. At other times fire conveys offering portions to the gods. Liquid sacrifice, however, is interesting precisely because many liquid offerings are frequently *not* heated with fire at all. For example, the blood used in Jewish sacrifice is applied to the altar almost immediately after it is shed from the victim. There are a number of possible explanations for this. First, we could conclude that cooking—that is, heating over a flame as preparation for consumption—is unnecessary in certain sacrificial contexts, and so fire is simply omitted from the ritual procedure. The blood that is spattered on the altar is not consumed by any ritual participants. Consequently, there is no need to cook the offering, so heating is omitted. Alternatively, we could conclude that heating is accomplished by some means other than fire. The fire is supplanted by another medium, a medium that "heats" the offering substance without the use of fire. For example, the soma juice used in Vedic sacrifice is "cooked" when it is mixed with milk because the milk is Agni's (the fire god's) sperm. Caroline Humphrey and James Laidlaw describe the transformation of heating in Vedic thought:

> In the *Rg Veda* the ancient god of fire, Agni, who is also the sacrificial fire itself, consumes demonic energies by heat (*tapas*). In later literature the expulsion of the demons is directly correlated with purification, of both the sacrificial objects and the sacrifice itself. Reference to the god Agni becomes progressively more symbolic and figurative, and increasingly it is *tapas*, the creative/destructive power of heat, which itself comes to be seen as the power of purification. The *Brahmana* texts emphasize the need for purification of the sacrificer himself. He is rendered "fit for the sacrifice" through *diksha* (initiation) which is attained through *tapas*. *Tapas* is self-imposed suffering and pain which generates an inner heat. . . . In particu-

> lar fasting, sexual abstinence, and regulated breathing are means of generating "heat" within the body. The fire imagery remains. Kaelber quotes the *Jaiminiya Upanishad-Brahmana* as saying that breath is man's essence or inner self, this inner self is *tapas*, and fire is the essence of *tapas*.[86]

The process of heating is transposed so that it becomes an internalized process. *Tapas*, one's internal spiritual-corporal heat, generated by spiritual and physical disciplines, replaces physical flames as the ritually significant manifestation of heat. Once this shift occurs, there is no need for fire. This shift from a literal to a symbolic heating process opens the door to other manifestations of heat. Heating in this context is reinterpreted so that the ritual concept remains but its form and procedure change. These permutations signify that elements of sacrificial procedure can be transposed or recast as time passes, adapting their formal manifestation to new religio-cultural contexts.

The Vedic and Jewish traditions differ in their attitudes toward the human consumption of their principal liquid offerings. It is tempting to leap to the general conclusion that blood as a liquid offering may not be consumed simply because it is blood. However, this prohibition is not universal. For example, W. Robertson Smith records that ritual participants drink the blood of a sacrificed camel in "the oldest known form of Arabian sacrifice."[87] Blood, then, is not universally prohibited from human ritual consumption. What, then, determines whether the principal offering can be consumed? The differing standards regarding the consumption of soma juice and blood are best understood as differences in the Vedic and Jewish views on humanity's status in relationship to "life essences." Vedic soma ritual participants consume the soma juice in addition to consigning part of it to the appropriate deities. Thus the Vedic tradition is comfortable with the human consumption of an offering's life essence within the ritual arena. The Jewish sacrificial tradition, in contrast, strictly forbids the consumption of any animal blood on pain of death. Prohibitions against the human consumption of blood are invariably coupled with implications that YHWH alone is to receive blood offerings. A brief overview suggests that blood is restricted to the gods in traditions in which it is seen as the locus of life. The Greeks, for example, prohibit the consumption of animal blood "because it is reserved for the divine."[88] As in Jewish sacrifice, the blood has to be released in such a way that the gods receive it but humans do not. Jean-Louis Durand argues that the visual

representation of animal sacrifice on Greek pottery emphasizes this point by omitting any depiction of the bloodletting. "The deed that actually drenches the blade and altar in blood is never pictured."[89] Various moments in the sacrificial process are represented, but the actual bloodletting is omitted because "the moment the blood gushes, belongs to the gods."[90] Similarly, in Judaism, YHWH alone has the right to receive the life essence contained in the blood.

Just as blood contains the life essence of animals in Jewish thought, breath is viewed as the life essence of animals in Vedic thought, and plant juice is viewed as the life essence of plants. Therefore, when a plant offering is crushed or pounded, it is considered "killed" just as an animal victim would have been. Consequently, the juice of the soma plant, extracted from the plant in the course of the sacrifice, parallels the extraction of an animal victim's blood in Jewish sacrifice. In both traditions the life essence of the creature is exposed to public view and ritual manipulation through its host's death.

It may be most accurate to argue that whatever substance contains the life essence of its host animal or plant must be released in a controlled fashion. Usually this life essence is released to the gods, although sometimes ritual participants also partake of this substance. The blood of Jewish sacrifices is given to YHWH. In contrast, we note that the Vedic gods seem to take little interest in blood. Instead, a sacrificial animal's breath is closely controlled during Vedic sacrifice and released in a controlled manner after its death, and soma juice is distributed to the gods and to ritual participants. Although these three substances—blood, soma juice, and breath—are dissimilar in physical consistency and form, they are similar in that they are the physical manifestations of life essence. Consequently their handling and consumption are strictly regulated.

In the previous pages, I have attempted to demonstrate two things. First, liquid offerings should be recognized as important sacrificial offerings, subject to the same types of manipulation that animal and vegetal offerings undergo. We have seen that Vedic and Jewish sacrifice incorporate animal, vegetal, and liquid offerings within their sacrificial systems, often combining them. Therefore, any ritual theorizing that focuses solely on animal offerings, or even animal and vegetal offerings, offers only a partial picture of sacrifice. By now it should seem reasonable to consider liquid offerings along with animal and vegetal offerings as principal offering substances and to incorporate all these offering substances in our

general theorizing. Second, sacrifices driven by liquid substances offer their own unique combinations of sacrificial procedures. Certain variations appear, including changes in the sequence of sacrificial activity, the absence of—and explicit prohibitions against—certain procedures, and the application of certain procedures (identification, killing) to new objects. My hope is that these variations will not eliminate liquid substances from consideration as sacrificial offerings but rather provoke renewed examination of our general assumptions about the nature of sacrifice.

CHAPTER FIVE

The Apportionment of Sacrificial Offerings

In this chapter I focus on one type of sacrificial activity, the apportionment (division and distribution of ritually valued substances in specified ways) of an offering. I examine the procedures involved in dividing the traditional Vedic and Jewish animal victims and then touch briefly on parallels in the treatment of grain-cake offerings. I hope to demonstrate that the apportionment of sacrificial offerings deserves more scholarly attention than it has received to date for several reasons. First, apportionment activities underscore the correlation between vegetal offerings and animal victims by subjecting both offerings to similar strictly controlled procedures. Portions of sacrificial grain cakes are explicitly compared with animal body parts, and the manipulation of these grain cakes parallels the manipulation of animal victims. As a result, vegetal offerings are presented as ritually equivalent to animal offerings. Second, the division of an offering generates new multiple discrete entities from a single, undifferentiated whole. This transformation of a single ritual offering into multiple parts often replicates cosmogonic activity, linking the activity of a handful of humans with creative activity on a cosmic scale. Third, division of an

animal victim generates a classifiable microcosm within the animal's body which parallels classificatory orders in other realms, including the sociocultic realm. Fourth, the guidelines that govern apportionment suggest a moral dimension to activity in ritual and social realms. Finally, the division of a traditional substantial offering is easily transposed into metaphoric or internalized sacrifice. The process of apportionment persists in internalized and symbolic sacrifice, allowing the language and authority of sacrifice to shift seamlessly into other streams of various religious traditions and ultimately into modern living.

All these elements reflect the importance of apportionment as a sacrificial activity. They also highlight the creative—rather than destructive—nature of apportionment in particular and sacrifice in general. Apportionment, rather than destroying an offering, rearranges and redistributes it. From this perspective, apportionment is a constructive, organizing activity that propels sacrificial ritual forward.

A note about my choice of the term *apportionment*. Some might challenge this term as too mechanical or clinical, arguing that it minimizes the violence done to a victim's body during the course of sacrifice. Terms such as *dismemberment* or *dissection* might be suggested as better alternatives. I use *apportionment* because the indigenous terms most frequently used to describe the process do *not* connote violence. For example, the Sanskrit verbs *bhaj-* and *vibhaj-* connote the division of offerings according to ritual guidelines, not the violent destruction of an animal body. The Hebrew verb *šāḥāṭ* (slitting the throat) suggests a specific slaughtering technique that, as fleshed out in later rabbinic writing, is intended to minimize the pain a sacrificial victim experiences. Israelite animal sacrifice, as Jonathan Klawans notes, "proceeds only in a very orderly and controlled way."[1] Although I certainly do not feel bound to analyze ritual practice solely in terms of an indigenous community's worldview, it will be helpful for the purposes of this essay to begin with the priestly characterizations of sacrificial apportionment that permeate brahmanical Hindu and biblical and rabbinic Jewish literature.

Apportionment within Vedic and Jewish Animal Sacrifice

The Vedic animal sacrifice (*paśubandha*) is performed independently (as a *nirudhapaśubandha*) or as a part of any soma sacrifice (as the *saumiya* rite). The *nirudhapaśubandha* is supposed to be performed annually

during the rainy season (at the new or full moon), although it may be performed twice yearly. In the *paśubandha* the animal victim (typically a male goat) is killed by strangulation. Afterward, it is cut up in an elaborate, predetermined sequence in which six priests participate, including the *adhvaryu* (who performs most of the ritual activity); the *āgnīdhra* ("the lighter of the fire"); the *pratipasthātra* (the *adhvaryu*'s assistant); the *hotra* (who performs most of the ritual chanting); the *maitrāvaruṇa* (the *hotra*'s assistant); and the *brahman* (who oversees the ritual activity and performs expiatory rites when necessary). In addition, the *yajamāna* (the ritual sponsor and the one who benefits from the sacrifice) and his wife (the *patnī*) participate under the *adhvaryu*'s direction. The ritual involves numerous offerings, but the three major phases involve the preparation of the omentum (*vāpa*), preparation of the internal organs that accompany a grain-cake, or *paśupuroḍāśa*, offering, and preparation of the heart as a primary oblation (*havis*). The following is a brief summary of the division and distribution of the animal offering.

After having been strangled or suffocated, the goat is ritually bathed and then placed on the ground, belly side up.[2] A blade of *darbha* grass is placed on the animal's stomach, and an incision is made through the blade and the stomach approximately four finger breadths below the navel. The omentum is removed, placed on two sticks, and roasted on the *āhavaniya* fire with *ājya* (clarified butter) poured over it (KŚS 6.6.15).[3] Once the omentum is roasted, it is cast into fire for Indrāgnī (or, less frequently, the Sun-god or Prajāpati). A series of *ājya* offerings are then performed. Some texts note that a priest should hold the stomach closed throughout this initial phase until the omentum has been offered.

At this point, the goat is dissected and the various *aṅgas* ("limbs" or animal parts) are distributed in specific ways. In this second phase of the rite, the *adhvaryu* priest removes various parts of the victim, and the *śāmitra* cooks them. The *pratipasthātra* directs the *śāmitra*'s activity, saying,

> O śāmitṛ, do you (extract from the animal's body and) put together the heart, the tongue, and the sternum; put together the liver and the two kidneys; keep aside the left forefoot; place the two thoracic walls separately; keep aside the right buttock and the testis with penis; put together the three organs, namely, the right forefoot, the left buttock, and the thin part of the rectum with anus; put down separately the large intestine and the tail; provide ample broth, shuffle (the various organs of) the animal)

> three times; place the heart uppermost (among the organs of) the animal which have been shuffled.[4]

The heart may either be cooked in a pot with the other organs or cooked separately on a spit on the *śāmitra* fire (KŚS 6.7.14). If it is cooked separately, the cooked heart is placed on top of the boiled parts in the pot later (6.8.2).

When the organs are cooked, the *śāmitra* is asked three times, "Are the organs cooked?" (*srṣṭam*), and he replies affirmatively (KŚS 6.8.1). A mixture of curds and clarified butter is poured over the organs and the heart,[5] and the organs are taken to the altar. The *adhvaryu* distributes the organs between three containers, the *juhū*, the *upabhṛt*, and the *iḍā*. The oily part of the flesh should be placed in another container (the *vasāhomahavanī*). The largest part of the entrails is presented as the *upayaj* offering (KŚS 6.7.8). The *upayaj* involves the division and distribution of the rectum, and this process accompanies the eleven *anuyagas* or "after-offerings."[6]

Subsequently the heart and other organs are divided into multiple portions and distributed to various ritual participants, including the priests: "[T]he Adhvaryu gives the part of the entrail to the Āgnīdhra. The part above the udder of the animal he gives to the Hotṛ" (KŚS 6.9.4–5).[7] Finally, the priests prepare the offering for the "wives of the gods" (*patnīsaṃyāja*), cutting sections from the lower part of the tail.[8] According to some texts, the *patnī* should give a portion of the tail to the *adhvaryu* and the upper part of the foreleg to the *śāmitra*.[9] Other texts prescribe that a portion cut from the upper part of the tail be given to the *agnīdhra*.[10]

In summary, over the course of the rite, the animal victim is divided into many pieces and distributed among all the ritual participants according to ritual guidelines. These pieces must be placed in a specific order in specific locations within the sacrificial arena, and designated priests must perform certain activities for the sacrifice to be correct. The apportionment of the animal victim is the most elaborate procedure in the *paśubandha* rite, requiring a considerable amount of time and concentration to be completed correctly.

Similarly, Jewish sacrifice also involves the elaborate division and distribution of animal offerings in the *ʿōlâ*, the *ḥaṭṭāʾt*, the *ʾāšām*, and the *šĕlāmîm* rites. Victims are selected "from the herd or from the flock" (*min habbāqār ûmin haṣṣōʾn*), that is, bulls, sheep, or goats (the sheep is the most common offering). During a sacrifice one part of the animal is set aside from other parts according to prescribed procedures. After the se-

lected animal has been presented near the altar and identified with an individual or the community as a whole, it is executed by having its throat cut. Immediately afterward, the animal is skinned, and its head and limbs are removed. The body is quartered, and a layman or a priest (depending upon whether this is a personal or communal offering) removes the parts that are to be arranged and offered on the altar or distributed among the ritual participants. Milgrom notes that the animal is divided along "the natural divisions of the animal's bone structure."[11] The following lengthy quotation from M. Tamid 4.2–3 describes the dismemberment procedure in the daily animal offering:

> He slit the carcass and the whole of it was laid open before him. He took out the fat and put it above where the head had been cut off; he took out the inwards and gave them to [the priest] who had gained the privilege to rinse them. . . . [The slaughterer] took up the knife and cut away the lungs from the liver and the finger-like strip of the liver from the liver, but he did not remove it from its position. He cut open the breast and gave it to [the priest] who had gained the privilege to [take] it. He came up to the right flank and cut downward up to the backbone, but he did not touch the backbone until he reached the two small ribs; he cut it [the flank] off together with the liver attached to it, and gave it to [the priest] who had gained the privilege to take it. He came to the neck and left with it two ribs on the [right] side and two ribs at the [left] side; he cut it off and gave it, together with the windpipe, heart, and lungs attached to it, to [the priest] who had gained the privilege to [take] it. He came to the left flank and left there two thin ribs above [by the tail] and two thin ribs below [at the breast], and in the same way he left [ribs] on the right flank. In this way we find that he left with the two flanks two pairs [of ribs] above and two pairs below; he cut this off, and gave this [section], together with the backbone and spleen attached to it, to [the priest] who gained the privilege to [take] it. This was the larger [portion], but they used to call the right [flank] the larger [portion] because the liver was attached to it. He [the slaughterer] came to the haunch, cut it off together with the fat tail, and the lobe of the liver and the two kidneys attached to it, and gave it to [the priest] who gained the privilege to [take] it. He took the left hind-leg and gave it to the [priest] who gained the privilege to [take] it.[12]

To paraphrase, once the slit has been made, the fat is removed, the entrails are removed and washed with water, various parts of the body are cut away

in discrete portions, and they are taken by priests to the altar fire to be burned.

If a bird (specifically a turtledove or a young pigeon, domesticated birds) is used instead of another animal for the *ʿōlâ*, the procedure changes somewhat for logistical reasons.[13] Obviously, no skin is removed; instead, the head is "pinched off" (*ûmālaq*). According to rabbinic tradition, the priest cuts the bird's throat with his fingernail, separating the head from the neck. Then the head can be completely removed from the body.[14] The blood is drained against the altar, and then the priest removes "the crop, the feathers, and the innards that emerge with it" (M. Zeb. 6:5). In sum, this means that the entire digestive tract is removed and discarded. The bird is then cut open so that the chest cavity is split apart, with the wings still attached to the body and fully extended.[15] The entire bird is then offered on the altar. As much as practically possible, then, the division of a bird sacrifice mimics the division of an animal sacrifice.

Note, too, that certain portions are consumed by different ritual participants: YHWH (via the fire), the priests, and the laity. The exact distribution varies a bit from sacrifice to sacrifice, but YHWH alone receives the fat, and the blood is applied to the altar. The priests receive the animal's hide. As discussed in the Introduction, the distribution of the rest of the animal depends upon which rite is being performed.

Specific rules also govern the consumption of sacrificial meat after it has been distributed. The *ḥaṭṭāʾt* and *ʿāšām* offerings must be eaten before the next morning, within the confines of the Temple. The *šĕlāmîm* (a "less holy" offering) may be eaten over the subsequent two days in a ritually pure location by anyone who is himself pure. Milgrom notes, "The rabbis claim that priests' eating of the sacrifices is an integral part of the expiation process (Sifra, Shemini 2.4), which they derive from this verse: 'He has given it to you to remove the guilt of the community and to make expiation for them before the Lord.' (Lev. 10:17)."[16]

Even this quick overview of Jewish animal sacrifice suggests that apportionment is depicted as the most lengthy and elaborate ritual step according to the rabbis, much more time-consuming than the selection, association, identification, or slaughter of the animal. In addition, the careful apportionment of specific animal parts helps to distinguish one type of offering from another. For example, in the *ʿōlâ* all the victim's flesh is burned on the altar along with the fat, whereas in other rites the flesh is divided between the priests and the laity. In contrast, all animal victims are

killed in the same way, no matter what rite the animal is being used for. The fine distinctions between different apportionment procedures suggest that the division and distribution of animal victims was a significant element of the rite as a whole.

We see from this brief summary that the ritual apportionment of an animal offering in brahmanical Hinduism or in biblical or rabbinic Judaism is a highly complex, carefully orchestrated activity, which varies from one specific rite to another. Before we begin to explore the significance of apportionment, however, it is important to note that there is a similar level of sophistication in the apportionment of vegetal offerings.

Apportionment and Vegetal Offerings

As we have seen in previous chapters, Vedic and Jewish sacrificial traditions incorporate numerous vegetal—specifically grain-based—offerings. Vegetal offerings do not simply act as substitutes for their animal counterparts in the Vedic system; they exist independently and are listed as one of the three main offering types: animal, vegetal, and soma. Vegetal offerings occur far more frequently than animal offerings in Vedic practices, even as principal offerings. As Jan Gonda notes, "most *haviṃsi* [principal sacrificial offerings] are vegetarian."[17]

Certain passages explicitly associate grain with animal victims: "The omentum is the chief part of cattle; the strew is the chief [part] of plants" (TS 6.3.9.5). Another passage states, "The chaff is the hair, the bran is the skin, the bright side is the blood, the ground grain is the flesh, the solid grain is the bones" (AitBr 6.9). Aitareya Brāhmaṇa 2.9.1 associates the beard of a corncob with an animal victim's hair. An even more intimate connection is suggested by ŚB 3.8.3.1, which indicates that rice and barley are the "essence" (*medha*) of all animal victims. Most directly, ŚB 1.2.3.5 asserts, "[I]t is as an animal sacrifice that this grain-cake is offered."

In constructing these parallels, the texts explicitly compare vegetal offerings to animal offerings. In the Vedic tradition, the *puroḍāśa*, a flat grain cake made of pounded rice or barley flour, is the vegetal offering most closely associated with animal victims. It is shaped and then baked on one of the sacrificial fires. Once the grain cake has been formed and baked, it is divided with just as much precision as any animal offering. The division of the grain cake into specific portions is primarily an attempt to identify the grain cake with an animal victim, so that its presentation is understood to

carry the same ritual force. In other words, if one manipulates the grain cake in a fashion parallel to the manipulation of the animal victim, the grain offering takes on as much importance as the animal offering.[18]

As in animal sacrifice, portions of the grain cake are distributed to various ritual participants and the deities. After the cake is shaped and cooked, it is broken apart. The *adhvaryu* removes the cooked *puroḍāśa* from the potsherds with tongs and places it in a pan smeared with clarified butter. Then the *adhvaryu* breaks away two portions of the grain cake with his thumb and two forefingers, one from the eastern part of the grain cake and the second from the western portion of the cake. The sizes of these cuttings are specifically prescribed in the texts. For example, the portions for the deities are to be the size of the phalanx of the thumb (KŚS 1.9.6). All the oblation portions should be offered to the east of the first offering, "each succeeding oblation to the east of the preceding one and touching it."[19] These offerings, considered the principal part of the *darśapūrṇamāsa*, are offered into the *ahavaniya* fire in the name of the appropriate deities.

In the *svistakṛt* offering, a secondary offering to Agni, the priest is directed to remove a portion from the northern halves of the northern and southern cakes. The *svistakṛt* offerings should be one less than the number cut for the principal offering.[20] The *svistakṛt* is also supposed to be larger than the one for the principal offering, and the portion for the *iḍā* larger still (VārŚS 1.1.1.37–38). The first portion is to be taken from the middle of the grain cake and the second portion from the eastern half. Dandekar, paraphrasing the commentator Śālīki, explains, "[I]f one and the same oblation-material is poured out for preparing oblations to several divinities, those several oblations become mixed up together (at the time of pounding, etc. and, therefore, the assignment of the oblations to the respective divinity by touching separately each of these oblations, indeed, becomes necessary.)"[21] The act of division, working in concert with other manipulations, assures that each divinity receives the portion appropriate in the ritual context.

It is logical to expect an elaborate division of the grain-cake offering, since the procedures applied to the grain cake parallel those applied to an animal victim. The parallels are drawn specifically by creating differentiated portions within the grain cake which can be distributed to ritual participants and the deities just as the animal's organs are. Thus grain cakes, like animal victims, have discrete elements that need to be identified, separated from one another, and manipulated in specific ways in

order to generate an ordered universe. The language used in the texts is explicitly designed to persuade the reader to view the two offering substances as equivalent.

Israelite vegetal offerings, like their Vedic counterparts, are divided into multiple parts and distributed in different ways to achieve distinct purposes. After the appropriate ingredients for the *minḥâ* (grain-based offering) have been assembled and the grain cake has been prepared in one of several ways, the *minḥâ* is brought to the priest. The priest then takes a handful of the offering, puts it into a ritual vessel, and consigns it to the fire. The priest may not remove this portion randomly; the handful he removes must include all the frankincense that had been added previously, leaving none of it behind. As a result, the portion of the *minḥâ* placed on the fire conveys a fragrant aroma to YHWH.

If the entire *minḥâ* were thrown onto the altar fire, there would be, in effect, no "apportionment" procedure. But this is not the case. The bulk of the *minḥâ* is distributed among the priests for consumption. Thus all *minḥâ* offerings are divided into parts for YHWH and for the priests. Clearly the apportionment of the vegetal offering is much simpler than that of the animal offering. But in both cases the division of the offering into distinct segments is designed to make it possible for one offering substance—animal or vegetal—to fulfill multiple purposes. The "handful," although a vague term to our ears, came to designate a very specific amount by the time of the compilation of the Mishnah (ca. 220 CE). Blackman, in notes to his translation of M. Men. 1.2, comments, "He [the priest] dips his closed outstretched fingers into the meal and scoops up a handful; with the small finger he levels off the meal on that side, an with the thumb he evens it off on that side also, so that none drops off on either side. This was deemed a most difficult operation to ensure that there was neither excess nor deficiency in the quantity."[22] The mishnaic text Menāḥôt discusses at great length the potential risk to the sacrifice if the handful taken is incomplete. For example, M. Men. 3.5 states, "[T]he smallest portion [missing] from the handful impairs [the validity] of the greater portion." In other words, if the handful taken by the priest is too small, the entire offering is invalidated.

To make matters even more complicated, a "handful" of the offering grains cannot be removed randomly from the *minḥâ*. If frankincense has been included in the grain cake, it must *all* be included in the handful distributed to YHWH; otherwise the offering is invalid. In the animal

offerings, we saw that certain parts of the animal victim were reserved for YHWH. In a similar—although simpler—way, portions of the *minḥâ* are handled in distinct ways. One portion is reserved for YHWH, and another portion is given to the priests.

None of the *minḥâ* is distributed to the laity: "[T]the remainder of the grain-cake shall be for Aaron and his sons, a most holy portion from YHWH's offerings by fire" (Lev. 2:3). Why this restriction? The apportionment of the grain cake is tied to the purpose of the offering. Vegetal offerings, unlike animal offerings, are not expiatory. They do not atone for sin (unless they are functioning as substitutes for an animal offering). Instead they serve as a gift or tribute to YHWH. Under these circumstances it is not necessary (or even logical) for the laity to give a gift or tribute to themselves. The tribute is meant to show honor to YHWH in general and to the Temple cult in particular. Consequently, the offerings given in tribute have to be distributed between YHWH and his functionaries in the Temple, the priests.

The priests (rather than the laity) distribute the grain cakes. "This is the law of the grain offering. The sons of Aaron shall offer it before the Lord, in front of the altar. One shall take from it a handful of the fine flour of the grain offering with its oil and all the frankincense that is on the grain offering and burn this as a memorial portion" (Lev. 6:14–15). Just as the priests divide the animal victim, they also divide the grain cake. Their activity at the altar is choreographed just as closely for vegetal offerings as it is in the animal sacrifices, with just as much concern for precision. Mention is made in M. Men. 1.2 of some potential problems that can occur if the priests are not careful: "If the priest took the handful with his left hand [the offering] is invalid. . . . If, when taking the handful, he also took up a small stone or a bit of salt or a grain of frankincense, it becomes invalid, for they have said, the handful that is too large or too small is invalid. What is too much? If [the priest] took a heaped up handful. And what is too little? If he took the handful with his fingertips only. How should he do it? He must stretch his fingers over the palm of his hand." Many other potential restrictions are discussed as well. The point is that the same level of detail accompanies the handling of vegetal offerings as animal offerings, even though the priests are dealing with a simpler offering substance.

Why is it necessary for the priests (rather than the laity) to divide and distribute the grain offerings? Although one could argue that ritual exper-

tise and training would be necessary to supervise animal dismemberment, it hardly seems necessary to have trained ritual personnel distribute handfuls of grain. Yet the texts make it clear that the priests—and only the priests—are permitted to remove the memorial portion. The division and distribution of the *minḥâ* parallels the elaborate division of the animal offering. Like the animal offering, it requires the specialized expertise of the priest to apportion the offering correctly.

In addition, the fact that ritual experts must apportion the *minḥâ* offerings emphasizes the importance of vegetal offerings in the broader sacrificial system. This is particularly significant because in vegetal sacrifice other activities are often minimal; the key activity is the distribution of the offering. The priest, who is viewed as the ritual expert, performs this process in the sacrificial procedure. We have already seen that the application of similar procedures to Vedic animal and vegetal sacrifice reinforces the equivalent ritual status of a vegetal offering. I would argue that a similar parallel is being constructed in Jewish sacrifice. If a priest apportions an animal offering and then he also apportions the vegetal offering, the vegetal offering is accorded greater ritual significance than if a layperson divides and distributes the *minḥâ*. Parallel priestly activity reinforces the parallel between animal and vegetal rites and the importance of apportionment in the sacrificial system overall.

Apportionment and Cosmogony

Within Vedic thought the act of division associates the sacrificial realm with cosmogony. The connection between sacrifice and cosmogony has long been recognized by scholars of Vedic sacrifice, but let us review the basic elements. In the Vedic creation myths, the creator god Prajāpati emits undifferentiated substance from his own person and then divides and arranges that substance into the structured universe:

> Prajāpati emitted the sacrifice, and after the sacrifice the *brahman* power and the *kṣatra* power were emitted. After them were emitted those creatures who eat sacrificial oblations and those who don't. The Brahmins are those creatures who eat sacrificial oblations, the Rājanyas [Kshatriyas], Vaishya, and Shūdras those who don't.[23]

> Prajāpati at first was one. He desired, "may I emit food, may I be reproduced. He measured out the *paśus* from his breaths. From his mind

> [he measured out] the man; from his eye, the horse; from his breath, the cow; from his ear, the ram; from his voice, the goat. And since he measured them out from his breaths, they say "The *paśus* are the breaths." And since he measured out the man from his mind, they say "The man is the first, the most virile (*viryavattama*) of the *paśus*." The mind is all the breaths, for all the breaths are firmly established in the mind. And since he measured out the man from his mind, they say, "The man is all *paśus*," for they all become the man's.[24]

Sacrifice remembers and replicates the cosmogonic activity of Prajāpati, who is both the first sacrifice and the first sacrificer. The he-goat, the principal offering, is even said to have been born "from Prajāpati's heat" (ŚB 7.5.2.36). Brian K. Smith, however, offers a more fine-tuned understanding of Vedic cosmogony and, by extension, Vedic sacrifice. As mentioned in Chapter 3, Smith asserts that Vedic creation should be understood as a two-step process, involving first the emission of undifferentiated substance and only second the ordering and differentiation of that substance. He explains, "Cosmogony, the production of an ordered universe out of a generated potential, is a secondary act in the Prajāpati myths as form is carved out of or constructed from the formless emission."[25] Sacrifice parallels this two-step process. It involves first the acquisition of "formless emission," but, more important, it involves the subsequent ordering of that material.

In the context of sacrifice, the process of division parallels the second act of cosmogony because the apportionment of the offering produces a ritually reorganized sacrificial substance analogous to Prajāpati's production of an ordered universe. The body is organized in several ways. First, the body parts are removed according to a certain *sequence*, so they are withdrawn in a specific temporal order. Second, they are transformed physically, by being cooked and/or by being mixed with butter (understood by some to be a kind of cooking), so they experience a new *qualitative* order. Finally, they are physically manipulated and distributed to different parties, so they are ordered in a new *spatial* arrangement or pattern. Thus, apportionment takes a ritually chaotic victim's body and organizes that body into a ritually ordered microcosm. Chaos (the natural animal body) is transformed into ordered substance (the ritually arranged body).

The biblical story of creation, although markedly different from the

Vedic version, also includes a process of division and differentiation. Genesis 1 describes a six-day process in which YHWH creates the universe by differentiating one substance from another and setting those substances in orderly relationship with one another. Jonathan Klawans notes that Israelite sacrifice, more than being about destruction, is about *imitatio Dei*: "a fair amount of evidence can be marshaled in defense of the argument that the notion of *imitatio Dei* informed ancient Israelite approaches to sacrifice."[26] Klawans focuses on acts of consumption and burning, but I would argue that the apportionment of the sacrificial offering more clearly imitates YHWH's creative work. Apportionment of a sacrificial offering, therefore, is not primarily about destruction; rather, it is a fundamentally constructive activity.

Ultimately, apportionment procedures generate multiple discrete entities where there was once a single, undifferentiated whole. A single animal victim becomes a kind of ritual piñata, yielding numerous distinct offerings. When one entity becomes many, the entire sacrificial project becomes much more complex. Numerous offerings require numerous procedures, requiring a much more elaborate sacrificial event. The death of the victim may produce a compliant offering, but it leaves behind only the raw materials of sacrifice. Apportionment is the specific procedure that generates the discrete sacrificial offerings that make all the subsequent ritual activity possible. Consequently, division has tremendous sacrificial significance, with a number of social and cultic implications that we will explore below.

Apportionment and Classification

Apportionment does not reorder sacrificial substances arbitrarily. The Vedic worldview posits certain inherent connections between elements on different planes, and the Sanskrit term most frequently used to denote this inherent connection is *bandhu*.[27] The division and subsequent distribution of offerings reorients victims' bodies so that they are in proper relationship with elements on other planes, particularly the cosmic, natural, and social planes. The process of division, then, reflects a certain classificatory logic that assumes these inherent connections. Although never stated explicitly, the procedures associated with division classify elements on multiple planes into categories based on analogous relationships.

The Śrauta Sūtras prescribe elaborate orderings based on these implied

classificatory relationships. The texts are very specific about the sequence in which an animal offering must be cut apart, the manipulation required of each part, and the final distribution of each portion. For example, the omentum must be removed through an abdominal incision before anything else is removed, and then it is roasted on two spits (KŚS 6.6.8, 11, 26). Next, the remaining organs are removed in a designated order and manipulated in specific ways (bodily organs boiled in a pot, heart roasted on a spit). In addition, certain animal parts are always associated with specific subrites within the overall sacrifice. For example, the heart, tongue, part of the chest, top part of the left foreleg, two sides, liver, testicles, the middle part of the large intestine, and the right buttock are associated with the *juhū* oblation,[28] while the top part of the right foreleg, the thin third of the entrails and the left buttock are associated with the *upabhṛt* oblation.[29]

Specific manipulations correlate the victim's body parts with multiple planes of existence. First, the animal's body parallels the macrocosm of the universe. The Bṛhadāraṇyaka Upaniṣad, for example, describes the horse sacrificed in the *Aśvamedha*, comparing its head to the dawn, its eyes to the sun, its breath to the air, its jaw to the cosmic fire, its body to the year, its back to the heavens, its belly to the atmosphere, its limbs to the seasons, its bones to the stars, its arteries to the rivers, its hair to the plants and trees, and its urination to the rain (1.1.1). Thus the animal victim contains the cosmos in its anatomy. Directions regarding the initial placement of the *paśubandha* victim also indicate its correspondence with the natural world: "Direct its feet to the north. Make its eye go to the sun, let loose its breath to the wind, its life to the intermediate region, its hearing to the quarters, its bones to the earth" (ŚŚS 5.17.3). The body is ritually positioned to bring it into alignment with all parts of the natural world. Finally, individual animal parts are correlated with individual ritual participants. At specified times, ritual players receive certain animal portions as their part of the sacrifice. That portion is determined by the ritual office one holds. Apportionment thus reflects (and reinforces) the general organization of and individual placement within the cultic realm.

This system of apportionment derives from a specific way of understanding relationships between various elements in the natural world. This mode of thinking has been called analogic, homologic, or correlative by various thinkers. Brian K. Smith has argued that an impulse to classify according to analogic relations governed the Vedic mindset. In *Classifying the Universe* (1994), he notes that the Vedic thinkers developed numerous

elaborate cosmogonies and that each cosmogony correlated specific animals with specific social classes, hymns or chants, cardinal directions, cosmic elements, and deities.[30] Thus, specific animals were offered in certain sacrificial rites because they corresponded to the relevant deity, season, or *varṇa*.

I want to suggest that the process of analogic classification continues *within* the bodies of animal victims as well and that this process governs the division and subsequent manipulation of the animal victim. By dividing the animal into multiple parts, the sacrificer generates an entirely new cosmos. He then proceeds to align its constituent parts with corresponding elements in the social and natural cosmic realms. In so doing, he inscribes the "orderliness" of the universe onto the sacrificial victim's body, which, in the context of the sacrifice, has become the focal point of all activity. It is as if a magnifying lens has concentrated the ritual power of the universe onto the animal victim's body. Ritual manipulation of the animal in the ritual setting is, for all intents and purposes, ritual manipulation of the cosmos.

Mary Douglas has already hinted at some of the socioreligious significance of inscribing order onto the bodies of sacrificial victims in her own study of Jewish sacrifice. In *Leviticus as Literature* (1999), she argues that the animal offering described in Leviticus mirrors the temple as well as the sacred landscape and in so doing reinforces the socioreligious hierarchy as well. Referring to biblical sacrifice, she explains, "In the interior of the body is the pattern made by the suet covering the liver and the two kidneys, in the interior of the tabernacle is the pattern of its furnishings and activities, and both can be assimilated to the pattern of the holy mountain."[31] The impulse to classify within the context of sacrifice thus reflects a desire to conserve the tradition more broadly, to avoid and even obstruct change by reifying natural, social, and religious relations through ritually constructed connections to cosmology.

The cosmic hierarchy that is played out in the victim's body is then translated into the social realm. Sociocultic relationships are indicated by the animal and grain portions as they are distributed among ritual participants. First, YHWH receives the best parts of the animal (the fat or *ḥēleb*) and the grain cake (the portion with frankincense). The priests then receive good portions (the hide, the flesh) before the laypeople receive anything that remains. Saul Olyan points out that in 1 Sam. 9:22–24 "Saul, whom Yhwh has chosen to be king[,] . . . is not only given a place of honor

at the table, but also presented with an elite portion of meat" at a sacrificial meal—an acknowledgment of his high status.[32] The portions Saul receives reflect his rank within the community. In general, the "most holy" foods may be eaten only by ritually pure men in the priestly line; less holy offerings (such as the "heave" or *tĕnûpōt* offerings, oil, wine, and grain) are then available to lay men and women.[33]

In addition, cultic rank is indicated by who is permitted to handle specific elements of the sacrifice: priests handle fat, blood, and flesh: "The exclusive priestly claim to the presentation of blood and fat, the manipulation of blood on the altar, and the offering of incense to Yhwh secures for the priest his preeminent place in the life of the cult according to the biblical representations."[34]

The priests also demonstrate their ritual superiority in their consumption of the animal victim. Referring to Suzanne Langer's work on presentational thought, Douglas explains, "The carcass of an animal is a virtual space on which social distinctions are projected, and more than that, they are validated by giving the *right* portions of meat to the *right* people."[35] The priests have ritual *knowledge*, as seen through their handling of the victim. In addition they have ritual *priority*, as seen through their reception of choice portions of the animal victim. The portions the priests receive reflect their important ritual status: the ritual expert, who manipulates the blood and who controls the ritual proceedings on the fire, is also the one who receives the priestly (that is, the best) portions of the animal offering for himself. Sacrificial division encourages a particular understanding of right social order.

Similarly, the apportionment process within Vedic sacrifice arranges elements on the bodily, natural, social, and cosmic planes in such a way as to replicate and entrench established hierarchical relationships by carving them into the animal victim's body. As Smith explains, the Vedic authors had "an overarching and systematic method for drawing consistent 'equivalences' and connections between things and beings, for classifying the universe."[36] Within sacrifice, the process of division makes the constituent parts of the animal victim "classifiable" and thus, by implication, analogous to other elements on various planes of existence. For example, the distribution of offering portions is tied to the sociocultic hierarchy. Note that although a layperson may slaughter a sacrificial animal, the priests are required to supervise the elaborate handling of the victim after its death. I suspect that this requirement developed at least in part because

the apportionment of an animal offering is more complex and more carefully regulated than its slaughter. The division of ritual labor suggests that the priest's activities (or those he supervises) are more ritually significant than the activities left to the laity. Any layman can kill an animal, but a ritual expert is required to dismember a victim ritually correctly. Such concern for correct handling after death implies that slaughter is not the most significant ritual act; it can clearly be done ritually effectively by a layperson. The proper apportionment of an offering, however, must be guided by a ritual expert.

The division and distribution of an animal victim's body, then, is not primarily destructive. Rather, it is largely about constructing and reinforcing established relationships purportedly based in the cosmos. The apportionment of sacrificial offerings according to predetermined guidelines reinforces the notion that the various realms of human experience are, always have been, and always should be, ordered in a specific way.

Apportionment and Moral Order

The elaborate processes of sacrificial division and reclassification imply that the natural order is defective or incomplete, that it needs to have order imposed upon it. The specific guidelines governing apportionment imply that there is a right way—and therefore many wrong ways—in which to impose this order. Thus, the act of apportionment implies a moral dimension to the universe: one ought to do some things in certain ways, and one ought not to do others.

I want to be clear here that I am *not* arguing that sacrifice upholds a specific ethical code of conduct. Rather, I am arguing that the foundational notion that there *is* a right way (and a wrong way) to handle certain offerings (and not other offerings) by certain people (and not others) at certain times and place (and not others) suggests a sense of "ought" in the community's worldview. Apportionment implies a "should" dimension to human behavior. Here, at the most fundamental level, is where ritual practice contributes an important sense of "ought" to human culture—not at the level of minutia, in individual actions, but at a deeper level, with the very presence of imperatives governing and directing human behavior and interaction with the natural world.

Within the sacrificial arena, this reference to moral order is not articulated explicitly; rather, it is presented indirectly, with the animal victim as

a key visual aid. Specifically, moral order is implied through the manipulation of a designated sacrificial offering within a prescribed ritual arena and demonstrated through the proper apportionment of sacrificial substances. As Douglas notes, "truth is vindicated not by its match with ancient history or with the demands of morality, but in a strict framing of time and space."[37] Truth and moral order are not abstract concepts in the Vedic mind-set. Though invested with transcendental authority, they are presented and vindicated in specific temporal, spatial, and substantial forms.

The sacrificial texts themselves indicate that a world without sacrificial order is not only wrong; it is also dangerous. The Pancaviṃśa Brāhmaṇa states, "Prajāpati emitted the creatures. They were undifferentiated, at odds with each other, and they ate each other" (24.11.2). A disordered, unclassified universe results in disaster. The Vedic sacrificial setting allows —no, requires—human participants to avert potential disaster by imposing religiously prescribed order upon the created world. In so doing, humans imitate the powerful, constructive activity of Prajāpati. It puts humans at the top of the moral hierarchy, acting as agents of right relationships on all levels of existence.

Elaborate rules governing proper versus improper behavior not only set humans apart from other living creatures; they also distinguish certain humans from other humans, emphasizing the ritual expertise of the priests.[38] Part of the priests' authority derives from their ability to protect the *yajamāna* from the dangers of the ritual animal. In one well-known ritual sequence, the animal victim, just prior to its execution, is paraded within the sacrificial arena. The *pratiprasthātra* walks behind the animal, touching it with two tree branches. The *adhvaryu* follows behind the *pratipasthātra*, and the *yajamāna* walks behind the *adhvaryu* (KŚS 6.5.5–8). The priests both connect the ritual patron to and protect him from the dangers associated with an animal victim prior to its completed ritual manipulation.

Apportionment, then, presumes, reflects, and reinforces an "ought to be" dimension to the universe. Things are not good enough the way they are; someone needs to bring about order. By presenting themselves as ritual experts, the priests not only present a specific ordered universe; they also establish their role—and the role of the laity—in maintaining that universe.

Concluding Thoughts

Having reviewed numerous examples of how offerings are apportioned, we need to think about the significance of this procedure. Why is apportionment important in the overall scheme of sacrificial activity? I would suggest that each procedure included in the matrix of sacrificial activity addresses an authoritative concern within religious practice. Sacrifice as a whole "works" because each element of sacrifice addresses an issue that has authoritative import for the socioreligious life of the community. The question we need to address now is, what concern in particular does apportionment address?

The actions involved in dividing and distributing portions of an offering substance are important in several ways. First, as we have seen, they generate multiple wholes from one whole, in effect multiplying a single offering so that it goes further. Durkheim explains, "[W]hen a sacred thing is subdivided, each of its parts remains equal to the thing itself. . . . [T]he part is equal to the whole; it has the same powers, the same efficacy."[39] Thus the thigh of an animal has as much power as the animal itself; the smallest drop of soma juice is as effective as the entire stalk would be. The ritual potency of an offering can be multiplied in the ritual economy through the apportionment of the offering itself.

Second, the division (and subsequent distribution) of various parts of an offering substance reflects and affirms distinctions between the ritual participants themselves. The gods receive certain portions from the offerings, usually the choicest; at times the gods are the only recipients of an offering. On certain occasions the priests share an offering among themselves, and on other occasions the sacrificer himself partakes of the offering. The apportionment of an offering frequently reflects a complex socioreligious hierarchy. Détienne, for example, notes, "The choice pieces—thigh, hindquarter, shoulder, and tongue—are given to the priest, king, or high magistrates of the city."[40] The distribution of the offering simultaneously reflects and reinforces socioreligious roles.

Finally, the redistribution of an offering substance to ritual participants creates a kind of ritual order where previously there had been disorder. Before the offering substance is distributed to the appropriate ritual participant or placed in the appropriate ritual location, it is not in its rightful place. That is, there is no correspondence in this realm to the cosmic realm above. Ritually, there is a kind of disorder. Once the offering had been

manipulated and distributed properly, however, religio-cultic order has been created, and the sacrifice can continue. Only then can the sacrifice be valid or efficacious. In the act of apportionment, ritual order replaces ritual chaos.

The practice of division, then, addresses a variety of concerns regarding the construction of order. Distribution procedures reflect and reinforce social roles, emphasizing the superiority of certain individuals over other individuals and the superiority of humans over the natural world. The underlying assumption is that the ritual order improves upon the natural order, and the division and distribution of ritual offerings forms a significant part of the construction of ritual order.

Hubert and Mauss, the grandfathers of sacrificial studies within religious studies, characterized sacrifice as fundamentally destructive. It is clear, however, that a closer study of sacrifice, even when it involves the division of a sacrificial offering, is largely *constructive*. Sacrifice brings order out of chaos, and the procedures associated with the division of the animal victim (and its corollary, the vegetal grain cake) have a great deal to do with this. Durkheim argues, "when a sacred thing is subdivided, each of its parts remains equal to the thing itself. . . . [T]he part is equal to the whole; it has the same powers, the same efficacy."[41] Thus the thigh of an animal can have as much power as the animal itself; the smallest drop of soma juice can be as effective as the entire stalk. Through division, the ritual potency of an offering can be multiplied in the ritual economy through the division of the offering itself. Ananda K. Coomaraswamy notes, "And what is essential in the Sacrifice? In the first place, to divide, and in the second to reunite."[42] While I hesitate to identify any element of sacrifice as "essential," I agree with Coomaraswamy that apportionment, according to prescribed cosmic paradigms, is very much at the heart of Vedic and Israelite sacrifice.

Apportionment also draws attention to the fact that certain procedures within sacrifice are linked to other procedures. Who consumes what is determined, at least in part, by who apportions what. Within Israelite sacrifice, the person who controls the flow of blood and apportions the animal victim receives a specific share in the sacrificial offering. How one participates early in the rite determines when one will consume a portion of the rite—and the portion itself. Sacrificial procedures are interrelated.

Fundamentally, division also highlights the fact that sacrality is constructed. Scholars of religion have long noted that humans construct sacred

time and sacred place. In the context of sacrifice humans also generate sacred substances, specifically by orienting them in analogous relationships with the cosmic, temporal, spatial, and social worlds. Apportionment leads to the creation of ritually formed, distinct sacrificial offerings from the raw material of the original offering. For the academic scholar of religion, sacred times and places have human origins, and the same is true of sacred substances. Close examination of apportionment procedures in particular can yield insights into how multiple sacred substances are generated within the sacrificial arena.

Finally, an examination of division within the context of sacrifice forces us to confront the fact that sacrifice is not simply a "primitive" exercise. From the ancient past to the very present, cultures have marked some substances as "sacred" and apportioned these substances in various ways. In ordering and reordering material substances, humans locate themselves in and take charge of the natural world. This is true beyond the realm of animal sacrifices or grain cakes. Although modern cultures often eschew animal offerings, they do set aside other substances. When we divide and distribute our time, talent, financial resources, and even our lives, we often characterize this activity as "sacrifice," investing our actions with the same authority that traditional sacrifice held in the brahmanical Hindu and biblical and rabbinic Jewish traditions. Certain aspects of traditional sacrifice may fall aside (i.e., slaughter), but other aspects of traditional sacrifice persist, the most notable of which are the controlled division and distribution of valuable elements of our lives. By continuing the practice of ordering and reordering material substances, modern humans continue to orient themselves in terms of centuries-old categories of sacrifice. As a result, apportionment translates sacrificial practice into a modern context while maintaining its traditional cultural role as an authoritative religious category.

Conclusion

> Solidarity is only gesture when it involves no sacrifice.
>
> —MARY DOUGLAS

In the previous chapters I have focused on sacrifice in the brahmanical Hindu and the biblical and tannaitic Jewish texts.[1] I have argued that sacrifice needs to be re-imagined in a polythetic way—that is, without a single, essential, defining characteristic. Indeed, sacrificial events need to be understood as complex combinations of the various activities we have explored in the previous pages: selection of a prescribed offering substance, association of that offering with the appropriate god(s), identification of the offering with the ritual sponsor(s), killing of the offering, apportionment of the offering, heating of some or all of the offering portions, and consumption of some or all of these offering portions by the ritual participants and/or the god(s). Specific sacrificial events involve some or all of these activities, in various sequences and combinations. While some sacrifices involve all these activities, others incorporate only a few.

When we recognize the polythetic nature of sacrifice, a number of implications come to light. We realize that individual rites are often more complicated than they appear at first. Many sacrificial events involve literally hundreds of manipulations (e.g., the *agnicayana*, the most compli-

cated soma sacrifice in the Vedic tradition). It is tempting to search for a single theme or overarching activity that encompasses all these manipulations, an activity that can serve as a kind of "umbrella" for the full complexity of the rite, thus making unfamiliar rituals seem more accessible to the outsider. For example, it may be tempting to think of sacrifice as killing—but then we brush aside other activities, dismissing them as preliminary or secondary to the heart of sacrifice. Similarly, it may be easy to think of sacrifice as consumption or "cuisine"—and then to marginalize nonculinary actions or force them arbitrarily into a culinary interpretive metaphor. But we have seen in the previous pages that the priestly traditions themselves rarely make such neat distinctions between primary and secondary sacrificial actions. Rather, the traditional ritual texts describe rich, complex sacrificial events involving multiple intricate procedures, often performed over lengthy periods of time. Consequently, we must conclude that when we grant primary importance to certain activities (and simultaneously minimize the importance of others), we skew our understanding of sacrifice, often by oversimplifying it.

I have also argued in the previous pages that the different activities performed in sacrificial events are intimately related to one another. No single activity—identification, heating, consumption, and so forth—is inherently sacrificial. Rather, each activity is inextricably bound up with the others. Consequently no one or two or even three activities constitute a sacrifice by their mere presence. Rather, individual activities become increasingly sacrificial as they become procedurally intertwined with other activities. For example, killing an animal does not mean that an animal has been sacrificed. However, killing an animal that has been selected for specific physical features, associated with a deity, identified with a ritual sponsor, apportioned into prescribed portions, heated in a particular way over a particular fire, and consumed by specific ritual participants is more reasonably understood as sacrificial. Thus, the interplay and interdependence of certain activities in more or less formal relationships make particular ritual events more or less sacrificial.

In developing these notions I have been focusing on what I would call, for lack of a better term, "traditional" sacrifice. Traditional sacrifice is performed with material offering substances, it is controlled by a body of ritual elite, and it is prescribed and described in the authoritative textual (oral or written) tradition. In the previous chapters we have seen that a polythetic approach to sacrifice yields benefits for the study of traditional

forms of sacrifice. But just as important, such an approach may yield useful insights for "nontraditional" forms of sacrifice as well. In these concluding pages I want to draw attention to two arenas outside traditional sacrifice in which a polythetic approach may be useful. First, a polythetic perspective may be helpful when examining symbolic, metaphoric, or internalized forms of sacrifice that develop subsequently or in reaction to traditional sacrifice within specific religious systems. Second, a polythetic perspective may help when examining the use of sacrificial language and imagery beyond the traditional sphere of religion, such as in national public discourse. In each of these arenas, sacrificial practice generates authority within specific communities.

Beyond Traditional Sacrifice

A brief glance at Hindu and Jewish texts reveals that sacrificial language is often applied to activities that are not traditional sacrifice. Scholars have often referred to these activities as "symbolic," "metaphoric," or "internalized" sacrifice. Yael Bentor summarizes, "The term 'interiorization of ritual' bears a multitude of meanings. It may pertain to a mental performance of the ritual; to the replacement of the ritual with a continuous process of life, such as breathing or eating; to a particular way of life, such as renunciation; to an actual performance with an inner interpretation; to the replacement of the external ritual with an internal one, and so forth."[2] In other words, a wide variety of activities are characterized as "sacrifice" even when they don't fit the criteria of traditional sacrifice. For example, in discussing rabbinic Judaism, Gregory Spinner notes, "It is true that in the absence of the Temple, the actual practice of sacrifice has been suspended; however, thinking about that practice has continued on, the priestly cult being so thoroughly enshrined in both the Written and Oral Torah. Ideas about sacrifice, so bound up with underlying notions of *covenant* and *atonement*, could not simply disappear, but were displaced onto other ritual activities (prayer and fasting, study and charity). . . . I maintain that sacrifice, as a canonical category, remains entrenched in the rabbinic imagination."[3] When Temple sacrifice (traditional sacrifice) was no longer possible, prayer, fasting, and Torah study became equated with sacrifice in rabbinic teaching (symbolic sacrifice). As a result, symbolic or metaphoric sacrifice persists in both Hinduism and Judaism as an authoritative category of religious experience beyond traditional sacrifice.

I suggest that this persistence of sacrifice as an authoritative category is possible, in part, because certain procedures that were part of traditional sacrifice persist in internalized sacrifice. Whereas priests and even a material offering substance become unnecessary, certain sacrificial *procedures* continue. I am not suggesting that this persistence of procedures is the only way in which sacrifice makes the successful leap from traditional to metaphoric or symbolic forms. Clearly, sacrifice has been successfully reinvented in metaphoric and symbolic forms for many reasons. I am arguing only that *one* way sacrifice survives as a useful religious category is through the continued presence of the procedures that we have discussed in the preceding pages. Even when the material offering disappears (or is translated into symbolic or internalized form), some of the procedures traditionally applied to the sacrificial offering continue, albeit in interiorized or metaphoric forms. Since the presence of these procedures in traditional forms of sacrifice has not received adequate attention to date, it is understandable that they have been overlooked in studies of metaphoric or internalized sacrificial systems, but the translation of sacrificial procedures from traditional to metaphoric forms of sacrifice is one stream of continuity within religious traditions.

It will be helpful to turn to some concrete examples at this point.[4] Students of Hinduism are well aware that several distinct traditions developed in India in reaction to the Vedic system. Buddhism and classical Hinduism developed at least in part as reactions to the elaborate priestly system of Vedic sacrifice. Certain streams of Hinduism, although setting aside actual traditional sacrifice, employ sacrificial language and imagery as a way of appropriating the authority of the Vedic system to justify alternative practices. For example, Bentor notes, "In presenting their new practices in terms of the vedic sacrifice, the renunciation movements characterized the classical vedic ritualists by the word *devayājin*, 'sacrificer[s] to the gods,' while calling their own practitioners *āmayājin*, 'sacrificer[s] to one's self.' "[5] In one stream of Hinduism an internalization of sacrifice develops in which the body itself is understood to generate an internal heat that consumes certain physical and spiritual elements. The term *tapas* is used in this context to refer to the internalized heat generated by austere devotional practices, and the practices associated with generating *tapas* can be understood in part as an internalization of sacrificial practice.

Walter Kaelber has done extensive study on the concept of *tapas*. He demonstrates that the concept of *tapas* extends as far back as the Ṛg Veda.

It is intimately involved with sacrifice, particularly with issues concerning purity but also with issues concerning pain and injury: "Agni, as the fire, destroys or consumes through *tapas*."[6] The sacrificial fire, which initially seems destructive, is also constructive, according to Kaelber, because it is purificatory. In addition, certain Vedic passages suggest that the sacrificer himself generates internal heat in the course of the ritual, which is also purificatory. Over time, Vedic conceptions of *tapas* that center on purification by means of fire offerings evolve into later Hindu conceptions of *tapas* that associate physical austerities with personal purification. Kaelber observes, "Only the imagery of fire remains when the later law book of Manu, for example, notes that: 'Whatever evil [i.e. *enas*] men commit by thoughts, words, or deeds, that they speedily *burn away by tapas*.'"[7]

Tapas is also associated with pain. Specific practices characterize *tapas*: abstaining from food, surviving on "fast-milk" alone, breath restraint (*prāṇāyāma*), and so on. Often the body reflects this pain through the loss of hair, body weight, and so forth—all of which are signs of the pain the practitioner is experiencing. The voluntary taking on of physical injury—originally understood as self-imposed painful heat—results in the purification of the self: "The human body because it is impure must be symbolically consumed through the heat of asceticism in order that a requisite purity—correlated with a divine state—may be attained. Once again, the word *tapas* (as asceticism) can easily convey this sense of a symbolic 'consuming' of the 'human' body precisely because of its 'earlier' meaning of a destructive heat which consumes in the literal sense."[8] Most important for our purposes, Kaelber comments on the long-term connection between *tapas* and heating:

> The Sanskrit noun *tapas* assumes various convergent and divergent loads of meaning in the Vedic literature. Central to all such meanings, however, is the notion of "heat" or "warmth." *Tapas* thus refers to natural heat, such as that emitted by the sun or fire. It refers also to the natural heat associated with biological conception, embryonic "maturation," and birth. Thus the heat of sexual desire, the heat of sexual excitation, and the heat generated during sexual intercourse are all rendered by the term *tapas*. *Tapas*, however, also refers to the heat of ascetism, to the heat generated by austerities, and thus to a voluntary and "nonnatural" heat. Relatedly, *tapas* refers not only to the heat generated through asceticism but to the practice of asceticism itself.[9]

I want to argue that this understanding of *tapas* as an alternative form of sacrifice is more than a clever use of language. Rather, devotional practices that are understood to generate a kind of spiritual heat are, in effect, replicating one of the activities performed in traditional sacrifice: heating, which is, of course, simultaneously destructive and constructive. In traditional sacrifice a distinct material substance is heated on an outdoor altar. In devotional practices an internalized, subtle substance is heated by devotional practices within the body. If certain devotional practices can be successfully characterized as sharing procedures of traditional sacrifice, they have the potential to share the religious acceptability and authority of traditional sacrifice. In other words, if symbolic sacrifice employs some of the same procedures as traditional sacrifice, then it may wield the same authority as well.

Symbolic or metaphoric sacrifice is not limited to Hindu traditions. As is commonly known, ancient Israelite worship was largely driven by sacrifice. Abraham, the original patriarch, performed a sacrifice at the instigation of the covenant with YHWH (Gen. 15). Biblical sacrifice was a significant component of the covenant given at Sinai around 1300 BCE. Over time, sacrificial activity was centralized in the Temple at Jerusalem, and it continued to be an important element of Jewish identity through Roman occupation until the Temple was razed in 70 CE.

Judaism is remarkable because, as a relatively small and localized religious tradition, it not only survived the destruction of its central sanctuary but actually developed into one of the world's major religions—partly because the tradition was able to transfer the authority of traditional sacrifice to other practices. Despite some marginal contemporary efforts to rebuild the Temple in Jerusalem, Judaism flourishes today as a global religion based largely on the Torah, observance of the *mitzvoth,* and prayer. A number of scholars have traced the transformation of Judaism in the early centuries of the common era, and I will not attempt to summarize their thoughtful, painstaking work here.[10] Rather, I want to focus on one means by which Judaism survived. The rabbinic stream of Judaism developed in the ancient Near East and then flourished in Diaspora at least in part because certain elements of sacrificial activity persisted in rabbinic thought. As a result, sacrifice—in symbolic form—continued as an authoritative category within the tradition.

Sacrifice also continued to be significant in the mythology of Judaism beyond the second Temple period. Most obvious, Jewish mythology in-

cludes the Akedah, the story of the near sacrifice of Isaac. In *The Last Trial*, Shalom Spiegel explains that several midrashic traditions developed around the Akedah story, including versions in which Isaac was actually sacrificed and then resurrected.[11] These midrashic versions became touchstones for persecuted Jews throughout Jewish history, particularly in the Middle Ages. Spiegel quotes from a prayer recited on the eve of Rosh HaShanah:

> Women bared their necks to one another in order to be offered up for the Unification of the Name. So a man treated his own son and his own brother; so a brother his own sister; so a woman her own son and daughter; so a man his neighbor and comrade, bridegroom his bride, lover his beloved—here is one sacrificing and himself being sacrificed. . . . Ask he now and see, was there ever such a holocaust as this since the days of Adam? When were there ever a thousand and a hundred sacrifices in one day, *each and every one of them like the Akedah of Isaac son of Abraham*?[12]

Jews who were martyred or who watched their family members be martyred found comfort and meaning by understanding those deaths as sacrifice. Their deaths, obviously, did not involve the Temple or priests or any of the other elements of traditional sacrifice. They also did not involve the identification of the "offering" with a ritual patron, the apportionment of offering parts, or the consumption of any offering substances. But one could argue that the Jews who were killed were associated with YHWH in the minds of their persecutors, and they were selected for execution on the basis of that association. Consequently, Jewish communities recognized certain procedures involved in martyrdom—association and killing—as reminiscent of Temple sacrifice. By transferring the authority and meaning of traditional sacrifice to the deaths of these martyrs, Jewish communities were able to imagine individual deaths as sacrificial and therefore meaningful.

The strategy of interpreting certain activities as sacrifice also occurred in other contexts. Torah study and prayer were self-consciously characterized as sacrifice as well. Spinner argues that sacrifice is "symbolized" in the rabbinic imagination in a number of ways. For example, "the proper way to atone for the sins which have brought on sickness, and thus the effective means to remedy the illness, is by sacrifice. This more homiletic theme of divine punishment and sacrificial atonement continues as the text [Midrash Tadshe] examines the destruction of the Temple, which rabbinic

tradition attributes to the sins of Israel, and more specifically to cultic infractions."[13] In other words, just as animal offerings were sacrificed in the Temple to avert physical sickness, an offering of the Temple itself has been required by God to atone for the spiritual sickness of all Israel.

But how is it that the rabbis can make the leap from traditional sacrifice *in* the Temple to a symbolic sacrifice *of* the Temple? Why does this "work"? I suggest that various activities involved in the destruction of the Temple are reminiscent of traditional sacrifice, making this symbolic reinterpretation of destruction as sacrifice acceptable to a broad spectrum of the community. First, the Temple itself, like sacrificial animals, fit certain selection criteria: it was unblemished, and it fit specific physical specifications. (For example, Spinner notes that there are several numerical homologies that link the Temple with other macrocosmic elements.) Second, the Temple (like traditional sacrificial offerings) was clearly associated with YHWH, the deity who must accept the offering. Third, the Temple had been publicly identified with its "ritual sponsor" (the Jewish people) through the initial consecration rites. Finally, the Temple was heated in the flames that destroyed it. As the object of these traditional sacrificial procedures, the destruction of the Temple can easily be read as a symbolic sacrifice.

I do not want to oversimplify the transformations and developments that occur in these major world traditions. Clearly, elements were present in brahmanical Hinduism and in biblical and tannaitic Judaism which challenged or supplemented traditional sacrificial activity and which came to greater prominence in the postbrahmanical and rabbinic periods. I simply want to draw attention to one point: sacrifice continues as an authoritative category in each of these traditions, and we have to be able to explain why. It is not enough simply to argue that metaphoric or symbolic sacrifice replaces traditional sacrifice. One has to answer the question, how does this happen? What is it that allows certain activities to be read as sacrificial? What is the overarching mechanism that facilitates the shift from actual, traditional sacrifice to symbolic, internalized sacrifice? Obviously, a number of factors are at play here, but I suggest that when we understand traditional sacrifice as a polythetic activity, we can see that metaphoric or symbolic sacrifice often replicates some of the procedures that were performed during traditional sacrifice.

Sacrifice in National Discourse

Why does any of this matter? What do the hundreds of pages I have just spent reviewing traditional sacrifice have to do with life today? Is it, in fact, helpful or even interesting to study sacrifice when many of us move in a world that largely dismisses or minimizes the importance of traditional sacrifice? I suggest that sacrifice continues to be an important category in the contemporary world precisely because of the possibilities for transformation that we have just reviewed. Traditional forms of sacrifice are continually being transformed into metaphoric sacrifice through new configurations of the various sacrificial procedures we have examined. In addition, sacrificial imagery and rhetoric carry tremendous weight beyond religious arenas. Perhaps most important, sacrifice functions as an authoritative category in national or civic discourse as well as in religious life. National sacrificial imagery often wields the same cultural weight as traditional sacrifice, not simply because it has successfully appropriated the *language and rhetoric* of traditional sacrifice but because it often appropriates some of the same *procedures and activity* of traditional sacrifice.

The fact that sacrifice is an important symbol and metaphor in national discourse is noteworthy for two reasons. The successful use of sacrificial language in public discourse infuses certain civil and national activities with religious authority. Consequently, the nation carries the the same weight as—and often more weight than—religion for many people. Conversely, the national appropriation of sacrifice shapes how we imagine religious sacrifice. That is, our understanding of ancient traditional sacrifice is shaped in part by our own personal experiences of sacrifice—which are largely secular and nationalistic. The study of sacrifice takes place in a context, and that context affects how we imagine traditional sacrifice. Let's explore each of these points in turn.

First, the seemingly timeless and transcendent authority of sacrifice is often used as a tool for creating national identity and loyalty. Ivan Strenski observes, "[T]he idea of sacrifice itself seems precisely one of those religious notions especially prone to migrate into politics. Notions like ritual and cultic giving—sacrifice—bear a natural affinity for civic giving."[14] As part of his own research on theories of sacrifice, Strenski argues that prevailing Roman Catholic understandings of sacrifice as the "complete giving of self" conditioned French political culture at the end of the nineteenth century. True French patriotism involved the willingness to give

oneself entirely for the nation, including one's life. The religious views of sacrifice (Roman Catholic) were appropriated by the nation (France) to encourage French citizens to give themselves to the country as one would give oneself in sacrifice to a religious cause.[15]

In *Blood Sacrifice and the Nation,* Carolyn Marvin and David W. Ingle also argue that sacrifice—particularly violent blood sacrifice—is used to create powerful national identity in the United States: "Though nationalism does not qualify as religion in the familiar sense, it shares with sectarian religions the worship of killing authority, which we claim is central to religious practice and belief. . . . Americans have rarely bled, sacrificed or died for Christianity or any other sectarian faith. Americans have often bled, sacrificed and died for their country. This fact is an important clue to its religious power."[16] According to Marvin and Ingle, nations integrate sacrifice into their foundational mythology, and certain national "totems" (such as the American flag) can be used to trigger a willingness to sacrifice. National institutions demonstrate and wield authority over individuals by claiming the right to demand sacrifice. In so doing they lay claim to their citizens' lives and loyalty. True citizens are characterized as those who would willingly lay down their own lives for their country whenever required.

As a side note, it is interesting that Marvin and Ingle, like so many others I have reviewed in this book, focus on a single activity involved in sacrifice. For example, Marvin and Ingle characterize sacrifice as violent bloodshed. In terms of the language I have been using throughout this book, Marvin and Ingle emphasize killing procedures. What is helpful for our thinking at this point, however, is that while these scholars understand sacrifice monolithically, they all recognize sacrifice as an important authoritative category for national as well as religious identity.

Sacrificial language connected with the nation has come into common public discourse particularly in the past few years. In his book *Holy Terrors* (2003), Bruce Lincoln examines the sacrificial language used by Al Qaeda terrorists in describing the events of September 11, 2001. Lincoln reviews instructions discovered after the attacks on the World Trade Center towers, instructions that encourage the hijackers to view the plane crew and passengers as sacrificial victims: "You must make your knife sharp and must not discomfort your animal during the slaughter."[17] Also, "If you slaughter, do not cause the discomfort of those you are killing, because this is one of the practices of the prophet, peace be upon him."[18] Ob-

viously, most American readers have a problem with viewing the attacks of September 11 as a sacrifice. They do not wish to validate this action by viewing the hijackers as sacrificial players. However, it is clear that the hijackers were encouraged to think along these lines. The question for us is, what procedures other than killing may indicate the sacrificial nature of the hijackers' activity?

The hijackers were encouraged to associate themselves with God verbally: "When the hour of reality approaches, the zero hour, [unclear] and wholeheartedly welcome death for the sake of God. Always be remembering God. Either end your life while praying, seconds before the target, or make your last words: 'There is no God but God. Muhammad is His messenger.'"[19] Specific "victims" were chosen: not just the individuals who perished but also the American jets and the World Trade Center, both of which carry specific connotations for Al Qaeda. The victims, planes, and towers were consumed in flames, igniting a symbolic fire as well as an actual one. Clearly, the acts of September 11 can be understood as sacrifice based on a number of actions performed on that day.

In a different way, Americans have also invoked their own sacrificial language when describing September 11. First, of course, the victims of the attacks are imagined by Americans as innocent victims, selected on the basis of perceived allegiance to America or, at the very least, participation in American society. In addition, in the wake of the terrorist attacks, President George W. Bush used sacrificial imagery to describe the activities of millions of Americans in response to the attack on the twin towers. Standing in the National Cathedral a few days after the attacks, he made the following remarks: "In this trial, we have been reminded, and the world has seen, that our fellow Americans are generous and kind, resourceful and brave. We see our national character in rescuers working past exhaustion; in long lines of blood donors; in thousands of citizens who have asked to work and serve in any way possible. And we have seen our national character *in eloquent acts of sacrifice.*"[20] In a subsequent address to the country on October 7, 2001, in which he announced military strikes against Al Qaeda terrorist training camps, Bush included the following:

> I recently received a touching letter that says a lot about the state of America in these difficult times—a letter from a 4th grade girl, with a father in the military. "As much as I don't want my Dad to fight," she wrote, *"I'm*

willing to give him to you." This is a precious gift, the greatest gift she could give. This young girl knows what America is all about.

Since September 11, an entire generation of young Americans has gained new understanding of the value of freedom, and its cost in duty and in sacrifice.[21]

In these speeches, Bush suggested that American patriotism requires sacrifice, specifically the setting aside of something that belongs to us (our time, our blood, our fathers) for the sake of the greater good (our country). In Bush's view sacrifice is not only about killing and death but also about apportioning time, energy, resources, and family members for the United States. If, in fact, only the people who shed blood are viewed as those who are making sacrifices, then the "thousands of citizens" and the fourth-grade girl, though moving, are not making true sacrifices. Bush's point, however, is precisely that they are. These Americans are making sacrifices that every truly patriotic American not only should acknowledge but also should imitate in some way. The only way to understand their actions as sacrifice is if citizens interpret sacrifice more broadly, as something beyond death.[22]

A broader understanding of sacrifice, which does not require blood sacrifice or killing, is tremendously helpful in national life. A broad interpretation of sacrifice allows greater participation in national crises by more citizens in more ways. Those who are able and willing to die may be called upon to do so; other citizens sacrifice in other ways. For example, individuals may participate in the corporate national sacrifice by identifying with sacrificial victims (soldiers, martyrs) or by apportioning resources (such as time or money) to the ritual elite (national or military leaders). By participating in one or more sacrificial activities, a wide range of individual citizens feel they are participants in the national sacrificial enterprise. Even a fourth-grader can do her part.

A broad, multivalent notion of sacrifice, then, can be an effective tool for reinforcing and representing national as well as religious identity. When it functions as such a tool, invoking sacrificial imagery invests national leaders with the same kind of authority and power as religious leaders. But it would be naive to imagine that religious conceptions of sacrifice remain untouched by their brush with civic discourse. The imagining of sacrifice in religious contexts is influenced by the national arenas in which the discourse takes place. In other words, understandings of

religious sacrifice are influenced by conceptions of national sacrifice, just as notions of national sacrifice are strengthened by the authority that underlies religious sacrifice. Ivan Strenski has recently argued that the way we study sacrifice in religious studies today has been largely influenced by the French society in which Henri Hubert and Marcel Mauss worked in the late 1800s and early 1900s. He notes that Hubert and Mauss were self-consciously challenging an understanding of sacrifice that derived from Roman Catholicism and that this understanding was being applied to French national identity.[23] Their academic approach to a phenomenon of religious experience was shaped largely by the sociopolitical climate in which they worked. The same is true today. Academic and religious interpretations of sacrifice are not isolated from the sociopolitical world in which academic and religious leaders live. Rather, their approaches to sacrifice reflect the social and political concerns of their times.

Sacrifice and the Study of Religion

Those of us who study religious communities and practices are well aware of the problems involved in imagining religion. For example, in commenting on Talal Asad's contributions to our field, Lincoln concludes, "Any definition that privileges one aspect, dimension, or component of the religious necessarily fails, for in so doing it normalizes some specific traditions (or tendencies therein), while simultaneously dismissing or stigmatizing others."[24] For example, we have all come to realize that definitions of religion that center on belief in a supreme being necessarily exclude (or at least marginalize) certain worldviews (e.g., some forms of Buddhism). The study of sacrifice continues to suffer from the same problem. A fresh perspective on traditional sacrifice which resists normalizing certain procedures while dismissing others may lead us to insights into the broader study of religion which have relevance today.

In this context, the comparative study of sacrifice matters. It matters because, as one form of ritual, sacrifice constitutes a particular mode of paying attention to time, space, and material substance.[25] In so doing, it reflects specific communities' understandings of the nature of the cosmos, the negotiation of earthly authority, and the mechanics of the relationship between human beings and the divine realm. Sacrifice also matters because the imagery and language of sacrifice are often applied to other

activities, invoking the authority of sacrificial practice and establishing continuity between sacrifice and other ritual practices. These practices often explicitly characterize themselves as a form of sacrifice (yogic disciplines in Hinduism, prayer and Torah study in classical Judaism, and nationalism in twenty-first-century American patriotism). By appropriating the language of traditional sacrifice, these movements implicitly acknowledge the authority that traditional sacrifice wields. The invocation of traditional sacrificial terminology suggests a resonance between traditional sacrifice and other activities that hope to take on the religious power and authority of traditional sacrifice. Consequently, an understanding of the nature and elements of sacrifice will shed light on other activities that self-consciously associate themselves with traditional sacrifice.

Finally, the study of sacrifice matters because of how we as scholars have been conditioned to understand its general nature. As I have noted repeatedly throughout this book, certain theoretical approaches have dominated comparative sacrificial studies. But why have these approaches flourished? I would argue that it is largely because religious studies as a discipline developed in the context of Christian studies and Protestant Christian practice. Within Christianity it may be perfectly appropriate to seek a single, definitive element in sacrifice and to argue that killing—particularly killing involving violence and bloodshed—is that definitive characteristic. The Vedic and Jewish sacrificial systems, however, present alternative bodies of data that do not necessarily fit with models developed under the umbrella of Protestant Christianity. Barbara Holdrege, in her own comparative study of brahmanical Hinduism and biblical and rabbinic Judaism, comments:

> The Protestant subtext of the dominant paradigms provides the implicit standard against which other religious traditions are compared and evaluated. While perhaps appropriate for the study of some religious traditions, such paradigms, together with the hierarchical taxonomies they perpetuate, become straitjackets when applied to other traditions. One of the tasks of the comparative study of religion in this context is to test and critique the prevailing paradigms, expose their inadequacies, and generate a range of possible models to account for the multiplicity of religious traditions. The comparative study of Hindu and Jewish traditions in particular serves to illustrate how two of the world's major religious traditions defy the classificatory schema associated with the prevailing Protestant-based paradigms.[26]

The investigation of these "alternative paradigms" is critical to the study of religion in the twenty-first century. Comparative work should not only contribute additional information to the academy but should also challenge the very categories that the academy uses to organize and interpret this information. The comparative study of sacrifice, particularly study that draws deeply from non-Western religious traditions, is an important element in this broader effort.

Notes

Acknowledgments

1. Earlier versions of Chapter 2 were presented at the American Academy of Religion conference in 2000 and published as "Death Be Not Proud: Reevaluating the Role of Killing in Sacrifice" in the *International Journal of Hindu Studies* 6, no. 3 (December 2002): 221–242. I gratefully acknowledge comments offered in response to these earlier works.

Introduction

Epigraphs: George W. Bush, speech at the National Cathedral on the National Day of Prayer and Remembrance, September 14, 2001. ŚB 1.7.1.5.

1. Reference is commonly made to Müller's *Introduction to the Science of Religion.*

2. Jensen, *Myth and Cult among Primitive Peoples.*

3. Henninger, "Sacrifice," 552.

4. See, e.g., Tylor, *Primitive Culture.*

5. Ivan Strenski argues convincingly that Durkheim and his students wrote also in response to a Catholic "annihilationist" notion of sacrifice by offering an alternative view that reflected sociopolitical as well as theological views of sacrifice in late nineteenth-century France. See his *Contesting Sacrifice.*

6. Mauss, *The Gift*, 16.

7. Braun and McCutcheon, *Guide to the Study of Religion*. Note that "ritual" is listed as a separate entry, suggesting that "sacrifice" (a subset of "exchange") is not included in ritual.

8. Alles, "Exchange," in Braun and McCutcheon, *Guide to the Study of Religion*, 111.

9. Ibid., 119.

10. Spiro, *Buddhism and Society*, 457–459.

11. Smith, *Lectures on the Religions of the Semites;* Tylor, *Primitive Culture.*

12. Détienne, "Culinary Practices and the Spirit of Sacrifice," in Détienne and Vernant, *Cuisine of Sacrifice among the Greeks*, 5.

13. Malamoud, *Cooking the World*, 34.

14. Lévi-Strauss, *Savage Mind*, 228.

15. Staal, *Rules without Meaning*, 131–132.
16. Ibid., 115.
17. Eggeling, *Śatapatha Brāhmana*, I:ix.
18. Staal, *Rules without Meaning*, 69.
19. Jamison, *Sacrificed Wife*, 6.
20. Jay, *Throughout Your Generations Forever*, xxiii.
21. See ibid., 128, for a more detailed discussion of "patriarchal presuppositions."
22. Jamison, *Sacrificed Wife*, 4.
23. Hubert and Mauss, *Sacrifice*, 19–20.
24. Ibid., 12.
25. Ibid., 13.
26. Girard, *Violence and the Sacred*, 1; Girard in Hamerton-Kelly, *Violent Origins*, 106; Girard, *Violence and the Sacred*, 4.
27. Girard, *Violence and the Sacred*, 8.
28. Girard, "Violence and the Sacred: Sacrifice," 243.
29. Burkert in Hamerton-Kelly, *Violent Origins*, 164.
30. Mack, "Introduction: Religion and Ritual," in Hamerton-Kelly, *Violent Origins*, 25, 27.
31. Hubert and Mauss, *Sacrifice*, 35.
32. Smith, *Drudgery Divine*, 53.
33. Jastrow, *The Study of Religion*, 28; see also Smith, "*Adde Parvum Magnus Acervus Erit*," chapter 11 of his *Map Is Not Territory*, 240–241; Smith, "In Comparison a Magic Dwells," chapter 2 of his *Imagining Religion*, 19–35, esp. 35.
34. Patton and Ray, *Magic Still Dwells*.
35. AGNI, 9.
36. Goodman, *Between Jerusalem and Banares*, 3.
37. Müller, *History of Ancient Sanskrit Literature*, 389; Lévi, *Le Doctrine du sacrifice dans les Brāhmaṇas*.
38. Smith, *Reflections*, 46.
39. Heesterman, *Broken World of Sacrifice*; Malamoud, *Cooking the World*; Smith, *Classifying the Universe*; Staal, *Rules without Meaning*. For a discussion of the debates between Staal, Heesterman, and Smith concerning the nature of Vedic ritual, see Holdrege's article "Meaningless Ritual, Agonistic Sacrifice, or Ritual Taxonomy?"
40. Milgrom, *Leviticus 1–16*, *Leviticus 17–22* and *Leviticus 23–27*; Levine, *In the Presence of the Lord*, and Levine, *Leviticus*.
41. Eilberg-Schwartz, *Savage in Judaism*, 3.
42. Ibid, 5, 6–7.
43. Paden, "Elements of a New Comparativism," 7.
44. Ibid., 5.

ONE: Re-imagining Sacrifice

Epigraph: Heesterman, *Broken World of Sacrifice*, 230n25.
1. Smith, *Imagining Religion*, 18.

2. Henninger, "Sacrifice," 544; emphasis mine. In Chapter 3 we will disagree with Henninger's claim that only human or animal offerings can be killed.

3. Holdrege, *Veda and Torah*, 3.

4. This point, of course, applies to the present study as well. We will return to the importance of historical context in historical theorizing at the conclusion of this work.

5. To distinguish between Jewish and Christian views of the divine, I use the tetragrammaton *YHWH* throughout this work to refer to the god worshiped in the Jewish tradition.

6. Milgrom, *Leviticus 1–16*, 155.

7. Malamoud, *Cooking the World*, 40.

8. Atri Smṛti 141–142 states, "By birth each man is a Śūdra, but through the performance of *upanaya* [ritual initiation] a man is called 'twice-born.'" The sacrificer is said to be "twice-born" in that he is born biologically and then born of the Veda through the ritual initiation process. The ritual second birth perfects the initially defective biological birth.

9. Śāstri, "Agnicayana in the Mīmāṃsā," in AGNI, II:179.

10. Various texts classify sacrifices in different ways. Malamoud notes that "the *Baudhāyana Śrauta Sūtras* distinguish five sorts of oblatory matter: plants (*auṣdha*), milk (*payas*), animal victims (*paśu*), *soma,* and clarified butter (*ājya* or *ghṛta*). The *Yajna Paribhāṣā Sūtras*, on their part, recognize two major groups: vegetal oblations, including granulated rice (*taṇḍula*), flour (*piṣṭa*), the rice cake (*puroḍāśa*), rice porridge (*odana*), gruel (*yavagu*), rice that has been ground after boiling (*pṛthuka*), etc. Animal oblations include milk (*payas*), curdled milk (*dadhi*), clarified butter (*ājya*), a mixture of curdled milk with boiled milk (*āmikṣā*), whey (*vājina*), the caul, or the membrane enveloping the viscera (*vapā*), the skin (*tvac*), the flesh (*māṃsa*), the blood (*lohita*), and the *paśura* (pith)." Malamoud, *Cooking the World*, 37. The Gautama Dharma Sūtra classifies sacrifices differently, as *Pāka-yajna-saṃsthā*, *Havir-yajna-saṃsthā,* or *Soma-saṃsthā* sacrifices. Singh, "Critical Study of the Kātyāyana-Śrauta-Sūtra," 71.

11. KŚS 6.3.18. Animals are used in some domestic sacrifices as well—for example, in the annual sacrifice to Rudra and the cow sacrifice to the ancestors. However, these domestic sacrifices are based on the *śrauta* rituals.

12. We should note that there are almost always multiple offering substances within any individual ritual. Therefore, even though a sacrifice may be classified according to the nature of its primary offering, the actual ritual includes multiple manipulations of multiple substances.

13. Milgrom comments that the fact that the Jewish sacrificial system was explained to and performed in front of all the Israelites "expose[s] the gaping chasm that separates Israel from its neighbors. . . . A colophon to a Mesopotamian ritual text states that the commoner was barred not only from viewing the ritual but from viewing the text of the ritual: 'This ritual which you perform, (only) the *qualified* person shall view. An outsider who has nothing to do with the ritual shall not view (it); if he does, may his remaining days be few!'" Milgrom, *Leviticus 1–16*, 143. See also Milgrom, "Sacrifices and Offerings, OT."

14. The following cities hosted temples prior to Jerusalem's establishment as the cultic center of Israel: Dan, Ophrah, Shiloh, Gilgal, Bethel, Mizpah, Gibeah for Saul, Nob, Bethlehem, Hebron, and possibly Arad. "It may be conjectured that after the first wave of settlement and the Israelite population began to expand into other parts of Canaan . . . the primary momentum of temple founding spent itself." Haran, *Temples and Temple Service in Ancient Israel*, 42.

15. In another classificatory schema the sacrifices are ranked in descending order of sanctity: the *ʿōlâ*, *ḥaṭṭāʾt*, *ʿāšām*, and *minḥâ* are the most sacred, as evidenced by the fact that they are consumed on the fire altar or by the priest. The *šĕlāmîm*, which is the only offering consumed by the laity, is considered less sacred.

16. See T. Menaḥ 10:2; Sipra, Nedaba 4:8. The Bible records several other reasons for an *ʿōlâ* offering (e.g., Judg. 20:26), but principally it expiated sin.

17. Milgrom, *Leviticus 1–16*, 149. It will quickly become apparent that differing interpretations of the basic sacrificial rites have developed over the centuries, and controversies continue to this day. Since the present study focuses on the *how* of sacrifice rather than the *why*, we will allude to differences of interpretation only when necessary. Readers who are interested in more detailed discussions of the varying interpretations of Jewish sacrifices should consult the bibliography of this work for relevant authors and titles.

18. Levine, *In the Presence of the Lord*, 22.

19. At times the *ʿōlâ*, the *minḥâ*, and, rarely, the *šĕlāmîm* function as expiatory offerings, but not always.

20. See Lev. 4:2, 13, 22, 27.

21. Lev. 16. I discuss the problem of the live goat sent into the wilderness on Yom Kippur later in this book.

22. See Lev. 5:1–6 for lists of individual transgressions that require a *ḥaṭṭāʾt*.

23. Lev. 4:1–35; see also Num. 15:27 for variant offerings for a communal *ḥaṭṭāʾt*: an *ʿōlâ* bull and a *ḥaṭṭāʾt* male goat.

24. Impurity can result only from a violation of a prohibitive commandment, not the omission of a commanded act.

25. Lev. 20:3. See also other contaminating acts: Lev. 15:31; Num. 19:13.

26. See, in particular, Levine's work in *In the Presence of the Lord* and Milgrom's work in *Cult and Conscience*, "The Function of the *Hatta't* Sacrifice" (Heb.), "Sacrifices and Offerings, OT," and *Studies in Cultic Theology and Terminology*.

27. Specifically, "the noun *ʿāšām* is the restitution for desecration by either composition or sacrifice and should be rendered 'reparation' and 'reparation offering,' respectively. The verb *ʿāšam* is a stative. When it is followed by the preposition *l* and a personal object it means 'to incur liability to' someone for reparation; without an object, it refers to the inner experience of this liability, meaning 'to feel guilt.' " Milgrom, *Leviticus 1–16*, 339.

28. Num. 5:6–7a; see also Lev. 5:15, 21; Ezra 10:10, 19.

29. Different interpretations of the significance of the *šĕlāmîm* have been put

forward. W. Robertson Smith argues that this particular sacrifice brought YHWH and the sacrificer together and should be understood as a kind of communion (rather than expiation) offering. Martin Noth argues that the *šĕlāmîm* "was meant to establish or strengthen the community between God and the participants" (Noth, *Leviticus*, 39), although the Bible does not strongly support this interpretation (See Judg. 6:18–21, 13–16; Ps. 50:12–13). Levine argues that "in the framework of temple ritual the term *šulmānu* connotes present objects as well as sacrificial animals" (Levine, *In the Presence of the Lord*, 16). Others have argued that the offering is more of a thanksgiving presented by the sacrificer out of gratitude for his well-being or wholeness (*slm*).

30. Levine argues that the *šĕlāmîm* probably entered Jewish practice relatively early on and that it was originally associated with kings. Only later was it appropriated for worship of YHWH. See, in particular, 1 Sam. 11:14–15. See Levine's discussion of the *šĕlāmîm* in *In the Presence of the Lord.*

31. Milgrom, *Studies in Cultic Theology and Terminology*, 100.

32. As a result the thanksgiving, freewill, votive, and Passover offerings are included in the category of *šĕlāmîm* sacrifices, since they do not act as expiations. "The precise sense of the term *šelāmīm* has eluded even the most recent scholars, and ascertaining the character and function of the rite so designated has constituted a crux in the study of biblical religion since late antiquity." Levine, *In the Presence of the Lord*, 3.

33. Various scholars have noted that it was unusual in the Near Eastern context for laypeople to have such open access to the ritual space and to the sacrificial performance itself. The Israelites were unique in their exposure to the ritual process and in the level of participation they enjoyed in the sacrifices. Milgrom, *Leviticus 1–16*, 147.

34. Milgrom, *Leviticus 1–16*, 156.

35. This area was also open to women: Lev. 12:6, 15:29; Num. 5:16, 18, 25, 6:10.

36. See M. Kelim 1.9, Sipre Zuta on Num. 5.2.

37. Lev. 16; there is, of course, as mentioned in an earlier note, also a live goat sent off to Azazel during the Yom Kippur ritual. We will discuss this in more detail later in the section on animals, since the inclusion of a live goat raises questions about the role of killing in sacrifice.

TWO: Reevaluating the Role of Killing in Sacrifice

Epigraph: Burkert, "Problem of Ritual Killing," 164.

1. To be fair, some theorists have focused on other aspects of sacrificial activity, especially the cooking and eating of sacrificial offerings. See, e.g., Détienne and Vernant, *Cuisine of Sacrifice among the Greeks*; Malamoud, *Cooking the World*; Smith, *Lectures on the Religion of the Semites*. Although these works offer an important balance to theories that overemphasize killing, they still tend to emphasize one sacrificial procedure—eating—and minimize or overlook others.

2. Bourdillon, introduction to Bourdillon and Fortes, *Sacrifice*, 16–17.

3. Hubert and Mauss, *Sacrifice*, 32.

4. Burkert, "Problem of Ritual Killing," 164.

5. Girard, *Violence and the Sacred*, 1.

6. Ibid., 8.

7. I have already mentioned Hubert and Maus's interest in Vedic sacrifice. Scholars of Vedic sacrifice should also be familiar with Heesterman, *Broken World of Sacrifice*; Jamison, *Sacrificed Wife*; Malamoud, *Cooking the World*; Patton, *Authority, Anxiety, and Canon*; Smith, *Reflections*; and Staal, *Rules without Meaning*. Each of these works has made significant contributions to the study of sacrifice in general by close examination of the Vedic sacrificial system.

8. The soma plant is no longer available in India, so a variety of substitutes are currently used in Vedic ritual. Ranade argues that the Pūtikā is normally used as a substitute. *Kātyāyana Śrauta Sūtra*, iv. Staal lists several potential substitutes, including "Ephedra, Sarcostemma, and other creepers and plants without particularly remarkable properties." AGNI, 109. Brian K. Smith has gone so far as to suggest that perhaps there was no original soma plant: "That an 'original' *soma* never existed at all is a speculation that has not been put forward by Indologists and perhaps deserves consideration." Smith, *Reflections*, 181n30.

9. Malamoud, *Cooking the World*, 40.

10. Kane explains, "Soma sacrifices are classified into those that are finished in one day (and so called ekāha), those that are celebrated for more than one day up to twelve (and so called ahīna), [and] those that extend over more than twelve days (and are called Sattra)." *HD*, 1133.

11. "The Agniṣṭoma is the model (prakṛti) of all soma sacrifices. The Agniṣṭoma is a one day (aikahika or ekāha) sacrifice and it is an integral part of the Jyotistoma so much so that the two are often identified." Ibid.

12. For example, the first offering of the evening session is offered to the Ādityas. The offering itself is made from leftover soma from the morning pressing and so is appropriately offered to beings who were, themselves, created from "leftovers." For a more extended discussion of the soma pressing, see *HD*, 1163–1165.

13. ŚB 3.9.4.17. See also 3.3.2.6

14. Malamoud, conversation with the author, April 20, 1999, University of California, Santa Barbara.

15. Dandekar, *Śrautakośa Encyclopedia of Vedic Sacrificial Ritual*, vol. 2, pt. 1, English section, 411, discussing BŚS 14.4.

16. See ŚB 3.8.2.15; BŚS 4.6–7, 15.28. Houben notes, "In the Aśvamedha the horse was suffocated by means of a cloth saturated with clarified butter (*tārpya*), a device which apparently functioned like a plastic bag preventing the horse from getting fresh air." Houben, "To Kill or Not to Kill," 118n21.

17. Other terms, such as *tamayanti* and *saṃjñapta* found in KŚS 6.5.15–22, e.g., also prescribe death by stopping of the breath.

18. Temple Grandin, who has developed relatively painless slaughtering methods for the beef industry, notes that the absence of "vocalization" is a reliable indicator that the animal is not in pain or experiencing trauma. See

Zwerdling, "Kill Them with Kindness." Perhaps the "quiet" required at the sacrifice of a Vedic goat is intended as an indicator that the animal died a nonpainful death. In other words, rather than seeing the texts as denying reality by describing a quiet death, perhaps we should view them as attempting to set a standard for real activity.

19. Heesterman, *Broken World of Sacrifice*, 72.

20. RV 1.162.9; Houben, "To Kill or Not to Kill," 119.

21. Houben, "To Kill or Not to Kill," 123.

22. Ibid., esp. 146.

23. See, e.g., the later text ChāndUp 8.15: *ahiṃsan sarvabhūtāni*. Houben, "To Kill or Not to Kill," 146.

24. Houben, "To Kill or Not to Kill," 115.

25. Heesterman, *Broken World of Sacrifice*, 10, 73. Staal's model of "meaningless" ritual recognizes the flatness of ritual as well as its intricacies. Although I disagree with Staal's conclusions regarding the nature of ritual in general, his emphasis on the internal order, complexity, and "grammar" of ritual is very much in accord with a polythetic model.

26. TS 6.3.8.3; ŚŚS 5.17.11. There is some debate as to whether the priests can kill the animal victim (see, e.g., KŚS 6.67.1–2), but it is clear that the killing of the animal is *not* the critical activity the priests perform.

27. *HD*, 1122.

28. See also VārŚS 1.4.4.15.

29. See BŚS 2.11.

30. Malamoud, *Cooking the World*, 183.

31. Quotation from Smith, *Reflections*, 51.

32. *HD*, 1122–1123.

33. For detailed discussions of the Jewish sacrificial system, I recommend the works of Milgrom, especially *Leviticus 1–16* in the Anchor Bible series, and Levine, especially the Jewish Publication Society commentary *Leviticus*.

34. There is actually a distinction between the biblical and the rabbinic understandings of "*zebāḥîm*." According to Milgrom, "biblical *zebaḥ* is limited to the meaning 'slain offering whose meat is eaten by the worshiper.' . . . In rabbinic Hebrew *zebāḥim* refers to all slain offerings." *Leviticus 1–16*, 218.

35. A grain offering can be used as a substitute offering substance in an *ʿāšām* when the ritual sponsor cannot afford an animal (Lev. 5:11), but the preferred offering is always a domesticated animal or bird.

36. Lev. 1:3, 10. Birds (turtledoves or pigeons) can also be used if the sacrificer cannot afford an offering from the herd or flock (Lev. 1:14). For obvious logistical reasons, birds are handled a bit differently.

37. During a sacrifice for an individual, the ritual sponsor skins his own offering (Lev. 1:6), but during a sacrifice performed on behalf of the congregation, the priest or Levites skinned the animal (2 Chron. 29:34).

38. An offering for the anointed priest or for the entire of community of Israel requires a young bull; an offering representing a ruler requires a male goat; and an offering representing the common Israelite requires a female goat. See Lev.

4:1–5:13. To complicate matters further, there is also a discussion in Lev. 5:1–13 of a "graduated *ḥaṭṭāʾt*" offering, which adapts the required offering according to the ritual sponsor's economic means. If one cannot afford a female sheep or goat (the preferred offering), one is permitted to bring two turtledoves or pigeons, and if one cannot afford these birds, one is permitted to bring a tenth of an *ephah* of semolina. Note that the system moves seamlessly from animal offerings to grain offerings.

39. Douglas, *Leviticus as Literature,* 91–92.

40. For a detailed discussion of the significance of blood manipulation in Jewish sacrifice, see Gilders, *Blood Ritual in the Hebrew Bible.*

41. See current writings that connect kosher slaughter with the work of Temple Grandin, an expert in the field of painless animal slaughter, such as Wolfson, "Kosher Slaughter," 16–17.

42. Hubert and Mauss, *Sacrifice,* 12.

43. Douglas, *Purity and Danger,* 67; my emphasis.

44. Ibid.

45. Ibid., 115.

46. *HD*, 1003.

47. Milgrom, *Leviticus 1–16,* 1018.

48. Douglas, *Purity and Danger,* 64.

THREE: Vegetal Offerings as Sacrifice

1. For example, toward the end of *Sacrifice,* Hubert and Mauss comment in a footnote, "It may cause surprise that in this scheme we have not mentioned those cases where the victim is not an animal. We might indeed have done so. . . . [I]t is possible to establish real symmetrical patterns between victims and sacrificial oblations. The preparation of the cakes, the way in which they were anointed with oil or butter, etc., corresponds to the preparation of the [animal] victim" (137n291).

2. The *ephah* was a standard unit of measurement, approximating 22.8 liters.

3. AGNI, 1:303, 2:464–465. Staal describes this substitution as an unprecedented aberration, brought on by "a great deal of publicity, popular sentiment, and official pressure," but he also notes that the rice flour was "folded in banana leaf in the same manner in which this is done at the śrāddha or funeral ceremonies, when the same substance also stands for an animal offering." Thus a precedent exists within the priestly tradition for the substitution of a grain-based product for an animal offering.

4. These rituals are also distinguished by the numbers of priests they use: four for the *iṣṭi*s, six for the *paśu*, and sixteen for the *soma.*

5. *HD*, 1107.

6. The *darśapūrṇamāsa* serves as the paradigm for a variety of *iṣṭi* sacrifices, including the *cāturmāsya*, the seasonal sacrifice, and the *āgrayaṇa*, the first-fruits offering. The scope of this study, however, prevents us from examining these variant rites. Simple *iṣṭi* rites also appear as subsidiary offerings in the *paśu-*

bandha and soma rituals. This chapter, however, focuses on the *iṣṭi* as an independent principal offering.

7. Veena Das notes that wild grasses are used in the preparation of the *vedi* (the "altar" constructed for the sacrifice) and in other aspects of the ritual but never as offering substances. This usage parallels the fact that a wild animal is incorporated into the ritual in the form of the dead antelope skin. In referring to the inclusion of the antelope skin and the wild grasses, Das argues that the realm of the wild is not entirely excluded from Vedic *śrauta* ritual. Das, "Language of Sacrifice," 2. Malamoud also challenges the assumption that only cultivated plants are used in Vedic offerings: "[W]hereas the vegetable substances which make up the offerings are, in theory, cultivated plants, there nevertheless exist certain rites (such as the *Sautrāmaṇī*) which prescribe the actual, and not merely simulated, use of wild plants." Malamoud, *Cooking the World*, 80.

8. *HD*, 1025. Every primary text that describes this procedure emphasizes the need for these extra grains.

9. Traditionally eight or eleven potsherds are arranged together to form a baking surface for the *puroḍāśa*, although different texts give different instructions. See, e.g., ŚB 1.62.5, ĀpŚS 1.22.23, and KŚS 2.4.27–34. More recently priests have begun to use one potsherd that has been divided with lines on its surface to simulate the placement of multiple potsherds.

10. KŚS 2.4.26; ĀpŚS 1.19–23 says that the grain cakes should be cooked either over the *āhavanīya* fire or over the *gārhapatya* fire.

11. *HD*, 1033.

12. Chakrabarti, *Paribhāṣas*, 172.

13. *HD*, 1023.

14. BŚS 1.4–6 as discussed in Dandekar, *Śrautakośa Encyclopedia of Vedic Sacrificial Ritual*, 265. The footnote reads, "Sāyaṇa, following ĀpŚS, prescribes it [the touching] for consecrating the poured out grains."

15. Vārāha 1.2.4 (as discussed in Dandekar, *Śrautakośa Encyclopedia of Vedic Sacrificial Ritual*, 271) says that the sacrificer touches the grains himself. If this occurs, then the *yajamāna* identifies himself directly with the offering substance.

16. KŚS 2.4.14–2.4.20; see also ŚB 1.1.4.13.

17. *HD*, 1030.

18. KB 2.7, translation in Smith, *Classifying the Universe*, 210.

19. Smith, *Classifying the Universe*, 253.

20. There is tremendous disagreement between scholars regarding whether vegetal offerings developed before, after, or simultaneously with animal offerings. For arguments from various perspectives, see Singh, "Critical Study of the Kātyāyana-Śrauta-Sūtra," 133.

21. See Lev. 1–7 for an overview of these rites. The term *minḥâ* probably comes from the root *mnḥ*, meaning "to give." The noun form that results from this root consequently means "tribute" or "gift." In the priestly writings we are focusing on in this study, *minḥâ* is usually translated more narrowly as "grain offering," referring specifically to the grain brought to the priests to be offered in the Temple. In the nonpriestly writings, the term *minḥâ* is occasionally used to

refer to animal offerings. For example, the sons of Eli (1 Sam. 2:29) are said to have treated a *minḥâ* (referring to an animal offering) irreverently. But the priestly literature clearly reflects an understanding of the *minḥâ* as a grain offering, and the rabbinic tradition picks up this understanding and develops it.

22. Smith, *Religion of the Semites.*

23. See Stager's argument that terraced-farming techniques allowed the Israelites to produce grain, enabling them to exist independent of the surrounding Canaanite grain economies. Stager, "Agriculture." Anderson argues that "Israel's very existence as an autonomous political unit depended on the grain produced on these terraced fields." Anderson, *Sacrifices and Offerings*, 23.

24. Milgrom notes that barley was less expensive than wheat and as a result was commonly used by the poor. Milgrom, *JPS Torah Commentary*, 38. Barley was also used in the "offering of remembrance," the grain offering used in the trial for adultery (Num. 5). In this context the barley was not mixed with oil or frankincense.

25. M. Abot 5.15; see also M. Sab. 7a, 10b, 17c; T. Menah 8.14.

26. M. Men. 8.1. The passage goes on to list two exceptions: the flour for the *ʿōmer* and for the two loaves must come from fresh produce within Israel. The Mishnah comments that it was popular to obtain flour from Michmas, Mezonichah (or Zanoach), and Charayim (or Afarayim).

27. "All measures used in the Temple were heaped up, excepting that of the High Priest, which in itself contained the equivalent of a heaped-up measure." M. Men. 9.5. This same passage describes liquid measures as holy but dry measures as nonholy.

28. Num. 28.5. A tenth of an *ephah* is also called an *ʿōmer* (Ex. 16.36) and is equivalent to 2.3 liters, which would have been considered equivalent to one person's daily bread ration.

29. Num. 28:9; see also Num. 15:4, Lev. 23:17, and Lev. 24:5.

30. A priest would prepare the *minḥâ* when it was meant as a gift from the community of Israel but never when it was meant as a gift from an individual Israelite.

31. The grain offering used in the adultery trial does not include oil or frankincense. See M. Men. 5.3.

32. Blackman's edition of the Mishnah, 112n12.

33. M. Men. 5.3 indicates that the showbread—which is not prepared in a vessel—includes frankincense but no oil.

34. M. Men. 5.3 notes that a grain offering "presented with a libation requires oil but not frankincense." We will discuss this more fully when we review the role of liquid offerings in Chapter 4.

35. Noth, *Leviticus*, 27.

36. Ibid., 29.

37. "The grain offering of an Israelite was 'folded over' into two [parts] and the two [folded again] into four, and separated, [but] the grain offering of the priests was 'folded over' into two [parts] and the two into four, but [the] crumbs were not separated." M. Men. 6.4.

38. For further discussion of *minḥâ* cooking techniques, see Noth, *Leviticus,* 28.

39. The wife is required to make physical contact with a grain cake with which her husband has had physical contact. One might infer that this mediated physical contact between husband and wife is part of what makes the test for adultery work.

40. Most scholars argue that Leviticus, an early text, presents the *minḥâ* as an independent rite, while Numbers reflects a later, postexilic date by describing the *minḥâ* as an accompaniment or supplement to the whole burnt offering.

41. In addition to the discussions of the various types of sacrifice found in Leviticus, see the discussions of the trial for adultery (Num. 5), the Nazirite's vow (Num. 6), the entry into the Land (Num. 15), and so on. M. Menāḥôt immediately follows Zebāḥîm in the fifth order, and discussions of *minḥâ* oblations are intermingled with discussions of animal oblations in tractates Ḥullin, Beḥoroth, Araḥin, Temurah, Kerithoth, Meilah, and Tamid.

42. Another popular explanation for the second-rate status of grain oblations is the story of Cain and Abel. Cain's offerings, which were vegetal, were unacceptable to YHWH, whereas Abel's animal offerings were acceptable. The Genesis story, then, seems to imply that grain offerings are certainly inferior to animal offerings, if not entirely unacceptable. The rabbinic tradition, however, explains that Cain's offering was unacceptable not because it was of grain but because Cain's intentions were not pure.

43. Milgrom notes that the use of grain as an alternative offering for the poor is not unique to Jewish sacrifice. There was a similar arrangement in Mesopotamia. See Milgrom, "Sacrifices and Offerings, OT," 769.

44. There are times when a grain offering cannot substitute for an animal offering. See Lev. 12:8, 14:21–32, 15:14.

45. See, e.g., TS 7.1.1.4–6, JB 1.68–69, PB 6.1.6–11, and ŚB 11.5.8.1–4.

46. Smith, *Classifying the Universe.*

47. Milgrom, *Leviticus 1–16*, 183.

48. Malamoud, *Cooking the World*, 39.

49. Ibid., 40.

50. Heesterman, *Broken World of Sacrifice*, 81.

51. I am grateful to Brian K. Smith for suggesting the use of these phrases in the present study.

52. Gen.1:11–12 discusses the creation of vegetal life, and Gen. 1:20–25 discusses the creation of animal life. Gen. 1:26–30 discusses the creation of humanity and YHWH's giving humanity dominance over vegetation and animals. The second creation story presented in Gen. 2:4b–24 differs markedly, of course, from the first one.

53. This order is taken from Baudhāyana's interpretation; Śālīki says that the *adhvaryu* should first cut a portion from the western half of the cake, then from the eastern half.

54. Dandekar, *Śrautakośa Encyclopedia of Vedic Sacrificial Ritual,* vol. 1, English section, Part 1, 366.

55. A *yajamāna* who has previously offered a soma sacrifice must, at this time, offer *sānnāya*, a milk offering, as well.

56. None of the *minḥâ* is distributed to the laity. These offerings are not expiatory. Rather, they are offered as a gift or tribute to YHWH. Consequently the offerings are distributed to YHWH and his cultic functionaries, the priests.

57. Blackman, *Mishnayoth*, 103n10.

58. This tractate discusses in great detail a variety of conditions that can invalidate the *minḥâ* offering, including both actions and intentions of the priests.

59. Girard, *Violence and the Sacred*, 11.

60. Hubert and Mauss, *Sacrifice*, 137n291.

FOUR: Liquid Sacrificial Offerings

1. The clearest example of using water to purify ritual personnel is the *avabhṛta*, the final ritual purificatory bath that the *yajamāna* and the *patnī* perform at the end of most *śrauta* rituals. Interestingly, there is also a container of water called "foot-washing water" (*pannejanī*) that never comes into contact with anyone's feet. Jamison argues that the name of the water indicates an earlier hospitality activity. See Jamison, *Sacrificed Wife*, 127–128.

Note that the soma sacrifice specifies different types of water to be used throughout the sacrifice: (1) *vasatīvarī* water, taken from a flowing stream, is used to extract the soma juice; (2) *nigrābhyā* water, poured over the soma stalks when they are pressed, specifies water in the *hotṛ* priest's cup; (3) *ekadhāna* water, used to extract soma juice, is taken from a pond or lake on the morning of the pressing day; and (4) water in the *maitrāvaruṇa* cup, poured into the *āhavanīya* trough, is also taken from a pond or lake on the morning of the pressing day.

In addition, water is used to "swell" (*āpyāyatām*) or revive the principal offerings. We have seen that water is applied to various parts of the dead animal's body. In the soma sacrifice water is also applied to the soma stalks, and the stalks are encouraged by mantras to swell, to expand. Jamison argues that we should "view this rehydration as a reanimation, a bringing back to life of a dry and apparently lifeless substance," much like the dead animal victim. The water brings life into the lifeless plant, but this time before the offering is killed, (re)animating the offering substance. Jamison, *Sacrificed Wife*, 148.

2. For example, in the *ʿōlâ* offering, "the entrails and the shins" of the animal are washed (Lev. 1:9); see also Lev. 1:13.

3. See, e.g., Lev. 16:14–19.

4. The one exception may be Sukkot. Rabbi Akiva, arguing from Num. 29:31, comments, "[T]here is a water libation on the Festival [Sukkot] in order that the year's rains will be blessed." Sif. Num. 150.

5. Minkowski, *Priesthood in Ancient India*, 22.

6. See, e.g., the discussion of after-offerings in KŚS 2.7.4–15.

7. Milk is not restricted, however, to Vedic sacrifice. The Greeks also offered libations of milk. Hubert and Mauss refer to these milk offerings, noting that "they are subject to the same distinctions as sacrifices" and that milk offerings, on occasion, "can even replace [animal sacrifices]"—yet the authors refuse to categorize milk libations as sacrifices. Hubert and Mauss, *Sacrifice*, 12.

8. ŚB 14.2.2.19 says that the *brahmin* priest "heals" the sacrifice.

9. Ranade, *Kātyāyana Śrauta Sūtras*, vii.

10. Jamison, *Sacrificed Wife*, 129.

11. Milgrom, *JPS Torah Commentary*, 118.

12. Ibid., 119. Note Milgrom's references to M. Suk. 4:9; Eccl. 50:15; Josephus, *Ant.* 2.234; Sif. Num. 107.

13. Chitrabhanu Sen defines a *haviryajña* as "a class of sacrifice in which offerings of *havis*: milk, butter, rice, barley and similar materials take place, as distinguished from *Soma*." Sen, *Dictionary of the Vedic Rituals*, 124. Kane comments, "According to Gau. VIII. 20 there are seven forms of *haviryajñas*, of which agnihotra is the second." *HD*, 998.

14. See Kane's summary of the *agnihotra* in *HD*, 998–1001.

15. Ibid., 1002–1006.

16. Ibid., 1001.

17. Ibid., 1001–1002.

18. Kane notes that there is some debate as to whether the milk should be boiled or simply heated. Ibid., 1002, referencing ŚB 2.3.1.14–16 and the commentary on KŚS 4.14.5.

19. A second portion of milk is always offered to Prajāpati, but there is no specific procedure that distinguishes the initial morning offering to Sūrya from the initial evening offering to Agni-Soma; the timing of the ritual (morning versus evening) seems to accomplish this distinction, along with the mantras spoken.

20. *HD*, 1005; see ĀpŚS 6.11.5, 6.12.2.

21. Heesterman, *Broken World of Sacrifice*, 211.

22. For a brief but substantive summary, see Kane's discussion of the Agnistoma in *HD*, 1133–1203; for more extensive discussion, see Caland and Henri's definitive work *L'Agniṣṭoma.*

23. Louis Renou, *Vocabulaire du ritual védique*, argues that this transaction supports the theory that soma was originally an illegal halucinogenic drug.

24. See Wasson, *Soma*, 286–298, and "Soma of the Rig-Veda."

25. Flattery and Schwartz, *Haoma and Harmaline.*

26. AGNI, 105.

27. Staal even argues that "the increasing complexity of the Soma rituals is a direct consequence of the decreasing availability of the original Soma." Ibid., 1:109.

28. Smith, *Reflections*, 181n30. Drury has suggested that the soma plant was originally a substitute for a human victim, "an enemy king or warrior whose life was forfeited by defeat, and whose essence must be partaken of because of the belief that the partaking of the remains of a powerful man (or god) transfers his power to oneself." Drury, *Sacrificial Ritual in the Śatapatha Brāhmaṇa*, 37.

29. Holdrege, "The Agniṣṭoma," 21.

30. Dandekar, *Śrautakośa Encyclopedia of Vedic Sacrificial Ritual*, vol. 2, English section, Part 1, 361.

31. *HD*, 1143. See also ĀpŚS 10.25.1.

32. Dandekar, *Śrautakośa Encyclopedia of Vedic Sacrificial Ritual*, vol. 2, English section, Part 1, 373.

33. Ibid., 373.

34. Malamoud further explains, "The figures obviously have a symbolic value: 2+3+4 makes nine, and nine, in one way of counting, is the number of vital breaths animating man." Malamoud, *Cooking the World*, 176.

35. For example, the first offering of the evening pressing is offered to the Ādityas. This offering is made from leftover soma from the morning pressing and so is appropriately offered to beings who were themselves created from "leftovers." Jamison makes the argument that "leftovers" are linked to fertility in Vedic sacrifice, including in this particular rite. Jamison, *Sacrificed Wife*, 133–134.

36. KŚS 9.4.15; see also ĀpŚS 12.10.4–8, 9; 12.12.8–9.

37. Dandekar, *Śrautakośa Encyclopedia of Vedic Sacrificial Ritual*, 411, discussing BŚS 14.4.

38. The priests' actions can generate a wide range of results, including rain, the prevention of rain, and the exorcism of a demon. See, e.g., ĀpŚS 12.9.1–11.10. In addition, the ritual texts prescribe changes the priest can make to the ritual of a *yajamāna* he hates. For example, a priest is encouraged to break the flow of soma juice for a patron he hates, when the stream should run uninterrupted.

39. ŚŚS 2.7.3–4; see also ĀpŚS 12.13.12.

40. KŚS 9.2.5–6; see also VārŚS 15.1–3.

41. ĀpŚS 12.16.9; KŚS 9.6.25.

42. Malamoud, *Cooking the World*, 39.

43. Ibid., 39–40.

44. Ibid., 38.

45. ŚB 2.2.4.15. Malamoud explains further, "The primal cooking that is milk's special prerogative makes it into something that is in fact neither an excretion nor even a secretion, and which is not impure like the other humours which emanate from the body." Malamoud, *Cooking the World*, 273n52.

46. Smith, *Reflections*, 185. See also ĀpŚS 9.3.3–16; BhŚS 9.4.5–9; HŚS 15.1.51–64.

47. Dandekar, *Śrautakośa Encyclopedia of Vedic Sacrificial Ritual*, 433, discussing ĀpŚS 12.13.5–13.

48. Except in the case of the *manthin* cup; its remains are poured into the sacrificial fire.

49. By distinguishing between "cooking" and "heating," I choose to use a different term than Malamoud's because the shift in language highlights the differences between the two processes. I agree, however, with Malamoud's reasoning, although I use a different term for the purposes of this analysis.

50. In contrast to Jewish practice, blood is rarely used in Vedic sacrifice In general, animal blood is considered inauspicious in a ritual setting, even impure and dangerous. As a result, blood is usually disposed of outside the ritual space, and its handling is minimized in the texts (see ĀpŚS 7.16.1; 7.18.4; ĀśvŚS 3.3.1). Occasionally, however, some ritual blood manipulation is described. For example, in the Āśvamedha (horse sacrifice), "he [the *adhvaryu*] places the blood oblations into the opening of the throat of a *gomṛga* ox, into the hoof of the horse, and into a pot made of copper. . . . The blood of the animals belonging to Prajāpati should be placed into reed branches, or the horse's own blood should

be placed into reed branches" (KŚS 20.8.1–3). In the *gopitṛyajña*, the animal sacrifice in honor of the ancestors, cow's blood is offered to the demons. In these cases, blood is given as a share to the *rakṣa*s, the demons, not to the primary Vedic gods (Agni, Indra, or Soma) who traditionally receive Vedic offerings (ĀśvŚS 3.3.1; see also ĀpŚS 7.18.14; TS 1.3.9.2; 6.3.9.2; KŚS 6.6.11). Consequently, it would be misleading to present blood as a significant liquid offering substance in Vedic sacrifice.

51. For a detailed discussion of this point, see Milgrom, "Prolegomenon to Leviticus 17:11,"152–156.

52. Lev. 17:11. See Gilders's discussions regarding whether to translate the phrase "life is in the blood" or "life is the blood" in "Representation and Interpretation," 60–63, 251–253. Gilders's dissertation has been published as *Blood Ritual in the Hebrew Bible: Meaning and Power.*

53. Lev. 1:4; see also Lev. 3:2, 8, 12, 4:4, 15, 24, 29, 33, and 8:22.

54. McCarthy, "Further Notes on the Symbolism of Blood and Sacrifice," 206.

55. See Gilders's discussion of these scholars' positions in "Representation and Interpretation," 123–127.

56. Indirectly, of course, the participants benefit from the blood sacrifice as well because they are able to continue a cultic relationship with YHWH. But that benefit accrues only because the blood has performed its primary function, purging the sanctuary of contamination.

57. Hubert and Mauss distinguish between personal and objective sacrifices, arguing that sacrificial activity may affect not only the sacrificer but also "certain objects with which he is concerned." Hubert and Mauss, *Sacrifice*, 13.

58. Mishandling blood can invalidate a sacrifice. For example, M. Zeb. 2.1 states, "If the blood were poured [straight from the animal's neck] on the pavement and the priest gathered it up, it is invalid as an offering. If the priest flung it on the ramp leading up to the altar and not against the base of the altar, or if he flung above what he should have flung below, or if what should have been flung within were flung outside, or if what should have been flung outside were flung within, the offering becomes invalid." This description of mishandling is another indication that blood manipulation is an important feature of Jewish sacrifice.

59. In addition to Milgrom's and Levine's writings on blood manipulation, see Brichto, "On Slaughter and Sacrifice," 19–55; Dion, "Early Evidence for the Ritual Significance of the 'Base of the Altar,' " 487–490; Grintz, " 'Do Not Eat on the Blood,' " 78–105.

60. I also wish to express appreciation for the numerous spirited conversations Gilders and I have had regarding Leviticus and M. Zebāḥîm.

61. Lev. 1:15. The priests collected the blood in special bowls, called *mizrāqôt*, and then conveyed them to the altar. See also Ex. 38:3; Num. 41:14; M. Kin. 1.1.

62. Lev. 4:6–7; my emphasis. See also 4:18. The *ḥaṭṭā't* is the only offering in which blood is poured out at the base of the altar.

63. I agree with Milgrom's interpretation here. See his presentation and refutation of other explanations of different blood manipulations by Kaufman and Levine in *Leviticus 1–16*, 261–263. See also Brichto, "On Slaughter and Sacrifice," 19–56.

64. W. Robertson Smith argued that the sprinkling of blood on worshipers had "the same meaning" as consumption would have had in Jewish sacrifice." Smith, *Religion of the Semites*, 344. According to Smith, sprinkling was, in effect, a substitute for and equivalent to eating. But we will recall that Smith was arguing for a general understanding of sacrifice as a kind of communion between humans and deities. If, in fact, an offering substance was not consumed, then he had to come up with some other way to locate "communion" in sacrificial blood manipulation. His interpretation, however, is not supported by the textual material.

65. See Gilders's discussion of these terms in "Representation and Interpretation," 42–46.

66. Milgrom, *Leviticus 1–16*, 239.

67. Ibid., 260; see also Milgrom, "Israel's Sanctuary," 75–84.

68. Levine, *In the Presence of the Lord*, 74.

69. Brichto, "On Slaughter and Sacrifice," 29.

70. Lev. 14 discusses the one situation in which blood seems to purify an individual, the one who has scale disease (*šāraʿat*). The procedure requires that blood be daubed on "the lobe of the right ear of the one who is being purified and on the thumb of his right hand and on the big toe of his right foot" (Lev. 14:14). A similar procedure is performed in the ordination of Aaron and his sons in Lev. 8. Blood placed on the body's extremities signifies the purification of the entire body. It seems clear from the biblical context, however, that the procedure in both these situations was meant not so much to cleanse the body as to prevent the body from contaminating the sanctuary when these individuals entered the ritual space. Thus, even the direct placement of blood on the body was meant primarily to protect the sanctuary, not to cleanse the individual. See Lev. 14 for the discussion of scale disease and Lev. 8 for the discussion of the priests' ordination. See also Levine, *In the Presence of the Lord*, 74, for his interpretation of the placement of blood on individuals.

71. "There were seven wet measures in the Temple: the *hin*, the half-*hin*, the third of a *hin*, the quarter-*hin*, the log, the half-log, and the quarter-log." M. Men. 9.2.

72. Certain passages indicate that a priest stirred the blood in its basin so that it would not congeal. See, e.g., M. Yoma 4.3.

73. This sequence makes logical sense and is also supported by M. Yoma 3.5.

74. The one ritual in which blood is heated is the offering of the red heifer, described in Num. 19. The heifer is slaughtered and burned, and its ashes are mixed with water and used to cleanse any individual who touches a corpse. Contact with a dead body contaminates an individual; contact with water mixed with animal blood removes or nullifies the contamination. The red heifer ritual is somewhat distinct from the other rituals we have examined for several reasons. Note that the ritual involving the red heifer is treated differently than other sacrifices, primarily because of the location—outside camp. P, the priestly redactor of this strand of biblical material, restricts spatial holiness to the sanctuary. The fact that the red heifer ritual is performed outside the sanctuary signals that

this rite had a different function in the life of the community than did any other animal slaughter. Milgrom notes other differences: "The rabbis find the Red Cow anomalous for another reason: all communal sacrifices are male animals (Pesiq. Rab Kah. 4:8; cf. M. Tem. II 1), and they hold that the Red Cow is purchased from a public fund (Sif. Zut. 19.2)." Milgrom, *Studies in Cultic Theology and Terminology*. Finally, the red heifer is not subjected to many of the sacrificial procedures we have identified. No attempt is made to associate the animal with YHWH; no individual places his hands upon the heifer's head to identify with it; no priest apportions the slaughtered animal into parts; and no ritual participant (including YHWH) consumes any of the offering. Consequently, the red heifer rite is substantially less sacrificial than any of the other blood manipulations we have examined.

75. Certain passages suggest that laypeople thought that sacrificial blood acquired magical properties from its contact with the altar. M. Yoma 5.6 explains that blood from the Yom Kippur sacrifices flowed from the Temple altar "into the Brook of Kidron. It was sold to gardeners as fertilizer, and the law of making inappropriate use of sacred property applied to it." In other words, blood that had made contact with the altar on Yom Kippur was seen to have special properties. The priests prohibited the sale of this sacred mixture and developed a general prohibition against the postcultic use of sacred substances.

76. Lev. 17:10–14. See also Deut. 12:16, 23–24.

77. See, e.g., the note to Lev. 7:20 in May and Metzger, *New Oxford Annotated Bible with the Apocrypha (RSV)*, 129.

78. Bergmann, *In the Shadow of Moloch*, 35.

79. Grintz, " 'Do Not Eat on the Blood,' " 85.

80. Milgrom, *Studies in Cultic Theology and Terminology*, 79.

81. Hubert and Mauss, *Sacrifice*, 32; my emphasis.

82. Van Baal, "Offering, Sacrifice and Gift," 277; my emphasis.

83. Smith, *Religion of the Semites*, 339. Smith also refers to similar practices in certain Syrian sacrifices.

84. Hubert and Mauss, *Sacrifice*, 36; see further references in note 213 of the same page.

85. Grimes, "Breaking the Glass Barrier," 239.

86. Humphrey and Laidlaw, *Archetypal Actions of Ritual*, 252.

87. Smith, *Religion of the Semites*, 338. Smith refers to Nilus's description of this sacrifice.

88. Durand, "Greek Animals: Toward a Typology of Edible Bodies," in Détienne and Vernant, *Cuisine of Sacrifice among the Greeks*, 90.

89. Ibid., 91.

90. Ibid.

FIVE: The Apportionment of Sacrificial Offerings

1. Klawans, "Pure Violence," 145.

2. Minor variations occur throughout the procedure, but the general se-

quence is fairly standardized. The procedures outlined here follow the Kātyāyana Śrauta Sūtra, probably the latest of the Śrauta Sūtras.

3. Some traditions indicate that the omentum should be offered with gold pieces.

4. Dandekar, *Śrautakośa Encyclopedia of Vedic Sacrificial Ritual,* vol. 1, English section, Part 2, 831–832.

5. KŚS 6.8.6; see also ŚB 3.8.3.8–9.

6. In contrast, the midsection of the entrails is associated with the *juhū* (KŚS 6.7.9).

7. "There is an optional enjoining of the avāntara iḍā (portion of clarified butter from the Iḍā-vessel to be applied to the forefinger to be licked by the Hotṛ) for the part above the udder (to be given to be [*sic*] Hotṛ as the Hotṛ-portion of the Iḍā)" KŚS 6.9.6. Trans. Ranade.

8. KŚS 6.9.14–15; see also ŚB 3.8.5.6–7.

9. Dandekar, *Śrautakośa Encyclopedia of Vedic Sacrificial Ritual,* vol. 1, English section, Part 2, 772.

10. KŚS 6.9.17.

11. Milgrom, *Leviticus 1–16*, 157.

12. M. Yoma 2.3–7 discusses how the priests divided the labors associated with animal sacrifice.

13. Lev. 1:14; see also 5:8.

14. See Milgrom's summary of a taxidermist's description in *Leviticus 1–16*, 169.

15. Milgrom notes that the purpose of this "may be to increase its size and give the appearance of a more substantial gift." Milgrom, *Leviticus 1–16*, 172.

16. Milgrom, "Sacrifices and Offerings, OT," 766. Note, however, that Milgrom himself disagrees with the rabbis here in the next sentence: "However, this interpretation is unlikely, since expiation is not the function of all sacrifices." Instead he views the flesh as a reward for participating in the expiation process.

17. Gonda, *Haviryajnāḥ Somāh*, 43.

18. Note that in ŚB 6.2.2.12, Prajāpati's body is said to have been reconstituted by a grain cake.

19. Dandekar, *Śrautakośa Encyclopedia of Vedic Sacrificial Ritual,* vol. 1, English section, Part 1, 366.

20. KŚS 1.9.9; see also 3.3.25.

21. Dandekar, *Śrautakośa Encyclopedia of Vedic Sacrificial Ritual,* vol. 1, English section, pt. 1, 285–286.

22. Blackman's edition of M. Men., 103.

23. AitBr 7.19, trans. Smith in his *Reflections*, 67.

24. ŚB 7.5.4.6, trans. Smith in his *Classifying the Universe*, 249.

25. Smith, *Reflections*, 62.

26. Klawans, "Pure Violence," 148.

27. Clooney notes how the Vedic concept of inherent connection continues in later Mīmāṃsā thought in the term *sambandha.* Clooney, *Thinking Ritually*, 102–104.

28. KŚS 6.7.6; see also ŚB 3.8.3.5.

29. KŚS 6.7.7; see also ŚB 3.8.3.13, 18.

30. Smith, *Classifying the Universe*, 81.

31. Douglas, *Leviticus as Literature*, 78.

32. Olyan, *Rites and Rank*, 12.

33. The Levites seem to fill a middle role: "Their superiority to the populace is evident in their reception of the tithe; their inferiority to the priests results from their having to give to the priests the holy portion, or 'fat part,' of the tithe." Ibid., 33.

34. Ibid., 30.

35. Douglas, *Leviticus as Literature*, 25; my emphasis.

36. Smith, *Classifying the Universe*, 14.

37. Douglas, *Leviticus as Literature*, 28.

38. Note, too, that this expertise is *not* necessarily required to kill the victim (the *sūtras* vary on whether priests may or may not kill the animal victim) but to divide the victim into its ritually prescribed portions.

39. Durkheim, *Elementary Forms*, 261.

40. Détienne, "Culinary Practice," in Détienne and Vernant, *Cuisine of Sacrifice among the Greeks*, 13.

41. Durkheim, *Elementary Forms*, 261.

42. Coomaraswamy, "Ātmayajna," 396.

Conclusion

Epigraph: Douglas, *How Institutions Think*, 4.

1. Tannaitic refers to the earliest rabbinic commentaries on the Torah, including the Mishnah (ca. 220 CE) and early midrashim.

2. Bentor, "Interiorized Fire Rituals in India and in Tibet," 594.

3. Spinner, " Jerusalem Temple as *Imago Mundi*," 1.

4. For further scholarship on the interiorization of Vedic rituals, see Biardeau and Malamoud, *Le Sacrifice dans l'Inde ancienne*; Eliade, *Yoga, Immortality and Freedom*; Heesterman, *Inner Conflict of Tradition*.

5. Bentor, "Interiorized Fire Rituals in India and in Tibet," 595.

6. See, for example, Kaelber, "*Tapas* and Purification in Early Hinduism," 193.

7. Ibid., 197.

8. Ibid., 202–203.

9. Kaelber, "*Tapas*, Birth, and Spiritual Rebirth in the Veda," 343.

10. See, e.g., Cohen, *From the Maccabees to the Mishnah*; Neusner, *Way of Torah*; Schiffman, *From Text to Tradition*.

11. Spiegel, *Last Trial*.

12. Ibid., 19–20.

13. Spinner, " Jerusalem Temple as *Imago Mundi*," 6.

14. Strenski, *Contesting Sacrifice*, 9.

15. This point is particularly interesting in light of the strongly anticlerical stance of the French Revolution which came earlier.

16. Marvin and Ingle, *Blood Sacrifice and the Nation*, 9. Note that Marvin and Ingle characterize sacrifice as violent bloodshed, a characterization I have been combating throughout this book. For our purposes at this point, however, I share their belief that "sacrifice"—however it is conceived—is regularly invoked by national as well as religious communities.

17. Lincoln, *Holy Terrors*, 94.

18. Ibid., 97.

19. Ibid., 98.

20. George Bush, speech at the National Cathedral on the National Day of Prayer and Remembrance, September 14, 2001; my emphasis.

21. Lincoln, *Holy Terrors*, 101; my emphasis.

22. Most recently, Bush referred to sacrifice in his January 11, 2007, address to the nation regarding sending more than twenty thousand additional troops to Iraq: "Young Americans understand that our cause in Iraq is noble and necessary. . . . They serve far from their families, who make the quiet sacrifices of lonely holidays and empty chairs at the dinner table. . . . The year ahead will demand more patience, sacrifice and resolve."

23. See my review of Strenski's *Contesting Sacrifice* in *Journal of the American Academy of Religion* 72, no. 3 (2004): 798–799.

24. Lincoln, *Holy Terrors*, 5.

25. Regarding ritual as a "mode of paying attention," see Smith, *To Take Place*, 103.

26. Holdrege, "Beyond Hegemony."

Bibliography

INDOLOGICAL SOURCES

Primary Sources

Atharva-Veda Saṃhitā

Bandhu, Vishva, ed. 5 vols. Vishveshvaranand Indological Series, 13–17. Hoshiarpur, India: Vishveshvaranand Vedic Research Institute, 1960–1964.

Translations:

Bloomfield, Maurice, trans. *Hymns of the Atharva-Veda, Together with Extracts from the Ritual Books and Commentaries.* Sacred Books of the East, vol. 42. Oxford: Clarendon Press, 1897.

Whitney, William Dwight, trans. *Atharva-Veda Saṃhitā.* Revised and edited by Charles Rockwell Lanman. 2 vols. Harvard Oriental Series, vols. 7–8. Cambridge: Harvard University Press, 1905.

Taittirīya Saṃhitā

Röer, E. (vol. 1), E. B. Cowell (vols. 1–2), Maheśachandra Nyāyaratna (vols. 3–5), and the Satyavrata Sāmaśramī (vol. 6), eds. 6 vols. Bibliotheca Indica, no. 26. Calcutta: Society of Bengal, 1860–1899.

Translation:

Keith, Arthur B., trans. *The Veda of the Black Yajus School Entitled Taittiriya Samhita.* Harvard Oriental Series, vols. 18–19. Cambridge: Harvard University Press, 1914.

Vājasaneyi Saṃhitā

Weber, Albrecht, ed. Berlin: Ferd. Dümmler; London: Williams and Norgate, 1852.

Translation:

Griffith, Ralph T. H., trans. *The Texts of the White Yajur-Veda.* Benares, India: E. J. Lazarus, 1899.

Brāhmaṇas

Aitareya

Sāmaśramī, Satyavrata, ed. 4 vols. Bibliotheca Indica, no. 134. Calcutta: Asiatic Society of Bengal, 1895–1906.

Translation:

Keith, Arthur B., trans. *Rigveda Brāhmaṇas: The Aitareya and Kauṣītaki Brāhmaṇas of the Rigveda.* Harvard Oriental Series, vol. 25. Cambridge: Harvard University Press, 1920.

Jaiminīya

Vira, Raghu, and Lokesh Chandra, eds. Sarasvati-Vihara Series, vol. 31. Nagpur, India: International Academy of Indian Culture, 1954.

Translations:

Bodewitz, H. W., trans. *Jaiminīya Brāhmaṇa I. 1–65.* Leiden, Netherlands: E. J. Brill, 1973.

——, trans. *The Jyotiṣṭoma Ritual: Jaiminīya Brāhmaṇa I, 66–364.* Oriental Rheno-Traiectina, vol. 34. Leiden, Netherlands: E. J. Brill, 1990.

Kauṣītaki

Bhattacharya, Harinarayan, ed. Calcutta Sanskrit College Research Series, no. 73. Calcutta: Sanskrit College, 1970.

Translation:

Keith, Arthur B., trans. *Rigveda Brāhmaṇas: The Aitareya and Kauṣītaki Brāhmaṇas of the Rigveda.* Harvard Oriental Series, vol. 25. Cambridge: Harvard University Press, 1920.

Pañcaviṃśa

Vedāntavāgīśa, Ānandachandra, ed. 2 vols. Bibliotecha Indica, no. 62. Calcutta: Asiatic Society of Bengal, 1870–1874.

Translation:

Caland, W., trans. *Pañcaviṃśa-Brāhmaṇa: The Brāhmaṇa of Twenty Five Chapters.* Bibliotheca Indica, no. 255. Calcutta: Asiatic Society of Bengal, 1931.

Śatapatha Brāhmaṇa

Weber, Albrecht, ed. Berlin: Ferd. Dümmler; London: Williams and Norgate, 1855. Reprint, Chowkhamba Sanskrit Series, no. 96. Varanasi, India: Chowkhamba Sanskrit Series Office, 1964.

Translation:

Eggeling, Julius, trans. *The Śatapatha Brāhmaṇa according to the Text of the Mādhyandina School.* 5 vols. Sacred Books of the East, vols. 12, 26, 41, 43, 44. Oxford: Clarendon Press, 1882–1900. Reprint, Delhi: Motilal Banarsidass, 1963.

Śrauta Sūtras

Āpastamba Śrauta Sūtras

Garbe, R., ed., with Rudradatta's commentary. Bibliotheca Indica Series, no. 92. 3 vols. Calcutta: Asiatic Society, 1882–1902.

Mahadeva, A., ed. *Āpastamba Paribhāśā Sūtra.* With the commentaries of Haradatta and Kapardisvāmin. Mysore, India: Sastri, 1894.

Translation:

Caland, W., trans., in German. *Āpastamba Śrautasūtra.* 3 vols. Calcutta: Vandenhoeck and Ruprecht, 1921. Reprint, Wiesbaden: Dr. Martin Sändig, 1969.

Müller, Max, trans. and commentary. *Āpastamba Paribhāśā Sūtra.* Sacred Books of the East, vol. 30. Oxford: Clarendon Press, 1882–1900.

Āśvalāyana Śrauta Sūtra

Vidyaratna, R., ed. *Āśvalāyana Śrauta Sūtra.* Calcutta: Asiatic Society of Bengal, 1874.

Translation:

Ranade, H. G., trans. *Āśvalāyana Śrauta-sūtram.* Part 1. Sanskrit Dictionary Project. Poona, India: Deccan College, 1981.

Baudhāyana Śrauta Sūtra

Caland, W., ed. 3 vols. Calcutta: Asiatic Society of Bengal, 1904–1924. Reprint, New Delhi: Munshiram Manoharlal, 1982.

Translation:

Kashikar, C. G., trans. *Baudhāyana Śrauta Sūtra* 3 vols. Delhi: Motilal Banarsidass, 2003.

Bhāradvāja Śrauta Sūtras

Kashikar, C. G., ed. and trans. 2 vols. Poona, India: Vaidika Saṃśodhana Maṇḍala, 1964.

Hiranyakeśi (Satyāsādha) Śrauta Sūtra

Agase, Kashinatha Sastri, and Sankara Sastri Marulakara, eds. Poona, India: Anandāśrama Sanskrit Series no. 53, 10 vols. Poona, India: 1907–1932.

Jaiminīya Śrauta Sūtra

Shastri, Premnidhi, ed. Included in *Jaiminīya-Śrauta-Sūtra-Vṛtti of Bhavatrāta.* Śata-Piṭaka Series, vol. 40. New Delhi: International Academy of Indian Culture, 1966.

Kātyāyana Śrauta Sūtra

Weber, Albrecht, ed. Reprint, Chowkhamba Sanskrit Series, no. 104. Varanasi, India: Chowkhamba Sanskrit Series Office, 1972.

Translation:

Ranade, H. G., trans. *Kātyāyana Śrauta Sūtra.* Pune, India: H. G. Ranade and R. H. Ranade, n.d.

Śāṇkhāyana Śrauta Sūtra

Hillebrandt, A., ed. 2 vols. Reprint, New Delhi: Meharchand Lachhmandas, 1981.

Translation:

Caland, W., trans. *Śāṇkhāyana-śrautasūtra.* Reprint, Delhi: Motilal Banarsidass, 1980.

Gonda, Jan. *The Haviryajñāḥ Somāḥ: The Interrelations of the Vedic Solemn Sacrifices.* Śāṇkhāyana Śrautasūtra 14, 1–13. Translation and notes. New York: North-Holland Publishing Co., 1982.

Dharmaśāstras

Manu Smṛti

Dave, J. H., ed. *Manu Smṛti.* 5 vols. Bhāratīya Vidyā Series. Bombay: Bhāratīya Vidyā Bhavan, 1972–1982.

Translations:

Buhler, Georg. *Manu Smṛti*. Sacred Books of the East, vol. 25. Oxford: Clarendon Press, 1886. Reprint, New York: Dover Publications, 1969.

Doniger, Wendy, with Brian K. Smith. *The Laws of Manu*. Translation with introduction. New York: Penguin Books, 1991.

Secondary Sources

Banerjea, A. C. *Studies in the Brahmanas.* New Delhi: Motilal Banarsidass, 1963.

Basu, J. *India in the Age of the Brahmanas*. Calcutta: Sanskrit Pustak Bhandar, 1969.

Bentor, Yael. "Interiorized Fire Rituals in India and in Tibet." *Journal of the American Oriental Society* 120, no. 4 (2000): 594–613.

Bhandarkar, D. R. "Were Women Entitled to Perform Śrauta Sacrifices?" *Proceedings of the All-India Oriental Conference*, Session 11, Benares, India, 1946.

Bhargava, P. L. *India in the Vedic Age: A History of Aryan Expansion in India.* 2d ed. Aminabad, India: Upper India Publishing House, 1971.

Bhattacharya, D. "Cosmogony and Rituo-Philosophical Integrity in the Atharvaveda." *Vishveshvaranand Indological Journal* 15 (March 1977): 1–12.

Bhide, V. V. *The Caturmasya Sacrifices.* Pune, India: University of Poona, 1979.

Biardeau, Madeleine, and C. Malamoud. *Le Sacrifice dans l'Inde ancienne.* Paris: Presses Universitaires de France, 1976.

Bloomfield, M. *A Vedic Concordance.* Harvard Oriental Series 10. 1906. Reprint, Delhi: Motilal Banarsidass, 1964.

Bodewitz, H. W. *The Daily Evening and Morning Offering (Agnihotra) According to the Brahmanas.* Leiden, Netherlands: E. J. Brill, 1976.

——. "The Fourth Priest (the Brahman) in Vedic Ritual." In *Selected Studies on Ritual in the Indian Religions: Essays to D. J. Hoens,* edited by Ria Kloppenborg. Leiden, Netherlands: E. J. Brill, 1983.

——. *The Jyotistoma Ritual: Jaiminiya Brahmana I, 66–364.* Leiden, Netherlands: E. J. Brill, 1990.

Brereton, Joel. *The RgVedic Adityas.* American Oriental Series 63. New Haven, CT: American Oriental Society, 1981.

Caland, Willem. *Das Jaiminiya-Brahmanas in Auswahl.* Text, Ubersetzung. Amsterdam: J. Mullers, 1919.

Caland, Willem, and V. Henri. *L'Agnistoma: Description complete de la forme normale du sacrifice de soma dans le culte vedique.* Paris: E. Leroux, 1906–1907.

Chakrabarti, Samiran Chandra. *The Paribhāṣās in the Śrautasūtras.* Calcutta: Sanskrit Pustak Bhandar, 1980.

Clooney, Francis X. *Thinking Ritually: Rediscovering the Purva Mīmāṃsā of Jaimini.* Leiden, Netherlands: E. J. Brill, 1990.

Coomaraswamy, Ananda K. "Ātmayajña: Self-Sacrifice." *Harvard Journal of Asiatic Studies* 6 (1941): 358–398.

Dandekar, R. N., ed. *Śrautakośa Encyclopedia of Vedic Sacrificial Ritual.* 2 vols. Poona, India: Vaidika Saṃśodhana Maṇḍala, 1958–1982.

Das, Veena. "The Language of Sacrifice." Paper read for the Henry Myers Lecture, Royal Anthropological Institute, London, April 21, 1982.

Drury, Naama. *The Sacrificial Ritual in the Śatapatha Brāhmaṇa.* Delhi: Motilal Banarsidass, 1981.

Dumezil, Georges. *L'Ideologie tripartite des Indo-Europeans.* Brussels: Collection Latomus, 1958.

Dumont, P.-E. *L'Agnihotra: Description de l'agnihotra dans le ritual vedique d'apres les Srautasutras.* Baltimore: Johns Hopkins Press, 1939.

Eliade, Mircea. *Yoga, Immortality, and Freedom.* Princeton, NJ: Princeton University Press, 1969.

Flattery, David Stophlet, and Martin Schwartz. *Haoma and Harmaline: The Botanical Identity of the Indo-Iranian Sacred Hallucinogen "Soma" and Its Legacy in Religion, Language, and Middle Eastern Folklore.* Berkeley: University of California Press, 1989.

Gonda, Jan. *Change and Continuity in Indian Religion.* The Hague: Mouton, 1965.

——, trans. and ed. *The Haviryajñāḥ Somāḥ: The interrelations of the Vedic Solemn Sacrifices. Śāṇkhāyana Śrautasūtra 14, 1–13*. New York: North Holland Publishing Co., 1982.

——. "Purohita." In *Studia Indologica: Festschrift fur Willibald Kirfel*, edited by O. Spies. Bonn: Universitat Bonns, 1955.

——. *The Ritual Functions and Significance of Grasses in the Religion of the Veda.* Amsterdam: North-Holland, 1985.

——. *The Ritual Sūtras*. Vol. 1, fasc. 2 of *A History of Indian Literature*, edited by Jan Gonda. Wiesbaden: Otto Hanassowitz, 1977.

——. "Vedic Gods and the Sacrifice." *Numen* 30, no. 1 (1983): 1–34.

——. *Vedic Literature: Samhitas and Brahmanas A History of Indian Literature.* Vol. 1, pt. 1. Wiesbaden: Harrassowitz, 1975.

Harper, E. B. "Ritual Pollution, Caste, and Religion." In *Religion in South Asia*, edited by E. B. Harper. Seattle: University of Washington Press, 1964.

Heesterman, Jan C. *The Broken World of Sacrifice: An Essay in Ancient Indian Ritual.* Chicago: University of Chicago Press, 1977.

——. *The Inner Conflict of Tradition: Essays in Indian Ritual, Kingship, and Society.* Chicago: University of Chicago Press, 1985.

——. "Reflections on the Significance of the Daksina." *Indo-Iranian Journal* 3 (1959): 241–258.

——. "Vratya and Sacrifice." *Indo-Iranian Journal* 6 (1962): 1–37.

Holdrege, Barbara. "The Agniṣṭoma." Paper submitted at Harvard University, Cambridge.

——. "Meaningless Ritual, Agonistic Sacrifice, or Ritual Taxonomy? Contending Perspectives in Vedic Studies." *Critical Review of Books in Religion* 1997 (1998): 59–62.

Houben, J. E. M. "To Kill or Not to Kill the Sacrificial Animal (*Yajña-Paśu*)?" In *Violence Denied: Violence, Nonviolence, and the Nature of Violence: South Asian Cultural History*, edited by J. E. M. Houben and K. R. van Kooij. Boston: Brill, 1999.

Inden, Ronald. "Changes in the Vedic Priesthood." In *Ritual, State, and History in South Asia: Essays in Honor of J. C. Heesterman*, edited by A.W. Van den Hoek, D. H. A. Koeff, and M. S. Oort. Leiden, Netherlands: E. J. Brill, 1992.

Jamison, Stephanie. *Sacrificed Wife / Sacrificer's Wife: Women, Ritual and Hospitality in Ancient India*. New York: Oxford University Press, 1996.

Joshi, J. R. "Prajapati in Vedic Mythology and Ritual." *Annals of the Bhandarkar Oriental Research Institute* 53 (1972): 101–125.

Kaelber, Walter. "*Tapas* and Purification in Early Hinduism." *Numen* 26, no. 2 (1979): 192–214.

Kane, P. V. *History of Dharmaśāstra.* Vol. 2, pt. 2. Poona, India: Bhandarkar Oriental Research Institute, 1990.

Keith, Arthur Berriedale. *The Religion and Philosophy of the Veda and Upanishads.* 2 vols. Harvard Oriental Series, vols. 31 and 32. Cambridge: Harvard University Press, 1925. Reprint, Delhi: Motilal Banarsidass, 1976.

Knipe, David. *Hinduism: Experiments in the Sacred*. San Francisco: Harper San Francisco, 1991.

——. *In the Image of Fire: Vedic Experiences of Heat*. Delhi: Motilal Banarsidass, 1975.

Kuiper, F. B. J. "The Basic Concept of Vedic Religion." *History of Religion* 15 (November 1975): 107–120.

Lévi, Sylvain. *Le Doctrine du sacrifice dans les Brāhmaṇas*. Bibliotheque de l'École des Hautes École, Sciences religieuses, vol. 11. Paris: Ernest Leroux, 1898.

Macdonald, K. S. *The Brahmanas of the Vedas*. Reprint, Delhi: Bharatiya Book Corp., 1979.

Macdonell, A. A., and A. G. Keith. *Vedic Index of Names and Subjects*. 2 vols. London, 1912. Reprint, Delhi: Motilal Banarsidass, 1958.

Majumdar, Girijaprasanna. "Vedic Plants." In *B.C. Law Volume*, pt. 1, edited by D. R. Bhandarkar et al. Calcutta: Indian Research Institute, 1945.

Malamoud, Charles. *Cooking the World: Ritual and Thought in Ancient India*. Translated by David Gordon White. New York: Oxford University Press, 1996.

——, ed. *Debts and Debtors*. New Delhi: Vikas Publishing House, 1983.

Minkowski, Christopher. *The Priesthood in Ancient India: A Study of the Maitrāvaruṇa Priest*. Vienna: Sammburg de Nobili, 1991.

Müller, F. Max. *A History of Ancient Sanskrit Literature*, 2d ed. London: Williams and Norgate, 1860.

O'Flaherty, Wendy Doniger. *Tales of Sex and Violence: Folklore, Sacrifice, and Danger in the Jaiminiya Brahmana*. Chicago: University of Chicago Press, 1984.

Olivelle, Patrick. *The Asrama System: The History and Hermeneutics of a Religious Institution*. New York: Oxford University Press, 1993.

Parpola, Asko. "On the Symbol Concept of the Vedic Ritualists." In *Religious Symbols and Their Functions*, edited by H. Biezais. Stockholm: Almquist and Wiksell, 1979.

——. "The Pre-Vedic Indian Background of the Srauta Rituals." In *Agni: The Vedic Ritual of the Fire Altar*, vol. 2, edited by Frits Staal. Berkeley: Asian Humanities Press, 1983.

Patton, Laurie, ed. *Authority, Anxiety and Canon: Essays in Vedic Interpretation*. Albany: State University of New York Press, 1993.

Ranade, H. G. *Illustrated Dictionary of Vedic Rituals*. New Delhi: Aryan Books International, 2006.

Renou, Louis. *L'Inde Fundamentale*. Paris: Hermann, 1978.

——. *Religions of Ancient India*. London: Athlone Press, 1953.

——. *Vocabulaire du ritual védique*. Paris: Librairie C. Klincksieck, 1954.

Sauve, James L. "The Divine Victim: Aspects of Human Sacrifice in Viking Scandinavia and Vedic India." In *Myth and Law Among the Indo-Europeans*, edited by Jaan Puhvel. Los Angeles: University of California Press, 1973.

Sen, Chitrabhanu. *A Dictionary of the Vedic Rituals*. Delhi: Concept Publishing, 1978.

Shamashastry, R. *The Vedic Calendar*. Reprint, New Delhi: Ganga Publications, 1979.

Shende, N. J. "The *Hotṛ* and Other Priests in the Brāhmaṇas of the ṚgVeda." *Journal of the University of Bombay,* n.s., 32, no. 2 (1963): 48–88.

Singh, Kamla Prasad. "A Critical Study of the Kātyāyana-Śrauta-Sūtra." Ph.D. diss., Banaras Hindu University, 1969.

Smith, Brian K. *Classifying the Universe: The Ancient Indian Varṇa System and the Origins of Caste.* New York: Oxford University Press, 1994.

——. *Reflections on Resemblance, Ritual and Religion.* New York: Oxford University Press, 1989.

Smith, Brian K., and Wendy Doniger. "Sacrifice and Substitution: Ritual Mystification and Mythical Demystification." *Numen* 36, no. 2 (1989): 189–224.

Smith, Frederick M. *The Vedic Sacrifice in Transition: A Translation and Study of the Trikandamandana of Bhaskara Misra*. Bhandarkar Oriental Series, no. 22. Poona, India: University of Poona, 1987.

Sparreboom, M., and J. C. Heesterman. *The Ritual Setting Up of the Sacrificial Fires According to the Vadhula School (Vadhulasrautasutra 1.1–1.4)*. Vienna: Verlag University Press, 1952.

Spiro, Melford. *Buddhism and Society: A Great Tradition and Its Burmese Vicissitudes*. 2d ed. Berkeley: University of California Press, 1982.

Staal, Frits. *Agni: The Vedic Ritual of the Fire Altar.* 2 vols. Berkeley: Asian Humanity Press, 1983.

——. "Ritual Syntax." In *Sanskrit and Indian Studies*, edited by M. Nagotomie et al. Dordrecht, Netherlands: D. Reidel, 1979.

——. *Rules without Meaning.* Toronto Studies in Religion, 4. San Francisco: Peter Lang, 1990.

Thite, Ganesh. *Sacrifice in the Brahmana Texts*. Poona, India: University of Poona, 1975.

Upadhyay, Govind Prasad. *Brahmanas in Ancient India.* New Delhi: Munshiram Manoharlal, 1979.

Vesci, Uma Marina. *Heat and Sacrifice in the Vedas*. Delhi: Motilal Banarsidass, 1985.

Vyas, R. T. "The Concept of Prajapati in Vedic Literature." *Bharatiya Vidya* 38 (1978): 95–101.

Wasson, R. Gordon. *Soma: Divine Mushroom of Immortality*. New York: Harcourt Brace Jovanovitch, 1968.

——. "The Soma of the Rig-Veda: What Was It?" *Journal of the American Oriental Society* 91, no. 2 (1971): 169–187.

Wheelock, Wade. "The Problem of Ritual Language: From Information to Situation." *Journal of the American Academy of Religion* 50 (1982): 49–70.

——. "A Taxonomy of the Mantras in the New and Full-Moon Sacrifice." *History of Religions* 19, no. 4 (1980): 349–369.

JUDAIC SOURCES

Primary Sources

Bible

Hebrew Bible

Eliger, K., and W. Rudolph, eds. Stuttgart: Deutsche Bibelstiftung, 1977.

Translation:

May, Herbert G., and Bruce Metzger, eds. *The New Oxford Annotated Bible with the Apocrypha. Revised Standard Version.* New York: Oxford University Press, 1977.

Leviticus

Driver, S. R. *The Book of Leviticus.* Leipzig, Germany: J. C. Hinrichs, 1894.

Translation:

Driver, S. R. *The Book of Leviticus.* New York: Dodd, Mead, 1898.

Classical Rabbinic Texts

Babylonian Talmud

Epstein, I., ed. London: Soncino Press, 1960–.

Translation:

Epstein, I., ed. *The Babylonian Talmud.* 1935–1952. Reprint, 18 vols., London: Soncino Press, 1961.

Deuteronomy Rabbā

Hallevy, E. E., ed. In *Midrash Rabbāh*, vol. 8. Tel Aviv: Machbaroth Lesifrut, 1963.

Lieberman, Saul, ed. 3d ed. Jerusalem: Wahrman Books: 1974.

Translation:

Rabbinowitz, J., trans. In *The Midrash Rabbah*, edited by H. Freedman and Maurice Simon, vol. 3. London: Soncino Press, 1977.

Jerusalem Talmud

Krotoshin edition. New York: Yam Ha-Talmud/Shulsinger Bros., 1948.

Translation:

Neusner, Jacob, et al., trans. *The Talmud of the Land of Israel: A Preliminary Translation and Explanation.* 35 vols. Chicago Studies in the History of Judaism. Chicago: University of Chicago Press, 1982–1993.

Leviticus Rabbā

Margulies, Mordecai, ed. 5 vols. Jerusalem: American Academy for Jewish Research, 1953–1960.

Translation:

Israelstam, J., and Judah J. Slotki, trans. In *The Midrash Rabbah*, edited by H. Freedman and Maurice Simon, vol. 2. London: Soncino Press, 1977.

Mekilta de-Rabbi Ishmael

Horovitz, H. S., and I. A. Rabin, eds. 1931. 2d ed. Jerusalem: Bamberger and Wahrmann, 1960.

Lauterbach, Jacob Z., ed. 3 vols. Philadelphia: Jewish Publication Society, 1933–1935.

Translations:

Lauterbach, Jacob Z., trans. *Mekilta de-Rabbi Ishmael.* 3 vols. Philadelphia: Jewish Publication Society, 1933–1935.

Neusner, Jacob, trans. *Mekilta de-Rabbi Ishmael: An Analytical Translation.* 2 vols. Brown Judaic Studies, nos. 148, 154. Atlanta: Scholars Press, 1988.

Mishnah

Albeck, Chanoch, ed. 6 vols. Jerusalem: Mosad Bialik; Tel Aviv: Dvir, 1952–1958.

Blackman, Philip, ed. and trans. 2d rev. ed. 7 vols. New York: Judaica Press, 1963–1964.

Translations:

Danby, Herbert, trans. *The Mishnah.* Oxford: Oxford University Press, 1933.

Goldin, Judah, trans. *The Living Talmud: The Wisdom of the Fathers and Its Classical Commentaries.* New York: New America Library, 1957.

Neusner, Jacob, trans. *The Mishnah: A New Translation.* New Haven, CT: Yale University Press, 1988.

Numbers Rabbā

In *Midrash Rabbāh*, vol. 2. Vilna, Lithuania: Romm, 1887.

Hallevy, E. E., ed. In *Midrash Rabbāh*, vols. 6–7. Tel Aviv: Machbaroth Lesifrut, 1963.

Translation:

Slotki, Judah J., trans. In *The Midrash Rabbāh*, edited by H. Freedman and Maurice Simon, vol. 3. London: Soncino Press, 1977.

Pesikta de-Rav Kahana

Mandelbaum, Bernard, ed. 2 vols. New York: Jewish Theological Seminary of America, 1962.

Translation:

Braude, Willliam G., and Israel J. Kapstein, trans. *Pesikta de-Rab Kahana: R. Kahana's Compilation of Discourses for Sabbaths and Festal Days.* Philadelphia: Jewish Publication Society, 1975.

Pesikta Rabbati

Friedman, M., ed. Vienna: [privately published], 1880.

Translation:

Braude, William G., trans. *Pesikta Rabbati: Discourses for Feasts, Fasts, and Special Sabbaths.* 2 vols. Yale Judaica Series, vol. 18. New Haven, CT: Yale University Press, 1968.

Translation:

Friedlander, Gerald, trans. *Pirke de Rabbi Eliezer. (The Chapters of Rabbi Eliezer the Great).* 4th ed. New York: Sepher-Hermon Press, 1981.

Medieval Legal Codes

Mishneh Torah

Lewittes, Mendell, trans. *The Code of Maimonides.* Vol. 8. New Haven, CT: Yale University Press, 1957.

Secondary Sources

Albeck, H. *Commentary to the Mishnah, Holy Things.* Jerusalem: Bialik Institute, 1956.

Alon, G. *Studies in Jewish History in the Times of the Second Temple and the Temple.* Vol. 1. Translated by I. Abrahams. Jerusalem: Magnes, 1957.

Anderson, G. A. *Sacrifices and Offerings in Ancient Israel.* Atlanta: Scholars Press, 1987.

Barr, J. "Sacrifice and Offering." In *Dictionary of the Bible,* edited by J. Hastings. New York: Scribner's, 1963.

Baumgarten, A. I. "Josephus on Essene Sacrifice." *Journal of Jewish Studies* 45 (1994): 169–183.

Baumgarten, Joseph M. "The Red Cow Purification Rites in Qumran Texts." *Journal of Jewish Studies* 46, nos. 1–2 (1995): 112–119.

——. "Sacrifice and Worship among the Jewish Sectarians of the Dead Sea (Qumran) Scrolls." *Harvard Theological Review* 46 (1953): 141–159.

Bertholet, A. *Leviticus.* Tübingen, Germany: J. C. B. Mohr (P. Siebeck), 1901.

Biale, David. *Eros and the Jews: From Biblical Israel to Contemporary America.* New York: Basic Books, 1992.

Bleeker, C. J. "Guilt and Purification in Ancient Egypt." *Numen* 13, no. 2 (1966): 81–87.

Bloch, Maurice. "The Past and Present in the Present." *Man* 12, no. 1 (1977): 278–292.

Bloch, René. "Midrash." In *Approaches to Ancient Judaism,* edited by Jacob Neusner. Atlanta: Scholars Press, 1990.

Boyarin, Daniel. *Carnal Israel*. Berkeley: University of California Press, 1993.

——. *Intertextuality and the Reading of Midrash*. Bloomington: Indiana University Press, 1990.

Brichto, H. C. "On Slaughter and Sacrifice, Blood and Atonement." *Hebrew Union College Annual* 47 (1976): 19–55.

Brown, J. P. "The Sacrificial Cult and Its Critique in Greek and Hebrew, I." *Journal of Semitic Studies* 24 (1979): 159–173.

——. "The Sacrificial Cult and Its Critique in Greek and Hebrew, II." *Journal of Semitic Studies* 25 (1980): 1–21.

Buchler, A. *Studies in Sin and Atonement in the Rabbinic Literature of the First Century.* London: Oxford University Press, 1928.

Bulmer, Ralph. "The Uncleanness of the Birds of Leviticus and Deuteronomy." *Man,* n.s., 24, no. 2 (June 1989): 304–320.

Carnoy, A. J. "Purification." In *Encyclopedia of Religion and Ethics*, 10. Edinburgh: T & T Clark, 1919.

Chan, K.-K. "You Shall Not Eat These Abominable Things: An Examination of Different Interpretations of Deuteronomy 14:3–20." *East Asian Journal of Theology* 3 (1985): 88–106.

Cohen, Shaye. *From the Maccabees to the Mishnah*. Philadelphia: Westminster Press, 1987.

Cross, F. M. "The Priestly Tabernacle." *Biblical Archaeologist* 10 (1947): 45–68. Reprinted in the *Biblical Archaeologist Reader* 1 (1961): 201–228.

Davies, D. "An Interpretation of Sacrifice in Leviticus." *Zeitschrift fur die alttestamentliche Wissenshaft* 89 (1977): 387–398.

Dion, P. E. "Early Evidence for the Ritual Significance of the 'Base of the Altar.' " *Journal of Biblical Literature* 106 (1987): 487–490.

Douglas, Mary. *Leviticus as Literature*. New York: Oxford University Press, 1999.

Driver, S. R. *Deuteronomy.* International Critical Commentary series. New York: Scribner's, 1895.

——. "Offer, Offering, Oblation." In *Dictionary of the Bible*, vol. 3, edited by J. Hastings. New York: Scribner's, 1900.

Eilberg-Schwartz, Howard. *God's Phallus and Other Problems for Men and Monotheism*. Boston: Beacon: 1994.

——. *The Human Will in Judaism: The Mishnah's Philosophy of Intention.* Atlanta: Scholars Press, 1986.

——. "Israel in the Mirror of Nature: Animal Metaphors in the Ritual and Narratives of Ancient Israel." *Journal of Ritual Studies* 2, no. 1 (1988): 1–30.

——. *People of the Body: Jews and Judaism from an Embodied Perspective.* Albany: State University of New York Press, 1992.

——. *The Savage in Judaism*. Bloomington: Indiana University Press, 1990.

Engelhard, D. H. "Hittite Magical Practices: An Analysis." Ph.D. diss., Brandeis University, 1970.

Fishbane, M. *Biblical Interpretation in Ancient Israel.* Oxford: Clarendon Press, 1985.

Friedman, R. E. "The Tabernacle in the Temple." *Biblical Archaeologist* 43 (1980): 241–248.

Funkenstein, Amos. *Perceptions of Jewish History.* Berkeley: University of California Press, 1993.

Gaster, T. H. "Sacrifices and Offerings, OT." In *The International Dictionary of the Bible* 4. Nashville: Abingdon Press, 1962.

Gilders, William. *Blood Ritual in the Hebrew Bible: Meaning and Power.* Baltimore: Johns Hopkins University Press, 2004.

——. "Representation and Interpretation: Blood Manipulation in Ancient Israel and Early Judaism." Ph.D. diss., Brown University, 2001.

Gray, G. B. *Sacrifice in the Old Testament.* Oxford: Clarendon Press, 1925.

Grintz, Jehoshua. " 'Do Not Eat on the Blood': Reconsiderations in Settings and Dating of the Priestly Code (Lev. 19:26; I Sam. 14:31–35; Ez. 33:25)." *Annual of the Swedish Theological Institute* 8 (1970–71): 78–105.

Guttman, A. "The End of the Jewish Sacrificial Cult." *Hebrew Union College Annual* 38 (1967): 137–148.

Hallo, W. W. "The Origins of the Sacrificial Cult: New Evidence from Mesopotamia and Israel." In *Ancient Israelite Religio: Frank Moore Cross Festschrift,* edited by P. D. Miller et al. Philadelphia: Fortress Press, 1987.

Haran, M. "The Complex of Ritual Acts Performed inside the Tabernacle." *Scripta Hierosolymitana* 8 (1961): 272–302.

——. *Temples and Temple Service in Ancient Israel.* Oxford: Clarendon Press, 1978.

Hendel, R. S. "Sacrifice as a Cultural System: The Ritual Symbolism of Exodus 24, 3–8." *Zeitschrift fur die alttestamentliche Wissenschaft* 101 (1989): 366–390.

Henninger, J. "Pureté et impureté: L'Histoire des religions. Peuples sémitiques, animaux impurs; le sang." In *Supplément, Dictionnaire de la Bible,* 9. Paris: Letouzey & Ane, 1979.

Hurowitz, A. "The Priestly Account of the Building of the Tabernacle." *Journal of the American Oriental Society* 105 (1985): 21–30.

Janowski, B. "Azazel." In *Dictionary of Deities and Demons in the Bible,* edited by Karl van den Toorb, Bob Becking, and Pieter van der Horst. New York: E. J. Brill, 1995.

Kalisch, M. M. *Leviticus.* 2 vols. London: Longmans, 1867–1872.

Kapah, J., ed. *Mishnah with Maimonides' Commenary.* 3 vols. Jerusalem: Kook, 1963.

Kaufman, Y. *The Religion of Israel.* Translated and abridged by M. Greenberg. Chicago: University of Chicago Press, 1960.

Klawans, Jonathan. *Impurity and Sin in Ancient Judaism.* New York: Oxford University Press, 2000.

——. "Pure Violence: Sacrifice and Defilement in Ancient Israel." *Harvard Theological Review* 94, no. 2 (2001): 133–155.

Koleditzky, S., ed. *R. Hillel on the Sipra.* 2 vols. Jerusalem: published by the author, 1961.

Lagercrantz, S. "Forbidden Fish." *Orientalia Suecana* 2 (1953): 3–8.
Lauterbach, Jacob Z. *Rabbinic Essays.* Cincinnati: Hebrew Union College Press, 1957.
——. *Studies in Jewish Law, Custom and Folklore.* New York: KTAV Publishing House, 1970.
Leibovitch, J. "Une Scéne de sacrifice ritual chez les anciens Egyptiens." *Journal of Near Eastern Studies* 12 (1953): 59–60.
Levine, Baruch. *In the Presence of the Lord: A Study of Cult and Some Cultic Terms in Ancient Israel.* Studies in Judaism in Late Antiquity, vol. 5. Leiden, Netherlands: E. J. Brill, 1974.
——. *Leviticus.* Philadelphia: Jewish Publication Society, 1989.
Margoliot, M. *Midrash Leviticus Rabbah.* Jerusalem: Ararat, 1956.
Marx, A. "Sacrifice de réparation et rites de levée de sanction." *Zeitschrift fur die alttetamentliche Wissenschaft* 100 (1988): 183–198.
——. "Sacrifice pour les péchés ou rites de passage? Quelques réflexions sur la Function du ḥaṭṭā'ṭ." *Revue Biblique* 96 (1989): 27–48.
McCarthy, Dennis J. "Further Notes on the Symbolism of Blood and Sacrifice." *Journal of Biblical Literature* 92 (1973): 205–210
——. "The Symbolism of Blood and Sacrifice." *Journal of Biblical Literature* 88 (1969): 166–176.
Milgrom, Jacob. *Cult and Conscience: The Asham and the Priestly Doctrine of Repentance.* Studies in Judaism in Late Antiquity, vol. 18. Leiden, Netherlands: E. J. Brill, 1976.
——. "The Function of the Hatta't Sacrifice." *Tarbiz* 40 (1970): 1–8.
——. "The Graduated Purification Offering." *Journal of the American Oriental Society* 103 (1983): 249–254.
——. "Israel's Sanctuary: The Priestly 'Picture of Dorian Gray.'" *Revue Biblique* 83 (1976): 390–399.
——. *The JPS Torah Commentary: Numbers.* Philadelphia: Jewish Publication Society, 1990.
——. *Leviticus 1–16.* Anchor Bible series. New York: Doubleday, 1991.
——. *Leviticus 17–22.* Anchor Bible series. New York: Doubleday, 2000.
——. *Leviticus 23–27.* Anchor Bible series. New York: Doubleday, 2001.
——. "A Prolegomenon to Leviticus 17:11." *Journal of Biblical Literature* 90, pt. 2 (June 1971): 149–156.
——. "Sacrifices and Offerings, OT." In *The Interpreter's Dictionary of the Bible,* supplementary volume. Nashville: Abingdon Press, 1976.
——. *Studies in Cultic Theology and Terminology.* Studies in Judaism in Late Antiquity, vol. 36. Leiden, Netherlands: E. J. Brill, 1983.
Montefiore, C. G., and H. Loewe, eds. *A Rabbinic Anthology.* New York: Schocken Books, 1974.
Morgenstern, Julian. "The Ark, the Ephod and the Tent of Meeting." *Hebrew Union College Annual* 17 (1943): 153–265, and 18 (1944): 1–52.
——. "The Decalogue of the Holiness Code." *Hebrew Union College Annual* 26:1–28.

Moskowitz, Moshe. "Toward a Rehumanization of the Akedah and Other Sacrifices." *Judaism* 37 (1988): 288–293.

Neusner, Jacob. *A History of the Mishnaic Law of Holy Things*. Pt. 6 of *The Mishnaic System of Sacrifice and Sanctuary*. Leiden, Netherlands: E. J. Brill, 1980.

——. *Method and Meaning in Ancient Judaism*. 2d series. Ann Arbor, MI: Edwards, 1981.

——. *Sifra in Perspective: The Documentary Comparison of the Midrashim of Ancient Judaism*. Brown Judaic Studies 146. Atlanta: Scholars Press, 1988.

——. *The Way of Torah: An Introduction to Judaism*. Albany, NY: Wadsworth Publishing Co., 1997.

Noth, Martin. *Leviticus: A Commentary*. Translated by J. E. Anderson. The Old Testament Library. Philadelphia: Westminster Press, 1965.

Oesterly, W. O. E. *Sacrifices in Ancient Israel*. London: Hodder and Staughton, 1937.

Olyan, Saul. *Rites and Rank: Hierarchy in Biblical Representations of Cult*. Princeton, NJ: Princeton University Press, 2000.

Patai, Raphael. "Hebrew Installation Rites." *Hebrew Union College Annual* 20 (1947): 143–226.

Pritchard, J. B., ed. *Ancient Near Eastern Texts Relating to the Old Testament*. Princeton, NJ: Princeton University Press, 1969.

Rainey, A. "The Order of Sacrifices in Old Testament Ritual Texts." *Biblica* 51 (1970): 485–498.

Rubinstein, Richard. "Atonement and Sacrifice in Contemporary Jewish Liturgy." *Judaism* 11 (1962): 131–143.

Schiffman, Lawrence H. *From Text to Tradition: A History of Second Temple and Rabbinic Judaism*. Hoboken, NJ: KTAV Publishing House, 1991.

Segal, J. B. "Popular Religion in Ancient Israel." *Journal of Jewish Studies* 27, no. 1 (1976): 1–22.

Snaith, N. H. *Leviticus and Numbers*. London: Thomas Nelson, 1967.

Spiegel, Shalom. *The Last Trial*. New York: Schocken Books, 1967.

Spinner, Gregory. "The Jerusalem Temple as *Imago Mundi*." Paper presented at the American Academy of Religion national conference, Toronto, November 2002.

Stager, L. E. "Agriculture." In *The Interpreter's Dictionary of the Bible, Supplement*. Nashville: Abingdon Press, 1976.

Thompson, R. C. *Penitence and Sacrifice in Early Israel outside the Levitical Law*. Leiden, Netherlands: E. J. Brill, 1963.

Wallace, D. "The Essenes and Temple Sacrifice." *Theologische Zeitschrift* (Basel) 13 (1957): 335–338.

Wenham, G. J. *The Book of Leviticus*. Grand Rapids, MI: Eerdmans, 1979.

Wright, D. P. "The Gesture of Hand Placement in the Hebrew Bible and in Hittite Literature." *Journal of the American Oriental Society* 106 (1986):433–446.

Yerkes, R. K. *Sacrifice in Greek and Roman Religions and Early Judaism*. New York: Scribner's, 1952.

GENERAL WORKS

Bable, Lawrence A. *Absent Lord*. Berkeley: University of California Press, 1996.

Bell, Catherine. *Ritual Theory, Ritual Practice*. New York: Oxford University Press, 1992.

Bergmann, Martin S. *In the Shadow of Moloch: The Sacrifice of Children and Its Impact on Western Religions*. New York: Columbia University Press, 1992.

Bourdillon, M. F. C., and M. Fortes, ed. *Sacrifice*. New York: Academic Press, 1980.

Braun, Willi, and Russell T. McCutcheon, eds. *Guide to the Study of Religion*. New York: Cassell, 2000.

Burkert, Walter. "Greek Tragedy and Sacrificial Ritual." *Greek, Roman, and Byzantine Studies* 7 (1966): 87–121.

——. *Homo Necans: The Anthropology of Ancient Greek Sacrificial Ritual and Myth*. Translated by Peter Bing. 1972. Berkeley: University of California Press, 1983.

——. "The Problem of Ritual Killing." In *Violent Origins: Ritual Killing and Cultural Formation*, edited by Robert G. Hamerton-Kelly. Stanford, CA: Stanford University Press, 1987.

Camporesi, Piero. *Juice of Life: The Symbolic and Magic Significance of Blood*. Translated by Robert R. Barr. New York: Continuum, 1995.

Cassirer, Ernst. *Mythical Thought*. In *Philosophy of Symbolic Forms*, vol. 2. New Haven, CT: Yale University Press, 1955.

Daly, Robert J. *Christian Sacrifice*. Washington: Catholic University of America Press, 1978.

Détienne, Marcel, and Jean-Pierre Vernant. *The Cuisine of Sacrifice among the Greeks*. Translated by Paula Wissing. Chicago: University of Chicago Press, 1989.

Douglas, Mary. *How Institutions Think*. Syracuse, NY: Syracuse University, 1986.

——. *Purity and Danger: An Analysis of Concepts of Pollution and Taboo*. New York: Praeger, 1960.

Durkheim, Émile. *The Elementary Forms of the Religious Life*. Translated by Joseph Ward Swain. New York: Collier Books, 1961.

Ellen, Roy F., and David Reason. *Classifications in Their Social Contexts*. London: Academic Press, 1979.

Eliade, Mircea. *The Sacred and the Profane: The Nature of Religion*. Translated by Willard R. Trask. New York: Harper and Row, 1961.

Evans-Pritchard, E. E. *The Nuer Religion*. Oxford: Clarendon Press, 1956.

Freud, Sigmund. *Totem and Taboo*. Translated by James Strachey. New York: Norton, 1950.

Girard, René. "Generative Scapegoating." In *Violent Origins: Ritual Killing and Cultural Formation*, edited by Robert G. Hamerton-Kelly. Stanford, CA: Stanford University Press, 1987.

——. *Violence and the Sacred*. Translated by Patrick Gregory. Baltimore: Johns Hopkins University Press, 1977.

Goodman, Hananya, ed. *Between Jerusalem and Banares: Comparative Studies in Judaism and Hinduism*. Albany: State University of New York Press, 1994.

Grandin, Temple. "Principles of Abattoir Design to Improve Animal Welfare." In *Progress in Agricultural Physics and Engineering*, edited by J. Matthews. Wallingford, Oxon, UK: CAB International, 1991.

Grandin, Temple, and J. M. Regenstein. "Religious Slaughter and Animal Welfare: A Discussion for Meat Scientists." *Meat Focus International* (March 1994): 115–123.

Grimes, Ronald. "Breaking the Glass Barrier: The Power of Display." *Journal of Ritual Studies* 4, no. 2 (1990): 239–262.

——. *Readings in Ritual Studies*. Upper Saddle River, NJ: Prentice Hall, 1996.

Halverson, John. "Animal Categories and Terms of Abuse." *Man*, n.s., 11, no. 4 (1976): 505–516.

Hamerton-Kelly, Robert G., ed. *Violent Origins: Ritual Killing and Cultural Formation*. Stanford, CA: Stanford University Press, 1987.

Hecht, Richard. *Sacrifice, Comparative Study and Interpretation*. Ph.D. diss., University of California at Los Angeles, 1976.

——. "Studies on Sacrifice, 1970–1980." *Religious Studies Review* 8 (1982): 253–259.

Henninger, Joseph. "Sacrifice." In *The Encyclopedia of Religion*, vol. 12, translated by Matthew J. O'Connell. New York: Macmillan, 1987.

Holdrege, Barbara. "Beyond Hegemony? South Asia, the Middle East, and the Politics of Comparison." Paper presented at Conference on Comparative Studies of South Asia and the Middle East, University of California, Santa Barbara, May 17, 2003.

——. *Veda and Torah: Transcending the Textuality of Scripture*. Albany: State University of New York, 1996.

Hubert, Henri, and Marcel Mauss. *Sacrifice: Its Nature and Functions*. Translated by W. D. Halls. 1898. Chicago: University of Chicago Press, 1964.

Humphrey, Caroline, and James Laidlaw. *The Archetypal Actions of Ritual: A Theory of Ritual Illustrated by the Jain Rite of Worship*. Oxford: Clarendon Press, 1994.

James, E. O. *The Origins of Sacrifice*. London: John Murray, 1933.

Jastrow, Morris, Jr. *The Study of Religion*. Chicago: University of Chicago Press, 1902.

Jay, Nancy. *Throughout Your Generations Forever: Sacrifice, Religion and Paternity*. Chicago: University of Chicago Press, 1992.

Jensen, Adolph E. *Myth and Cult among Primitive Peoples*. Translated by Marianna Tax Choldin and Wolfgang Weissleder. Chicago: University of Chicago Press, 1963.

Katz, Nathan, et al. *Indo-Judaic Studies in the Twenty-First Century: A View from the Margins. The State of the Art in Indo-Judaic Studies*. New York: Palgrave Macmillan, forthcoming.

Kleeman, Terry F. *A God's Own Tale*. Albany: State University of New York Press, 1994.

Lawson, E. Thomas, and Robert N. McCauley. *Rethinking Religion: Connecting Cognition and Culture*. Cambridge: Cambridge University Press, 1990.

Levenson, Jon. D. *The Death and Resurrection of the Beloved Son: The Transformation of Sacrifice in Judaism and Christianity*. New Haven, CT: Yale University Press, 1993.

Levi-Strauss, Claude. *The Savage Mind*. Chicago: University of Chicago Press, 1966.

——. *Totemism*. Translated by Rodney Needham. Boston: Beacon Press, 1963.

Leinehardt, R. G. *Divinity and Experience: The Religion of the Dinka*. Oxford: Oxford University Press, 1961.

Lincoln, Bruce. *Authority, Construction, and Corrosion*. Chicago: University of Chicago Press, 1994.

——. *Death, War and Sacrifice: Studies in Ideology and Practice*. Chicago: University of Chicago Press, 1991.

——. *Discourse and the Construction of Society*. New York: Oxford University Press, 1989.

——. *Holy Terrors: Thinking about Religion after September 11*. Chicago: University of Chicago Press, 2003.

——. *Myth, Cosmos and Society: Indo-European Themes of Creation and Destruction*. Cambridge: Harvard University Press, 1986.

Lorenze, Konrad. *On Aggression*. Translated by Marjorie Kerr Wilson. New York: Harcourt Brace Jovanovich, 1966.

Mack, Burton. "Introduction: Religion and Ritual." In *Violent Origins: Ritual Killing and Cultural Formation*, edited by Robert G. Hamerton-Kelly. Stanford, CA: Stanford University Press, 1987.

Marvin, Carolyn, and David W. Ingle. *Blood Sacrifice and the Nation: Totem Rituals and the American Flag*. New York: Cambridge University Press, 1999.

Mauss, Marcel. *The Gift: Forms and Functions of Exchange in Arabic Societies*. Translated by Ian Cunnison. 1925. New York: Norton, 1967.

McClymond, Kathryn. Review of *Contesting Sacrifice: Religion, Nationalism, and Social Thought in France*. *Journal of the American Academy of Religion* 72, no. 3 (2004): 798–799.

Müller, Friedrich Max. *Introduction to the Science of Religion*. London: Longmans, Green, and Co., 1882. Reprint, London: Adamant Media Corp., 2001.

Needham, Rodney. "Polythetic Classification: Convergence and Consequences." *Man*, n.s., 10, no. 3 (1975): 349–369.

——. *Symbolic Classification*. Santa Monica, CA: Goodyear Publishing Co., 1979.

Nilson, Martin P. *Greek Piety*. New York: Norton, 1969.

Paden, William E. "Elements of a New Comparativism." *Method and Theory in the Study of Religion* 8, no. 1 (1996): 5–14.

——. *Religious Worlds: The Comparative Study of Religion*. Boston: Beacon Press, 1988.

Patton, Kimberly C. *Religion of the Gods: Ritual, Paradox, and Reflexivity*. New York: Oxford University Press, 2008.

Patton, Kimberly C., and Benjamin C. Ray, eds. *A Magic Still Dwells: Compara-*

tive Religion in the Postmodern Age. Berkeley: University of California Press, 2000.

Puhvel, Jaan. "Victimal Hierarchies in Indo-European Animal Sacrifice." *American Journal of Philology* 99 (1978): 354–362.

Smith, Jonathan Z. *Drudgery Divine: On the Comparison of Early Christianities and the Religions of Late Antiquity*. Chicago: University of Chicago Press, 1990.

——. *Imagining Religion: From Babylon to Jonestown*. Chicago: University of Chicago Press, 1982.

——. *Map Is Not Territory: Studies in the History of Religions*. Studies in Judaism in Late Antiquity, vol. 23. Leiden, Netherlands: E. J. Brill, 1978.

——. *To Take Place: Toward Theory in Ritual*. Chicago: University of Chicago Press, 1987.

Smith, W. Robertson. *Lectures on the Religion of the Semites*. 1889. New York: Meridian Books, 1957.

Spiro, Milford E. "Religion: Problems of Definition and Explanation." In *Anthropological Approaches to the Study of Religion*, edited by Michael Banton. A.S.A. Monographs, vol. 3. London: Tavistock, 1966.

Strenski, Ivan. *Contesting Sacrifice: Religion, Nationalism, and Social Thought in France*. Chicago: University of Chicago Press, 2002.

Turner, Victor. "Sacrifice as Quintessential Process: Prophylaxis or Abandonment?" *History of Religions* 16, no. 3 (1977): 189–215.

Tylor, E. B. *Primitive Culture: Researches in the Development of Mythology, Philosophy, Religion, Language, Arts, and Custom*. 3d ed. New York: H. Holt, 1873.

Urban, Hugh B. "The Remnants of Desire: Sacrificial Violence and Transgressive Sexuality in the Cult of the Kapalikas and in the Works of Georges Bataille." *Religion* 25, no. 1 (1995): 67–90.

Valeri, Valerio. *Kingship and Sacrifice: Ritual and Society in Ancient Hawaii*. Translated by Paula Wissing. Chicago: University of Chicago Press, 1985.

Van Baal, J. "Offering, Sacrifice, and Gift." *Numen* 23, no. 3 (1975): 161–178.

Van Baaren, T. P. "Theoretical Speculations on Sacrifice." *Numen* 11, no. 1 (1964): 1–12.

Wolfson, Ben. "Kosher Slaughter." *Mishpahah* 364 (August 1998): 16–17.

Zwerdling, Daniel. "Kill Them with Kindness." americanradioworks.publicradio.org/features/mcdonalds/grandin1.html.

Index